Politics
of
Change
in
Latin
America

POLITICS
OF
CHANGE
IN
LATIN
AMERICA

Edited by

Joseph Maier
Richard W. Weatherhead

FREDERICK A. PRAEGER, *Publisher*
New York

BOOKS THAT MATTER

Published in the United States of America in 1964
by Frederick A. Praeger, Inc., *Publisher*
111 Fourth Ave., New York 3, N.Y.

Library of Congress Catalog Card Number: 64–13382

Printed in the United States of America

To
FRANK TANNENBAUM

teacher, scholar, and colleague,
wise interpreter and friend of Latin America,
these essays are dedicated as tokens of
esteem and affection

Preface

The purpose of this book is to honor Frank Tannenbaum and to present to the reading public a group of useful essays on contemporary Latin America. The participants are men of distinction who have traveled and studied widely in Latin America and are intimate with the contemporary scene and its historical backgrounds. Their work is eminent without avoiding the risks of controversy. To them we want to express, with a full heart, our gratitude and praise. They gladly contributed their valuable time and thought to our undertaking and bravely withstood the editors' importunities.

The result of this collective effort, we hope, will be to stimulate new thoughts and to encourage new perspectives on the difficult and complex universe that is Latin America.

Any errors in translation and editorial revision can, alas, only be ours, but matters of judgment and substance will be the responsibility of each contributor.

We wish to thank those whose labors were indispensable in producing this book. E. Bradford Burns of the State University of New York in Buffalo, New York, gave worthy assistance in translating Gilberto Freyre's essay. To Frederick A. Praeger, our publisher, whose zeal for understanding world affairs and, especially, contemporary Latin America served always as a happy stimulus, we express both our appreciation and our gratitude. And, finally, to Mrs. Alice H. Maier we extend our affection and our warmest thanks for her encouragement, imagination, painstaking labors, and patience, which sustained us through the best and the worst moments.

THE EDITORS

Contents

Politics
of
Change
in
Latin
America

INTRODUCTION

Politics of Change in Latin America

Latin America is a society living under the stress of change. Everywhere the new is challenging the old. The twentieth century has
caused conflict within the traditional nineteenth-century molds.
The sweep of change is relentless, and change is the mark of the
time in Latin America.

The response to this change will determine the character of the
new society as it emerges today and tomorrow. We can no longer
afford to view this change as a simple contest between democratic
and totalitarian forms of life and government. Whether fortunately
or unfortunately, we are the witnesses of a deep transformation in
every single institution of traditional society.

The impact of change has permanently ended Latin America's
isolation from the forces at work in the world today. The nineteenth century preserved and prolonged the colonial substance of
Latin American society and merely gave it a democratic dressing
and a republican façade. The old was continued in different garb.
The modern state only appeared to exist; the reality was something
else. The colonial legacy, the imperial, hierarchical, and aristocratic
ways persisted, in spite of all the zealous attempts at reform and in
spite of all the civil wars. Even the great shock of independence
(1808–24) was not enough to uproot the old order and implant a
new one. The revolutionary concepts of the late eighteenth century
were new to Latin America, just as they were to the United States
and France; but in the latter they germinated with the people and
had foundations in popular assemblies, while in the old Spanish
colonies they became the civil protestations of an educated, well-

3

placed elite. The people's demands sometimes found articulation, but seldom were they truly fulfilled.

In the nineteenth century, Latin America's place in the world was one of isolation. Today, change has brought this area to the forefront of our world-wide preoccupations, and we can no longer speak of it as outside the mainstream of thought and change in the Western world. The last century was one of appearance; ours is one of reality. Our world is a difficult one to live in because it has grown terribly complex. And complexity is augmented, exacerbated, by the steady pressures brought forth by change.

Despite all the turmoil, bloodshed, *pronunciamientos, golpes de estado*, and a bewildering succession of idealistic constitutions in Latin American countries, no profound change was registered anywhere during the nineteenth century. After Simón Bolívar's death in 1830, Latin America returned to the traditional manner of life under the vigorous, individualistic rule of the *caudillos*, a brand of "bastard kings"—that is, rulers who had no patents of legitimacy and no sanctions in tradition. Their way was force and violence. But they kept society orderly and resistant to social change of any nature. The rule of the *caudillo* was no more than a political backwash of the colonial period. For Latin America, the nineteenth century was the twilight of the Middle Ages, the waning of feudal customs, the debilitation of the colonial legacy.

The Industrial Revolution, which began in Western Europe in the eighteenth century and spread rapidly across the Atlantic to the eastern seaboard of the United States, is only in our time significantly touching Latin American societies. Latin American economies have been characterized by a persistent mercantilism that lasted beyond the end of World War I, and in some places even beyond the great depression of the 1930's. Their economic growth depended upon the dynamism of foreign national economy. Capital and capitalists came to Latin America to exploit. Their concern was not to develop or aid these countries—as it is ours today—but rather to use them for their own purposes and profits. Monopolistic tendencies, whether foreign or national, were logical consequences of the mercantile outlook. The landholding systems—the hacienda, the *hato*, the *estancia*, or the fazenda—were both feudal and exclusive in their effect. Agriculture was landlocked by what seemed to be a perpetual system of latifundia—large tracts of land, or seigniories, where men played the part of medieval lords, and regarded their dependents as economic serfs or household chattels. The extractive-exportive arrangement of subsoil minerals tied the internal economies of Latin America to the vicissitudes of the world market.

The changes of this century have undone the apparent economic permanence of the last. The cries for social justice, the persistent demands of more vocal labor unions, the slow but sure development of responsible political parties, the dogma of class warfare, the whirlwind growth of cities where only villages had stood, the new communications that bring the tangible accomplishments of the middle class in other Western countries to the movie and television screens, and the unholy injustice of poverty and wealth in shameless juxtaposition—all these are factors that have undermined the economic and social *status quo* of 1900. The economies have been challenged by change, just as the states have been upset by it.

By the "traditional order of things" we mean the persistence of the colonial legacy, however modified or disguised by the mere trappings of reform. We mean, specifically, the vestiges of feudalism. The system of landholding and its exploitation through peonage are the outgrowths of medieval practices in Spain and Portugal. The encomienda is the historical antecedent of the hacienda, just as the *encomendero* is of the *hacendado*. The large estate (the latifundium) does not participate in the monetary economy of the nation. It is sometimes autarchic, sometimes it provides no more than a subsistence economy, and it is generally inefficient; instead of allowing the development of national unity, it frustrates the growth of the state by spawning a patchwork of principalities.

Political life in Latin America is always handicapped by the personalist tradition, unquestioning loyalty to the person of the leader rather than to the law of the republic. The *jefe político*, the local boss, is in the continuous line of the colonial figures, the cacique and the corregidor. The *jefe máximo* of this century and the *caudillo* of the last are throwbacks to the conquistador: All have seized authority without regard to scruple and have retained it by stealth and strength. The military caste is too often the final arbiter of constitutional processes, and a military career too surely leads to political power. Rivalries among military services and cliques within each service lead to incessant plotting, counterplotting, and periodic revolts, contributing yet another element of tension to the unstable political scene. It is the unsheathed sword of the soldier and not the secret ballot of the citizen that all too frequently decides the outcome of an election. And even when legality appears strong and the deputies are in the Chamber debating the issues before the nation, one must always wonder if the soldiers are in their barracks or in the streets. To be sure, modern concepts of popular democracy have influenced—or frightened—the military everywhere, but have the soldiers accepted subordination to civilian authority, or are they still the truculent guardians of the traditional order and the interests of their own caste?

The long shadow of the Church is still upon the land. The history of the nineteenth century in Latin America is, in effect, the history of the bitter contest between Church and state for absolute supremacy in society. But, while the Church is the great conserving institution, it is the institution most receptive to the forces of change. It has none of the brittleness of the latifundia or of the political and economic oligarchies. It has resisted change in order to ensure its eminence: It has held great extensions of land in the form of entailed estates; it controls its faithful; it dominates much of the educational system; it has formed and still maintains alliances with the traditional elites; it has masked conditions of poverty by giving alms and by extending spiritual refuge to the weary in body; and the brilliance of its architectural splendor has palliated without ameliorating the misery of the people. Withal, the Church is resilient and resourceful. It is adjusting to the forces of change more rapidly than are the traditional elites in Latin America. The Christian Democratic parties are an example of this adjustment. Their programs are committed to the twentieth century, and they are not exclusively Catholic. They are mass parties and not a secular arm of the ecclesiastical hierarchy.

The oligarchs of the land and of politics have been recalcitrant in accepting the change of this century. The Church, on the other hand, has recognized its legitimacy and its urgency, has absorbed it and, in large measure, become its advocate. The Church, from the promulgation of the *Rerum Novarum* (1892) to the *Mater et Magi-*

stra (1961) and *Pacem in Terris* (1963), has taken a firm and clear stand for reform leading to social justice.

The nineteenth century was a time of isolation and stagnation. As a historical experience of a people, it parallels the seventeenth century in the colonial period. Both were times of actual stasis and quietude, and both followed profound historical events. The seventeenth century succeeded the tremendous impetus of discovery, conquest, exploration, and peopling of virtually the entire American continent. Then, splendor in architecture, class and caste in social hierarchy, sophistry and scholasticism in letters and education, and bureaucracy—*empleomanía*—in government and empire became the overriding concerns of all. The nineteenth century, overlapping World War I, followed the great effort of political rupture with Spain and Portugal. Political ties had been severed with the mother country, but the colonial society of the metropolis remained. The king was gone, but not the tendency to monarchy.

Latin America's isolation can be illustrated by another example. The area is something like Japan before Perry's ironclad ships steamed into Tokyo Bay, bringing the impact of change, the stark confrontation of the old with the new, and thereby ending the 200-year rule of the Tokugawa. In the generation immediately following the Meiji Restoration (1868), Japan feverishly incorporated as much of Western progress as she could into her own previously feudalistic and now suddenly anachronistic inheritance. In effect, Japan imposed Western models of progress upon her Oriental and medieval society and successfully transformed it into a powerful industrial state. Just as Japan did after the arrival of Perry and the outside world in 1853, so Latin America is now questioning and attacking the foundations of its traditional society. Yesterday's sacrosanct has become today's evil, tomorrow's purgatory.

In most cases, however, Latin America cannot make the wholesale transformation carried out so thoroughly by the Japanese. Nor is it possible to do now what was accomplished so quickly in the Orient in the last century. Nor, perhaps, is it advisable. Yet, the predicament of resolving the acute problems of change is similar in both instances. The Japanese rulers early in the Meiji period realized that, if change is resisted, the consequence is often a holocaust for those currently in power. They faced change, the Western presence in their midst, by reaching a *modus vivendi* with it. Resistance to change may bring on a fatal collapse of the social order. Adaptation to it and transformation with it will most likely preserve the useful features and functions of traditional society.

The impact of change is seen in the city better than anywhere else. The city is the very focus of change. It is the catalyst between the old and the new in Latin America. It dramatizes the old injustices and precipitates the coming of the new. The city and the machine have brought irreversible change to the surface and the soul of Latin America. Poverty is cast into sharp relief because of their presence.

The city is the only place where there is light in Latin America—in a figurative as well as a literal sense. The traveler appreciates this as his airplane approaches any of the great Latin American cities. Beyond them is darkness, the endless stretches of land still unilluminated by the progress and change of this century, still obscured by the traditional medieval order of things.

The city holds out the promise of the twentieth century. It may be artificial, but it galvanizes men's hearts and draws them magnetically to its environs. The middle class is metropolitan and trained in a profession or a craft. The immigrants move from the feudal countryside to the contemporary city for the benefits it promises, but they are frustrated in participating in them because they are illiterate, unskilled, and uncouth. They are not yet of this century.

The city of the twentieth century conflicts with the siesta. The large metropolis of means and misery is discipline, progress, and tension. It means punctuality and organization. The city is man's response to the idea of material progress. It means reliance upon functional rather than personal relationships. The city means the breakdown of the traditional, patriarchal family. Functionalism has replaced splendor in the city of our time. Feudal splendor has become both profligate and anachronistic.

The city has been the birthplace of democracy. The machine is the means to egalitarian justice. The factory breaks down the superstition and subservience basic to the paternalistic framework. The machine demands a discipline and rationality of those who operate it and direct its uses. The factory, to exist, must be efficient and productive. The latifundia can be wasteful and dependent upon the caprice and improvidence of the *patrón*. The city has its laws, the countryside its folkways. The capitalist in his metropolitan existence has been restricted by labor laws, mass agitation and demogogic controls, corporate structures, and egalitarian codes in general. The land baron, the *hacendado*, is the lord of his domain: There can be no incursion upon his authority, on his land his fiat is absolute, obedience to him is total and personal. Only in the cities do the politics of change have their proper habitat.

Adjustment to radically new situations is the essence of the politics of change. The new cannot be held off by a blind reference to the past. We have cited Japan's experience in the last century under the Meiji and the Catholic Church's recent stand on political and social reforms as examples of successful response to the imperatives of change. The measure of any viable institution, or of any worthy man for that matter, is the capacity to adjust quickly and sensibly to the challenges of change. This, basically, is the problem of our relations with Latin America and the problem of Latin Americans themselves in their own societies. The imperatives of change will become the winds of revolution unless we and they devise a workable set of policies and politics for our changing times.

In the United States, we will never understand the nature of change in Latin America until we come to see it in Latin American terms and experience. We must forgo our ready use of extreme alternatives when we speak of this area. We have simplified their world beyond recognition by our language of absolutes: Communism or democracy, free enterprise or a state-controlled economy, progress or explosion, evolution or revolution. There is a kernel of truth in all these truisms—but no more than a kernel. Latin America, no matter what extravagant terms we use, will have its own peculiar development. We must learn to recognize the special characteristics of this development by the sympathetic act of understanding. Latin American societies are just now assuming their modern form, a form still unclear; they are moving forward with sometimes stunning velocity—or regressing with dismaying frequency. The final outcome of their course may not satisfy our cultural preferences or our political and economic strategy. But before we can influence any of them in any way, we must see them as entities different from our own society. In a world where difference is accepted, change is no longer a dismaying challenge, but a beckoning stimulus.

These will be hard ways for us to learn because we are used to the frozen politics of the Cold War. We may now for the first time be moving slowly out of its barren shadow. The Latin Americans, too, will face unexpected hardships and cruel frustrations in their adjustment to change. Recourse to the old will be useless or tragic. Resistance to change will be fatal. If we in this country must abandon our terminology of absolutes, they in Latin America must forswear their pantheons of demons. The new generation there will have to accept their heritage proudly, but dismiss much of its polemic and illogic. The tirades against the gringo, the extreme suspicion and cunning turned upon most foreigners, and the excessive xenophobia must be moderated by new knowledge, new experience, new insights. Latin Americans live in a world of international interdependence, social responsibility, and advancing technology. They face the ordeal of transforming their societies from top to bottom; but nationalism need not carry them into the excesses of a hate campaign against the United States—or any other nation. Nationalism awakens a people by stirring its patriotic sentiments, by calling upon the past to aid the present, and it has a thousand wise uses. Nationalism can be a tiger, too, and devour those who ride it irresponsibly for their own purposes.

Change confronts the new generation in Latin America with an increasingly wide world stage, a society in which only responsible action will repair ancient evils, and where modern science is fast gnawing away the façade and foundation of traditional society. If their politics of change are flexible and responsible, as ours should be too, the middle of the twentieth century can be the threshold of a coming great age in Latin America. Otherwise, it will be the tragic climax of a system that outlived its justification and was overwhelmed by the changing heralds of a new age.

JOSEPH MAIER
RICHARD W. WEATHERHEAD

I

THE FORCES OF CHANGE
AND CONTINUITY

1

Traditions of Conflict in Latin America

RICHARD W. WEATHERHEAD

Latin America, we are told daily, is a continent in crisis, a subcontinent in revolutionary ferment. Since 1958, the year of Vice President Nixon's hectic journey in South America, and even more since 1959, the year Fidel Castro came to power in Cuba, Latin America has been painfully present in the minds of us all. Our support is enlisted for such programs as the Alliance for Progress, even though eminent critics forecast its inevitable failure. Crisis comes upon crisis in domestic politics and international economic relationships, but, on the other hand, we read of increasing stability and steady development. We discover that more than half the total population is illiterate and, withal, there is a cultural renaissance stirring the Latin Americans everywhere. At best, we can say that the panorama of contemporary Latin America is a diverse one; at worst, we must admit confusion. Our serious concern to understand only augments our perplexity. Our efforts seem governed by the law of diminishing returns. We are, doubtless, more attentive than ever before, yet we see less. Perhaps we do not see the forest for the trees.

The good North American, ingenuous, altruistic, and genuinely well-meaning, cannot fathom the continuous outbursts of anti-Yankeeism. Why is he so pilloried when he is so sincere? Why are his best efforts as a citizen of the world so excoriated? Why is the Latin American Left so unrelenting in its antagonism? The answers to these questions, like the solutions to Latin America's complexity, are both subtle and diverse. We must learn to live in a complex world and at the same time derive some workable pattern to explain the course of its events.

The Latin American lives under the sign of paradox. He inherits a tradition of conflict that underlies his culture and his way of life. The very foundations of his existence are a series of basic antagonisms from which he can never escape. His life and his work, as well as his spiritual being, respond to these antagonisms. Whatever he affirms will somehow be fatally contradicted by its opposite. This rule will hold true no matter what he does, and no amount of logical consistency can overcome his burden of paradox.

There are four great themes that illustrate this tradition of conflict the Latin American inherits. There are other themes than these, but these four have been constant since the Wars of Independence in the early 1800's and are still the major ones today. They are: (1) the ideal of hemispheric unity and the reality of particularist disunity, (2) the quest for a distinct national character and the curse of insignificance in the modern world, (3) the nineteenth-century legacy and the revolutionary mystique, and (4) the dream of democracy and the practice of tyranny. Each theme, it will be noted, is really composed of antagonistic elements or, in other terms, of thesis and antithesis. They are cultural and political manifestations of the basic paradox that characterizes Latin American life.

What the Latin American creates surges from the clash implicit in each of these four themes. He finds his intellectual universe peopled by warring factions. His ideas find little support in a single, central, national tradition. Unless he turns to Europe, the United States, or the Communist countries, he lives suspended in an uncertain present. He seeks definition but is lost in ambiguities; he forges new forms and finds them to be artifacts from some other place. The cultural land he treads is shaky because its tradition is one of conflict and its present one of contradictions.

i

The first tradition of conflict is that of the antagonism between the universal ideal and the particularist reality. The earliest attempt at hemispheric unity in modern Latin American history is, of course, the Bolivarian experiment to forge continental unity at the Congress of Panama in 1826. Bolívar's intent was to preserve the Hispanic cohesion of the colonial period and to affirm politically the military successes recently achieved at the expense of Spain in South America. His invitation to the new American states to attend this Congress was meant to lay the lasting foundations for continental solidarity. The response to Bolívar's gesture was slight and faltering, for the newly independent nations were entering a stage of fragmentation and political anarchy.

The Congress at Panama stands as a curious first expression of the idealistic urge to continental unity. To find its title, Bolívar went back to Greek history and took the word *anfictionía*, which meant a consulting assembly of equal states meeting to discuss common problems. It was to be a recurrent assembly, with its agenda covering a wide range of issues created by the new configuration of the political world at the collapse of the Spanish Empire, the rise of European imperialism, and the growing influence of the United States. Bolívar, however, could not impose his great authority on the Congress, nor could he restrain the ambition of the *caudillos* who had been his lieutenants in the defeat of the Spaniards but who now clamored for control of their countries. Santa Cruz in Bolivia and Páez in Venezuela refused to admit any command higher than their own. They were suspicious of the real motives behind Bolívar's invitation to the Congress at Panama: Was he not cloaking his own political ambition for control of the northern tier of South America in the benign phrases of idealism?

From the beginning, the Congress of Panama was obstructed, and ultimately doomed, by the suspicions of Bolívar's former subordinates. The lure of absolute political power was too strong for the *caudillos* to resist. They did not actually view absolute rule as the legitimate booty that naturally comes to the victorious after the battle is won. They saw themselves as the only men capable of filling the political vacuum created at the fall of the Spanish Crown as effective head of Church, state, and society. They denied Bolívar's claim to ascendency over their countries, for, after all, to them he was an outsider, a foreigner, no matter what services he had given to all the Americas as the symbol of independence, as the Great Liberator. Bolívar did not realize the force of ambition in politics. With Spain defeated, the common front that had triumphed fell away into bits and pieces, and not infrequently into ferocious rivalries.

Bolívar's military greatness is owed in large measure to his stubborn rejection of the limitations imposed on his will by circumstance and nature. He was quixotic as the visionary and had the *hybris* of the hero. As a revealing insight into his character, one can cite any number of passages from his works, but for olympic defiance against whatever the odds and whatever the consequences, perhaps this is the best: "If nature opposes us, we will fight against her and we will defeat her." He may have been sincere in his idealism and it is best that we assume he was. We can say that he was a consummate egoist, but then, all true idealists always are. His egoism, however, thwarted his idealism, just as the nationalistic ambitions of the *caudillos* frustrated the realization of the Congress of Panama.

Bolívar's ideal was to keep the old colonial possessions of the Spanish Empire unified after the Wars of Independence had ended. But, on his death in 1830, his political creation, Great Colombia, was torn apart into the three states of Venezuela, Ecuador, and Colombia. Personal jealousies, the centrifugal attraction of regions, the drive to power of the many cunning *caudillos*, splintered Bolívar's universal ideal into senseless fragments of land, what are called in Spanish *la patria chica* (the small country), *la patria boba* (the silly country), *el terruño* (the small bit of land where one is born, lives, and dies), and *la política de campanario* (the politics of the clique and the cabal). Bolívar, despairing, broken in health by consumption, cried out in the agony of disillusion at the end of his life: "America is ungovernable. Those who have served the revolution [i.e., its independence] have plowed the sea." The universal ideal, the quixotic dream of continental unity, shattered against the harsh reality of particularism, that is, regionalist and personalist politics. The paradox was bitter, but it was also inevitable; it was, in another sense, the heart of the political matter.

The Bolivarian dream, even though it failed, was the early forerunner of Pan-Americanism, the Organization of American States (OAS), and Juscelino Kubitschek's proposal for Pan-American action, which later took shape as the Alliance for Progress. Politically, today as much as ever before, the concept of hemispheric unity is as alive in the hearts of the Latin Americans as it was when Bolívar first proclaimed it. It is still no more than an ideal, something distant on the horizon of hope that may move man to action, both good and bad, now as before. While this concept of hemispheric solidarity lies mostly in the realm of idealism, we must not dismiss its real political potency. Latin Americans are moved more by rhetoric than by reason, stirred more by "idealism" than by "pragmatism." They are concerned not so much with the program of an idea as with its purpose and its expounder. Thus, the force of Bolívar's dream is still with us, although its concrete results lie beyond our reach.

If we refer to the work of the Mexican *pensador* José Vasconcelos, we see clearly the attraction of the hemispheric ideal and its frustration by the particularist reality. In two long essays, *La Raza Cósmica* and *Indología*, Vasconcelos wrote with mystic and crusading zeal about the great new race, the "cosmic race," a racial integration of the best human factors.[1] It naturally took place in Latin America and was to become ultimately the area's lasting mark upon human history. Vasconcelos' concept is no more than the universal ideal translated into racial terms and expressed militantly against the supremacy of the Anglo-Saxon countries, especially the United States.

Vasconcelos was so allured by the brilliance of the universal dream that he spoke no longer merely in hemispheric terms but rather of the whole human cosmos. In spite of the appeal of the man and the cleverness of much of his supple prose, one sees that the "maestro" was completely unaware of the inner ironies that made his proposition in reality—not spiritually or idealistically—untenable. The basis of his cosmic race was the fusion of the principal ethnic elements in Latin America, especially the *mestizo*, a half-breed born of the Spaniard and the Indian. The *mestizo* is still an entity beset by ambiguity; he is an unstable composite of radically contradictory elements. Furthermore, the *mestizo* does not exist in every Latin American country; for example, his part of the total population in Argentina, Chile, Costa Rica, Haiti, and Uruguay is negligible. The *mestizo*, in effect, has no meaning in these countries and therefore the concept of cosmic race cannot be applied to Latin America as a whole. Racial fusion is a slow process, made difficult by tradition, prejudice, and ignorance. In Latin America there are myriads of racial enclaves, Indian, Negro, Caucasian, and many shades of the *mestizo*, all differing from one another almost as much as the Eskimo from the Pygmy.

The point to remember is that Vasconcelos was moved by the universal ideal and thwarted by its opposite—in this case, the presence of distinct and, as yet, unfused ethnic groups. Dream and reality were again in harsh conflict, and Vasconcelos, for reasons different from Bolívar's, died in despair and bitterness.

This almost fatal sign of paradox between ideal and reality is at work elsewhere, frustrating the dreams of men and leaving them, at the end of the road, with empty hands, disillusioned, and alone. Again, on the political level, we have the example of the APRA Party and its leader for a whole generation, Haya de la Torre.[2] The doctrine of the party, based largely on the various writings of José Carlos Mariátegui and the collected political essays of Haya de la Torre, is a form of liberal socialism whose purpose is to redeem the Indian and incorporate him into the new national structures of this century. While *aprismo* originated in Peru, its call is to all those countries where the indigenous population bulks politically and economically large—that is, where the Indian contributes to the racial and economic essence of the nation without having any real weight in or influence upon the course of governmental policy.

Aprismo is sentimental, idealistic, and international in its appeal. It reaches well beyond the fluctuating borders of Peru—for Peru is one of the Latin countries perpetually plagued by boundary squabbles with her neighbors—and might reach the point of hot polemics in such countries as Guatemala, Bolivia, Ecuador, and, although much less so, Mexico, where the Indian problem has been relieved by government action. It recalls the greatness of the Indian past, when sites of powerful civilizations flourished before the coming of the white man. It is a return to some of those pristine forms, such as the *ejido* in Mexico and the *ayllu* in Peru (systems of communal landholding and sharing), and a recovery of the Indian's just claim to responsible participation in the national life of his country. Even with its appeal to the dream of continental unity, its sentimental vision of lost aboriginal grandeur, and its blending of recent anthropological data with various shades of socialism advocating justice and reform, *aprismo*, as a workable hemispheric program of reform, and Haya de la Torre, as titular head of the *aprista* movement, have had only moderate effect beyond Peru.

The reasons why the *aprista* message never became a movement of continental reform are many. Just as Bolívar inspired more suspicion than loyalty with the Congress of Panama, so Haya de la Torre had critics who doubted his altruism. The Peruvian oligarchs saw the *aprista* movement as a radically socialist organization, if not a Communist front, and they thought that, if ever in power, it would destroy their models of capitalism. Haya was faced from the outset of his role as redeemer with frank, sometimes bloody, belligerency from the rulers of Peru who sought and still seek the continuance of their power at the expense of the Indian. As they see it, there is no means of compromise between their system, that which Peru has followed since independence, and the *aprista* solution. The only way out is for one eventually to destroy the other, by legitimate means if possible, by violence if necessary.

We have seen the effect of the conflict between the dream of continental unity and the reality of fierce sectionalism in the lives of Simón Bolívar, the great military genius and political seer of the Wars of Independence; José Vasconcelos, the *pensador* whose weapon of persuasion and controversy was the written word; and Haya de la Torre, the intellectual drawn into the political arena by the force of his own ideas and by the lure of a grandiose program. The same conflict is still with us. The Alliance for Progress and the OAS partake of it. If we say, as many impatient critics do nowadays, that all of these undertakings have been too idealistic, too bound up with the inspiration of handsome rhetoric and seldom concerned with the hard realities of a given situation, what can we say of the professional who not only believes in many of these continental concepts but places his expertise and experience at their service?

Today we give credence to our fondest dreams if the scientist, technician, or specialist endorses them. We feel that with specialized knowledge and fact, all ranged together at our service, we will attain an infallible condition of security and omniscience. This may or may not be so, but it does represent much of modern man's credo. And so, when the technician serves eagerly the realization of our dreams, we believe them, of a sudden, practicable things. Thus it is with such enterprises as the Common Market in Central America, the movement of economic integration in South America sponsored by the Economic Commission for Latin America (ECLA) of the United Nations, and the hemispheric alliance as seen in its many ramifications of the OAS.

Two men, one an economist, the other a banker, commit their names, talents, and the large funds of the institutions they direct to bring about plans for greater economic and political unity in this hemisphere. They are Raúl Prebisch,[3] an Argentine economist and director of ECLA, and Felipe Herrera, a former sociologist from Chile, today president of the Inter-American Development Bank. Both have written for years of the necessity of continental solidarity by means of political cooperation, economic development, and an integration of similar economic systems. Because their calls to unity are technically stated and framed in the language of economics, they are no less urgent than the others already discussed. The extent of their appeal is no doubt smaller, since their audience has to have at least some training in the rudiments of economic theory and practice and some awareness of the realities of the modern world. Their goal of unity, however, strikes no less against the bane of disunity.

The Common Market in Central America and the regional market in South America progress uncertainly and are hampered by local apprehensions of entering some all-embracing economic structure, thereby limiting prerogatives, privilege, and, worse, profits. These two men are not merely prophets in the desert, nor have their efforts been completely unsuccessful. Some success is patent, but judgment on the final outcome cannot be passed now. Unlike the other men who propounded similar undertakings, both Prebisch and Herrera receive the backing of some of the most powerful national and international agencies of modern times. If this support is consistent and lasts over a long, long period of time, the plans of economic integration and political cooperation might well come to reasonable fruition before this century ends.

All of these men were and are moved by the ideal of hemispheric unity in one form or another. They have placed their reputations in its service and, sometimes, they have risked life and limb in its fulfillment. Whether visionaries, displaced Don Quixotes, or modern experts, they have seen the dark reality of particularism. The obstacles in their paths have always been formidable: The region, the *caudillo*, local pride and egoism, and vendettas between factions have inhibited the realization of the universal ideal. Hemispheric unity, in whatever guise, is still the will-o'-the-wisp for the Latin American.

ii

The second tradition of conflict is posed by the quest for a distinct national character as against the curse of insignificance in the modern world. Since the end of World War II, the revelation of the might of the atom, and the Cold War, our world has been divided into two hostile camps. Each proclaims a doctrine radically incompatible with the other, so that "capitalist" and "Communist" view one another with much misgiving and mistrust. Only recently have the ice floes of the Cold War loosened, and now we can see some signs of flexibility on both sides. Today, happily, the world is no longer as excruciatingly simple as it once was; we see complexity on every hand, so much so, in fact, that our leaders are reluctant to act because they cannot see single motives for reprisal or war.

A large part of this change was brought on by what has been called the world-wide revolution, "the rising expectations" of the masses everywhere, and the appeal to social justice, nationalism, and the development of the economically backward. Latin America, although it cannot be easily compared with Asia or Africa, except on the most superficial levels, is generally put in this category of an underdeveloped area in need of the leavening action of broad social reforms. In other words, we say that Latin America has yet to reach those standards of general well-being in which we would class the countries of Western Europe, Japan, and the United States. The standards have a markedly Western bias and are in most cases arbitrary and misleading. This is not, here, the point of importance. The significance we must see in the application of these standards to the underdeveloped areas is that, willy-nilly, we relegate them to an inferior and dependent position vis-à-vis our own.

The distempered nationalism of the last few years, in all the underdeveloped areas, has been due largely to an increasing recognition of the division in the world between the wealth of the West and the misery elsewhere. Those who live elsewhere have grown restive and indignant; they no longer feel shackled by their age-old poverty, because the example of the West and modern science and technology have taught them that, with courage and will, poverty can be dispelled.

Poverty alone does not explain the extremities of anger and outrage that characterize much of contemporary nationalism. Poverty is, after all, man's unhappy but natural condition. General affluence on a large scale, such as has been achieved in the United States for example, is altogether new and artificial.

The crux of the matter lies, I think, with the idea of the nation-state and of its culmination in Western Europe and the United States. There is no doubt in the mind of a Frenchman that he is French and that France has known greatness in the past and will experience future glories, a confidence especially felt since the coming of De Gaulle. The same is generally true for the Englishman under Elizabeth II or the North American living through the days of the New Frontier. For each the nation-state represents something continuous and stable. An ordinary example will suffice to substantiate this point. In all these countries there is a sort of indignant reluctance to pay taxes and to put up with the annual burden and cost involved in them; but taxes are paid, even if grudgingly yielded up to the awesome figure of the tax collector. To evade taxes is considered not only wrongdoing but a form of *lèse-patrie*. The tax dodger, however clever he is, is looked upon as both a bad citizen and a bad patriot.

This is not the case in Latin America, where the concept of nationhood is still nebulous. The intense nationalism of the past generation certainly does not mean that the Latins have found a satisfactory definition of their countries or themselves. On the contrary, extreme nationalism is a clear sign of the frenetic search for identity in the modern world and for national personality.

That the concept of the nation-state originated in the West and that its broad success has not worked readily elsewhere have contributed to the flood tide running against Western colonialism and Western influence generally. Another way of describing this phenomenon is to say that we in the West have been successful too long, and success—a word better sensed than defined—apparently plagues the Western world. All this the underdeveloped peoples have recognized in the last twenty years, and clamor has replaced former inertia and lethargy. The nationalism of today finds its inner strength in a sense of outrage and a search for identity. It is a defiant struggle to overcome the curse of insignificance that has for generations hung upon their destinies.

The search for a true national personality has been a long and agonizing one for most of the Latin American countries. Begun during the Wars of Independence and continued through the parliamentary deliberations considering what political forms should be applied after independence was won, the quest has continued with increasing urgency down to the present. Nationalism is not a robust, confident affirmation of identity; it is a febrile, disjointed pursuit, at times taking on the exalted tones of fanaticism or mysticism. The nationalist has to do daily battle with an ambiguous past and an uncertain future, and, in the second third of the twentieth century, statistics and social injustice show him that he is woefully short on time. The quest has become more difficult today, for an element of urgency has been added: the rising population and the rising demands of the people. It has been complicated, furthermore, because the nationalist must define himself and the distinctive being of his country on the world's wide stage. His actions are gauged sometimes more for the effect they may have on a significant part of the world's audience than to define the essence of his people.

In Mexico, this probing of the national character began in the 1820's with Lorenzo Zavala, and a few years later with José Luis Mora[4] and Lucas Alamán.[5] These men were politicians, *pensadores*, and historians. They attempted to define Mexico as it should be— that is, what political forms should govern growth of the nation throughout the nineteenth century. They were concerned with the question of whether Mexico should be Catholic, Hispanic, and

centralist or develop along the more liberal lines of religious tolerance, the North American model of federation, and the principle
of free trade. They were what we might call seers, men who determined those social and political patterns that would best fit
Mexico's development. They wrote at the transitional point in
Mexican history, arguing the radical change from colonial government, in which monarchy was the central force of cohesion and
stability, to republican structures.

Similar concern can be found in the writings of the Honduran
Francisco Morazán,[6] in Alberdi[7] and Sarmiento[8] of Argentina, the
Brazilian José do Manoel Bomfim,[9] González Prada[10] of Peru, and
Eugenio María de Hostos[11] of Puerto Rico. Each sought the essence of what was "American," and each tried to formulate what
was special about his own land and people. Their works are not
mere sociological monographs; for that they were not prepared;
nor was academic equilibrium their goal. Their words were a spiritual summons to their compatriots to forge the real meaning of
their country in a never-ending search for it. Thus, the search becomes a crusade in which only those whose hearts are moved can
participate. The quest is more spiritual than analytical. Poetry, in
prose or verse, is more important to its realization than are analysis
or statistics. Latin American sociology has always been more intuitive than empirical.

This quest for a distinctive national character comes into conflict with "the curse of insignificance." Latin Americans feel their
special selves to the point of uniqueness, and yet they have never
been fully participating members of the Western world in the
same sense that, say, Germany, Ireland, or Norway have—even
though political independence was consummated in Latin America
before it was in these countries. Thus, the imperative of national
identity clashes with insignificance on the world stage.

Each region of each country in Latin America has cultural traits
considered superior to all other regions of the same country. The
same feeling of regional egoism and local pride exists as well on the
international level. A Colombian, for example, considers Bogotá
the "Athens of America," while any number of other cities vie
with each other for the title of "Paris of the New World." The
Spanish spoken in Mexico City is purer, more supple, richer in

nuance, than Spanish spoken anywhere else in the Americas—only for the Mexican, of course. The Peruvian and the Chilean have their own opinions, for the former is sure that Lima is the capital of culture and the latter is quick to remind us that Santiago is the real emporium of education.

Within individual countries, regions compete in song, dance, *fiestas*, polemics, political intrigue, and economic growth. The competition is not simply an instance of friendly rivalry against a background of cooperation, and there have been times when the bitterness of jealousy led to secession, revolt, and civil war. In Mexico, as a case in point, there are endless stories and songs that either corroborate or deny the superiority of one state over another. The *tapatío*, the *yucateco*, the *jarocho*, and the *chihuahuense* all lay equally adamant claim on having the best of what Mexico really is. The same intramural competition is found in Colombia between the *antioqueño* and the *bogotano* and in Brazil between the *carioca* and the *paulista*. One is born within a special mold of spiritual, aesthetic, moral, and political values. One's cultural basis is regional, not national. If one becomes nationally powerful by political cunning, by revolt, or by legitimate ascent, one imposes one's own regionalist loyalties and values upon the nation and its culture. Here, we come upon a substratum of conflict. The quest for national character is hampered by the *terruño*, deep ties to one's native land. For example, the nature of Brazilian government changes sharply as the presidential incumbent is from São Paulo, Rio de Janeiro, Belo Horizonte, Rio Grande do Sul, or Bahia. This pattern, with slight variations, is repeated in all the other countries.

These examples reveal the common preoccupation with forging and articulating a special national personality. It has a thousand daily manifestations in the wit and animation of a café, in student demonstrations in the university, in poetry recitals—a wonderfully civilized experience of human expression typical everywhere in Latin America—in popular song, or even on the silver screen in movie houses.

Such architectural or developmental adventures as *Peruvia* in the central massif of the Andes; the splendid effusion of modern architecture and indigenous motifs in the University of Mexico;

and the fabulous city of concrete and dream that is Brasília, the present-day capital of a Brazil that belongs to the future, materially attest to the force of this search. The last two feats of construction were built in great haste and are the symbols of the new Mexico and the new Brazil. Both of these audacious adventures are responses to the malaise of insignificance. They are an inspired defiance against what is traditionally thought possible and impossible. They are the Mexican's and the Brazilian's answer that nationalism can be carried out only at the crusader's pace.

The category of "underdeveloped" serves only to confirm the condition of insignificance. That is, the voice and vote of any of the Latin nations cannot be considered on a par with the English, the French, or the Italian. Expertise, manufactured and capital goods, education at its best, affluence and influence, all flow from the capitals of Western Europe and the United States toward Latin America. To rise above his status of "underdeveloped," and to cut the albatross of insignificance from his neck, the Latin American has to accept the tutelage of the West. We should hope that this tutelage will develop into a relationship of equals. The alternative is a relationship tantamount to servitude with the Sino-Soviet bloc. And tutelage, even if an irritant and a source of frequent frustrations, is obviously preferable to servitude. One allows eventual equality among the parties involved; the other permits only continued subservience.

In part, this is Castro's plight today. To create a distinctive revolution (as Cuban as the royal palms, he was wont to say in its early phases) he fanned the flames of anti-Yankeeism until they were red-hot, he purged the Cuban middle class, defied his former Yankee masters by hostile and arbitrary acts, and risked his life and that of his Cuba on the fate of his alliance with the Communists. Castro's error is obvious to most Latin Americans. His revolution no longer appears a vehicle to national definition. It is more a challenge to the United States and an alliance with the Sino-Soviet bloc than a distinctive expression of the Latin American revolutionary mystique. He let his outrage at Cuba's previously supine dependence on the United States lead him into the fury of the Cold War.

iii

The dilemma posed by Castro's revolution leads directly to the third tradition of conflict. In some ways, perhaps, this expression of the basic antagonism will appear more important than the others, if only because it seems more timely. This example is, nonetheless, only another manifestation of what I have described as the constant underlying theme of conflict in culture. Here, the conflict arises between the revolutionary mystique peculiar to Latin America and the legacy of the nineteenth century.

The Latin American of today is restless and rebellious. The world he lives in and its forms do not answer his yearnings. The condition of being underdeveloped, the "insignificant status" on the world stage, the absence of technological know-how and industrial "drive," the poverty and backwardness of his people, are bitter indications that something is amiss and has been so for too long. Commentators on Latin America always tell us that the area is one of marked contrasts; they tell us of the striking opposites one can see almost everywhere: the faithful, sure-footed donkey, that timeless beast of burden, alongside the sleek and speedy air-conditioned Greyhound bus; or, again, the hovels of a slum section pressing in upon the sparkling luxury and convenience of skyscraping apartment houses and office buildings. The point is, as we are made to see in these graphic examples, that the vestiges of feudalism practically overrun the outgrowths of modern technological and social advance. Feudalism and the legacy of the past conspire against the present and the future in a thousand seen and unseen ways.

This is, of course, nothing new in Latin America. The conflict of an unusable past—the epitome of anachronism, if you like—with the demands of a radically complex present is a theme going back as far as the Wars of Independence. Sarmiento, in *Facundo* (1845), says that the thirteenth century lives side by side with the nineteenth century and is equally as strong in cause and effect. We are again confronting one of the bedrock antagonisms in Latin American life, in this case as it happens in Argentina. This dualism is really the theme of Sarmiento's book, and he went to pains to make this clear in its subtitle, "Civilization and Barbarism," the two extremes within which the Argentine people had to develop.

What has given currency and urgency to all of these contrasts is the imported progress of the twentieth century with its social doctrines of leveling and egalitarianism. The contrasts have become unbearable, they cannot be rationalized, nor can they be covered up or hidden. Travelers no longer see these harsh contrasts and call them quaint aspects of a lovely civilization still untouched by the unpleasantnesses of materialism. Rather they cry out against them, pointing to them as abuses and brutal injustices. This was the reaction of William Benton, for example, in *The Voice of Latin America* (1961).[12]

The nineteenth-century legacy with its republican façade is no more than a mask for the colonial institutions and influences. It does not fit the demands of the twentieth century. It is an anachronistic and inflexible mold. It cannot come to terms, in full measure, with the industrial revolution and the popularist ideologies spawned in this century since Lenin and Roosevelt gave them two distinct social applications. It cannot absorb the welter of changes brought forward constantly by the progressive refinement of technology. The system of the nineteenth century is wobbly because it is inoperative: It does not respond to the needs of another age.

The rigidity of the nineteenth-century legacy pervades all of Latin America. It is the *caudillo* or the monolithic party that presides over the fortunes of political battle, regardless of political controversy and constitutional debate. The economy is arteriosclerotic, dependent on single commodity exports, such as oil, tin, bananas, grains, and meats. It is weakened by the nepotism of the *patrón* system and the onus of an unskilled bureaucracy, both clearly outdated contradictions of efficient management and efficient production. Economic growth is further hampered by a neurotic fear of what the foreign investor will or will not do and by the suspicion that every foreigner, especially the Yankee, is an imperialist wolf dressed in a trader's sheepskin.

All the models, all the ideas conceived so laboriously in the course of the preceding century, have suddenly become the iniquities of this century. In Latin America, the state is ineffective or inoperative in most countries. We speak of dominant castes, classes of privilege, and institutional legacies rather than the central government as the real sources of power, stability, change, or stagnation. The republican creations of the last century are, then, the artifacts of enlightened men who acted as they had to act, believing that the republican ideas they took from France, Spain, and the United States were the most apt means of implanting a stable political structure in their native soil. On the basis of these artificial, later anachronistic, instruments, there did, indeed, appear to be order and progress generally in Latin America. At the turn of the century, Porfirio Díaz controlled Mexico with a competent hand of iron; Augusto Leguía initiated reform and brought stability to Peru; Juan Vicente Gómez found black gold in the Maracaibo basin and brazenly imposed his rule of demagogic dictatorship on Venezuela; and even Brazil, Chile, and Argentina were outwardly calm with an appearance of progress and prosperity. And in Cuba our own proconsul, Leonard Wood, was putting the finishing touches on American colonialism and the Cuban Constitution, which was to last until the coming of Fidel Castro.

Yet, somewhere something had gone wrong. The republican experiments were not in accord with the social realities or with economic necessities. The quest for national self-identity, what we can call "revolutionary nationalism," is a protest against the nineteenth-century legacy. They are, in effect, today's political antipodes.

The rejection of the past implies a rejection of its models, its ethos, its structures, and its causes. The United States, because it served as an example for these nations in the last century, is unavoidably implicated in this rejection. Hence, to a large degree, the persistent illogic of anti-Yankeeism. The hate and suspicion directed against the North American of today is, in turn, obsolete. The Latin American repudiates the robber baron, the captain of industry, the manifest-destiny imperialist, the dollar diplomat, and the arrogant tourist. But so does the North American. The Yankee and the gringo as effective stereotypes ceased to exist twenty-five years ago. True, we have relapses, and our know-how can lead us to offensive bumptiousness or our fears can lead us to exposing our racial prejudices; but, on the whole, today's gringo is a civilized, well-balanced, constructive creature. Think, to take a few examples, of the earnest student who goes to Latin America to learn and discover, the altruistic adventurer of the Peace Corps, the businessman who accepts socialistic restriction of his enterprise and splits his total profits with the host government, and the increasing number of talented career men occupying more and more posts of authority in the State Department and the Foreign Service. These are certainly not imperialist myrmidons sent out to conquer the world and impose colonial shackles on oppressed native populations!

But, alas, confidence is won at a snail's pace and only by repeated example. We, too, in the United States are burdened by our own nineteenth-century legacy, and the stereotype of the gross, grasping gringo is perhaps our heaviest incubus, our most dogged bugbear.

This dissatisfaction with one's inherited, inescapable past can be seen in various ways. *Aprismo* in Peru, the Mexican Revolution and its 1917 Constitution, the Peronist *justicialismo*, the influences of Prestes and Julião in Brazil, the Arévalo-Arbenz experiment with Communism in Guatemala, the socialist-Indianist revolution in Bolivia, the social reforms of Muñoz Marín in Puerto Rico, the measures of expropriation and nationalization of key industries, not to mention *fidelismo* and the impact of that revolution, are all signs of deep disquietude with a past that is no longer usable. The only lesson the past can teach, it seems to many of our contemporaries in Latin America, is a sterile catechism without validity for this time and this generation.

Up to this point I have spoken of the conflict between the rigidities of the past and the complexities of the present. The resulting antagonism has been seen in a number of instances, in the material contrast visible to the traveler's eye, for example, and in the opposition of old ideas and new imperatives in politics and economics. Now we must examine a more difficult matter: that of the nature of the revolutionary mystique in Latin America.

In a sense, all modern societies are the children of revolutions. Revolution is the optimum political vehicle for national expression and unity—or so it seems. Revolution, furthermore, appears as a ready solution to the welter of complexities: It is quick and heroic and turns over the old, replacing it with the new—or so it seems.

Revolution, independence, and nationalism are the political trinity
under whose sign we live and whose force is greater in those lands
labeled "underdeveloped."

A key word to understanding the attraction of revolution in the
Latin American setting is *reivindicación*. It means "recovery," "replevin," and at first blush it seems as lifeless as so many legalisms
pronounced with crisp impartiality by lawyers. Yet, in Spanish, the
word catches fire and the concept behind it is supercharged with
emotional flammability. It is found in novels, proclamations, in
heated debate in cafés, and even amid the technicalities of economic tracts. It means the rejection of an inappropriate past, of
present misery, of the curse of insignificance and underdevelop-
ment in a world prizing prominence. It is a fighting and defiant
word. It is a bold statement of the febrile search for national
meaning and uniqueness. *Reivindicación* is a compendium of emotions and a program of defiant hopes. The Latin American leader
has the fanaticism of the mystic, the militancy of the crusader, and
the charisma of a messiah. His conviction inflames belief in
others, his rhetoric dispels doubt, and his past deeds are touted as
those of the great national hero. He is the herald of a new era,
and his followers are the torchbearers of the new order. Those who
oppose him stand against the sweep of history and the creation of
the *patria*. There is no alternative of dissent, for dissension becomes apostasy, the antithesis of the leader's crusading struggles:
It is, in a word, antirevolutionary. The man who, out of principle or
previous commitment, cannot join the revolution is ostracized as
if he were a heretic. The revolutionary process at this point becomes almost inquisitional, and, in fact, the crueler trappings of
the regime—indoctrination, surveillance, interrogation, and summary trial; the severe penalties for criticism or even doubt, imprisonment, torture, and death—are almost an exact replica of the
Holy Office of the sixteenth and seventeenth centuries made secular. The leader's struggles before he gains power give him the
mantle of the hero, while his movement is presented to the world
with all the religiosity of a crusade. On his victory, sense and virtue will return to the country and his oppressed people will breathe
freely, without the yoke of imperialism or feudalism. In the United
States, we say there will be a complete "house-cleaning" if one or

another candidate is successful at the polls. This metaphor, though, is too homey and domestic to convey the fervor involved in any Latin American revolution. Fervor and *fiesta*, I should add, for the elements of the *fiesta* are present in all Latin revolutions: the parades, the rallies, the swirling colors of people in movement, the blare of discordant trumpets, the air of expectancy about what will happen during the *fiesta's* fortuitous course. It is no coincidence either that *fiestas* are popular celebrations of saints or Church holidays. Take them from this religious setting, put them into the political life, and you have translated religious fervor into unquestioning political allegiance.

The leader is a man possessed by a shining ideal. He communicates the mysticism by which he is seized better than he defines the postulates of his movement. That is his role and his prerogative. Are not the rebel, the hero, and the redeemer men who reject the old, defy the established, and affirm what will come? At best, they will be constructive iconoclasts. This is what is most difficult for the Anglo-Saxon to understand. The Latin does not seek programmatic progress in his revolution. He wants, rather, to upset the *ancien régime*. Programs, parties, and postulates all take too long, they are impersonal and lack entirely the flamboyance and the spectacular ingredients of the crusade and its hero, the fervor and the *fiesta*.

The revolutionary hero is endowed with the might of his quixotic vision. He tilts against the windmills of the impossible. He has reverses, yes, but they do not count or they are contrived by that evil band of backsliders, the antirevolutionaries. The leader sees into the future of his people and therefore sees the real meaning of the nation he has come to save. His mission is that of the redeemer, his vision that of the mystic (the quixotic vision), his impassioned words, those of the fanatic, and his image that of the hero. His coming is a day of glory and *fiesta*, and even if after time works its corroding effect and his attributes tarnish and his support flags, he has the ultimate alternative of martyrdom. Such has been the experience of Simón Bolívar, Antonio Conselheiro, and Fidel Castro.

The leader must, of course, be a popular hero before he is anything else: He must have some meaningful, direct ties to his people. He leads them in pursuit of his quixotic vision, but he reflects as well their dominant characteristics. In the Latin American context, this means a manly body and a virile pose. The leader must be flamboyantly masculine, with wit and a flexible set of scruples for almost any circumstance, except those where his masculinity is doubted or his honor depreciated. The *macho* type has an irresistible charm for his people and a detonating cunning for his political adversaries. He must have, as we would say, more "savvy" than scrupulosity. Basically, the hero is *macho, muy macho,* and no amount of sociological sophistry can get around this fact of political life in Latin America, and perhaps in all the Latin lands, for that matter.

The degrees of *machismo* (manhood) and their varieties are endless, running from the sophisticated worldliness of Simón Bolívar to the sensual and ribald earthiness of Pancho Villa. In between these extremes of the spectrum of *machismo*, we find such prototypes as Juan Manuel Rosas and José Antonio Páez. The first was an Argentine gaucho, bred in the raw ways of ranching on the *pampas* in the early 1820's, who eventually was to rule over Argentina until he was overthrown in 1852. Páez, a combination of intrepid swashbuckler and rugged cowhand, spent his youth on the Venezuelan plains (*llanos*) and, in only a quasi-figurative sense, won his spurs during the Wars of Independence. He, like Rosas, ruled the destiny of his country until after mid-century.

Both were rough-and-ready cowhands, expert horsemen, possessed of unbelievable physical endurance, canny in the art of handling men, and completely ruthless in imposing their will on their followers. Although raised upon the land, near to the ways of nature and animal, they were not coarse in an ordinary sense. Their justice was intuitive and swift; in most cases, there were no appeals or pardons. They had the poetry of myth and music always about them, in the foreground or background of their deeds.

Neither the gaucho nor the *llanero* was intelligible without his *vihuela* or his *cuatro*—musical instruments similar to the guitar. The chronicle of exploits was kept by the improvised ballad and the guitar. Poetry and happenstance were fused by music and the hero lived on in popular legend. The popular ballad has always been one of the bonds between the hero and his people in the

Latin lands. In Spain, it is the *romance*; in Mexico, the *corrido*; only the accent and the narration vary, the idea remains the same.

If *machismo* is the nuclear attribute of the Latin American hero, we see clearly enough how this fundamental masculinity leads to a father image and the concomitant ties that exist between a father and his lesser, "minor" relatives. We speak, for instance, of *personalismo* as the overriding influence in politics—that is, the excessive influence of one man in the affairs of the state and a consequent dependence on him that is almost total. Thus, we have nepotism on a grand scale and untrained bureaucracy of gigantic proportions, because the hero is the commanding figure in any political drama. Socially, the bonds to the *macho* hero intertwine, producing a congeries of sentiments and obligations. The structure evolves into patriarchy, with feudalistic forms of living, such as the *ingenio* (sugar plantation), the hacienda, and, in Brazil, the fazenda. The structure over which the patriarch presides is stately, baronial, and to a decreasing degree in our modern world, autarchic. This is the significance of the exodus of the peasant from his rural milieu to the city. The leveling doctrines of the twentieth century and the march of technological refinements have weakened the grip of the patriarch on his dependents.

Two other facts of Latin American society reveal this retrogression from admiration of the *macho* hero to dependence on the father image, the patriarchal arrangement of life. One is the *patrón* system common throughout the continent and which we might well have treated as a part of the colonial aspects of the nineteenth-century legacy. No aspect of social endeavor is untouched by the *patrón* system: it is root and branch of the daily life of the Latin American. While it provides continuity for those who are variously attached to the *patrón*, it nevertheless represents an obstacle in the path of social development as we understand it today. It is the antithesis of economic liberalism and democratic guarantees as they have evolved in most countries of the Western world. It is a medieval outpost in the modern world: It is secure, but it is also stifling.

Similarly, and on a more intimate level, the *macho* hero is closely related to his followers by the bonds of *padrinazgo*. By this system he is involved in an ineffable series of connections ranging from actual godfather (which the word *padrino* literally means) to the more intangible ones of friend and sponsor. It is a word betokening intimacy and confidence, while its flexible application covers a wide range of sense and sinning.

We in the United States have never really understood this kind of leader or his revolutions. We simply are not sympathetic to them over a long period of time. Our history and our daily experience have conditioned us to expect other things. Our shock is greater than our admiration, for example, when we see blatant virility displayed in the *macho* hero. We are nonplused by gesture and deed if openly done. We desire more restraint in our political leaders, perhaps from our notions of respectable conformity or from a different standard of ethics and aesthetics. We have not yet grown used to the idea that Fidel Castro should continue to dress in his olive-drab uniform or wear a beard. We find his improvisation in government to be total disorganization and utter administrative chaos. His long speeches on television are frequent spates of verbose harangues. For a time we stand his outfit and behavior, but then it becomes suspect and finally disreputable.

By recourse to our comfortable prejudices and platitudes, we have failed to grasp much of the significance of what is going on in Cuba. We overlook the appeal Fidel still retains in Cuba and much of Latin America, and we do not see him as a product of the conflict between the nineteenth-century legacy and the emerging revolutionary mystique.

The uniqueness of the Cuban Revolution has been due to the "genial madness" of Fidel Castro—or to his *maña* and *malicia*, to use Spanish terms. He is the word and soul of the Cuban Revolution; he is its symbol of continuity, its hero, its messiah, and its absolute ruler. To be sure, his range of independent action is now limited because he is so committed to the Communist scheme of things. But as long as he remains the focus of revolutionary activity, the revolution keeps its basic identity as something begun before the Soviets came with aid and alliances or the United States with its invasion forces. Castro, as hero, is the continuum of the Cuban Revolution. His presence confirms the many links it will always have with the revolutionary mystique in Latin America. He alone arouses support for the Cuban experiment in Communism as a form of revolutionary change.

There is no one in Cuba who can replace Fidel Castro. His claim, like no one else's, to being the *jefe máximo* is absolute and inalienable. Eliminate him and you will have removed the native identity of his undertaking, his creation, and, in a way, his child. Raúl Castro, his brother; Ernesto Guevara, the Argentine revolutionary and Marxist mentor to Fidel; and Carlos Rafael Rodríguez, head of the agrarian reform institute (INRA), could never replace Fidel, for none of them can truly play the role of the *macho* hero. None of them is endowed with the ineffable and vital qualities of manhood that Fidel radiates.

iv

Finally, the Latin American world is shot through with the conflict between the dream of democracy and the practice of tyranny. The search for democracy, perhaps in too pristine and abstract a form, has been a never-ending chase after the will-o'-the-wisp. The Latin Americans have sought after it too much with their quixotic vision of the world and have not governed their pursuit enough by the lessons of experience. Democracy has all too often meant creating perfect forms in constitutions, proclamations, charters, and the like, while the daily functioning of democratic practice has been inadequate or lacking. This is not to say that the individual is totally without safeguards or that there is no relief from systematic oppression. Rather, the individual finds his guarantees in recourse to his protector (*padrino*), his boss or employer (*patrón*), or his political leader (*jefe*), and thus becomes a *fidelista, peronista, batistiano, varguista*, or, if the political party is absolute, as in Mexico, a *priísta*. This personal allegiance rewards the individual with status and varying degrees of security. The political party, if it exists, is an appendage of the leader and all its members are his minions. This is the case in Cuba, where, whatever monolithic party ultimately emerges, it will definitely be *fidelista* in cast and tone.

Political democracy has never meant in Latin America that interplay of tradition and compromise it has in the Anglo-Saxon lands. Tradition and institutions have always been the governing factors of our political contests. We do not, for example, effect change outside the extant political, social, and economic order. Our changes tend to be palliative. Our job as reformers, we think, is to correct as best we can the ills and excesses of our system rather than uproot the system itself and begin anew. We say we believe in evolution and not revolution, and by saying this we reveal our firm commitment to consensus by compromise. We will live within our institutions and by our traditions, and change and progress and stability will follow naturally: We will follow the rules of the game and settle the dispute by the art of fair play.

Our political tradition is much more that of the English trimmer than of the French Jacobin. We prefer compromise to revolution even in our world where the winds of revolutionary change blow so strong. Our solution to social injustice was fairly summed up in President Kennedy's program of the Alliance for Progress: change by evolution, material progress through self-help and cooperation, individual freedoms guaranteed by institutional permanence. The Communist solution is too extreme and too inappropriate to our ways and development. The Latin American revolutionary mystique is too volatile to be compressed into a system of progressive change. Withal, the Alliance for Progress stands as the trimmer's—the com-promiser's—answer to the need for change. Change, yes, but not violent change. Evolution and not revolution, for the institutions of compromise are not to be overturned by intransigence.

Tradition, institutional permanence, and the trimmer's craft of compromise all allow a free range of open political dissent. The sponsors of disagreement find diverse outlets of expression and their opposition is kept before the public conscience. Dissent and opposition form the integral part of our political dialogue. In England, there is the Queen's loyal opposition, and in the United States, recent Presidents have given members of the opposing party influential cabinet posts and have worked cheek by jowl with their opponents in Congress. Our code, again, is that of the trimmer: We think not of what we must sacrifice but of what we can salvage. The give and take of majority assent and minority dissent and the art of compromise are the keystones of our politics of evolution.

In Latin America, however, compromise as a political craft has little prestige and scant effectiveness. Indeed, compromise has clearly derogatory overtones. The verb *transigir*, broadly meaning "to compromise," implies giving in, in a prejudicial sense. A man gives up rather than gives in; he loses, surrenders, and sacrifices, and thereby his honor or strength or manhood is impugned. If a man appeals to compromise, it is because he no longer has the necessary strength. His recourse to conciliation is taken as proof of his weakness. Before the fall of the Díaz regime in Mexico, the Limantour negotiations with the rebellious *maderista* faction served only to indicate Don Porfirio no longer had the real power and that was why he sought a *détente*. The negotiations were confirmatory evidence of the *ancien régime's* decay and weakness.

If compromise is held in disrepute, then dissent is almost completely disallowed. In Latin America, the dissenter is forced to play one of three possible roles: that of the rebel, the apostate, or the exile. He can, at different times, play all these parts. But, in his own country, if he dissents and forms an opposition group, his acts are not the signs of social criticism; they are a direct challenge to the power of the "in group" and a threat to its established position in the society. Dissent is equated with disruption of the existing order of things. The dissenter in Latin America is always the enemy, and as such he must be eliminated from the political scene, muzzled as a spokesman of the potential opposition, or neutralized by exile. The trimmer, with his skills of compromise, has no place in the Latin American political game, where the rules are few and the political institutions brittle. The dissenter is always the Jacobin and the iconoclast.

We believe, on the other hand, that the degree of dissent allowed is the final measure of true democratic practice. We see that, where dissent is suppressed, it must inevitably burst forth as rebellion. This has been the political history of Latin America, in the large, since the Wars of Independence. Rebellion and anarchy have been the means of change and the alternatives to absolutism and despotic rule. The most recognizable figure on the Latin American political stage is, after all, the dissenter as the errant exile. His purpose may only be to reform; but to effect change at all, he must cause revolution. He has no recourse but to violence, for he has no access to public debate and, therefore, no chance of adjustment by compromise.

Much has been said recently of a swelling tide of democratic revolution sweeping across the entire Latin American continent.

Democracy has suddenly come to full maturity or at least is on the threshold of doing so, we are informed in newspaper and scholarly journal alike. There is some evidence to support this view. From 1948 onward, there has been a general movement against the old forms of government, dictatorial *caudillismo*, and against one of its apparent concomittants, the social injustice of acute, widespread poverty. The tyrants are passing away and the middle class is on the rise. The men born in this century are now coming to power for the first time. Elections have been held with remarkably little agitation or loss of life, and, with some exceptions, the results of the balloting have been adhered to by the power groups. Trujillo was assassinated and his cabal was ousted after more than thirty years of progress and corruption. Following clean, orderly elections, Juan Bosch became the new president. He was liberal, literate, a democrat, nationalistic, yet cooperative with the United States—and he soon fell, a victim of the traditional order. Rómulo Betancourt will be the first Venezuelan president to complete his full term in office without being overturned by barracks revolt since the country won its independence in the last century. This is part of the proof offered up as valid testimony that democracy has finally replaced, or is about to replace, the ways of rigid authoritarian rule.

But is it really so? The answer, I fear, must be negative, even though we are zealots—in the trimmer's sense—for spreading the wise practices of democracy abroad. Democracy does not leap contagiously, like the Asian flu, from border to border. It does not, in the long run, inflame men's hearts. Its effects are slow in showing themselves, for democracy is meaningless away from the halls of tradition and without the tones of compromise. It is true that, since 1948, the year José Figueres successfully opposed a military uprising and initiated a period of reform for Costa Rica, there has been a turning away from the selfish practices of a benighted oligarchy supporting an antediluvian dictator. The old pillars of continuity, the army, the oligarchs in land, natural resources, and industry, the Church, and the bureaucratic branches of the government, have been shorn of much of their respectability and have had to resist increasingly effective attacks from more liberal sectors. Most governments now pay more than lip service to the hackneyed phrases of social justice. The revolutionary mystique, Castro, Communism, the affluence and influence of the West, and the egalitarianism of the Christian ethic have been the leaven for this recent period of change and reform.

Change will come unavoidably to all the Latin American countries, for ours is the century of change *par excellence*. The question is how, when, and under what guise it will come. I would suggest, however, that it is grossly inaccurate to interpret forces of change, rife in our times everywhere, as certain proof of a process of democratic evolution afoot in Latin America. And this is not merely the last chant of the pessimist before his jeremiads are overwhelmed by a triumphant army of optimists. The cant of optimism fills our ears and we are made giddy by the do-gooder's hyperbole. We must see the world for what it is and not believe it to be what we would have it.

Latin American revolutions have been written by the exiles who finally end up leading them. The dissenter goes into the no man's land of exile to finally return to his fatherland and overthrow the *caudillo* or dictator he and his faction oppose. Abroad, he obtains aid and exhorts his compatriots to join his cause. Bolívar was at different times in exile and, in fact, during his stay in Jamaica, he wrote what is probably his most durable and penetrating political comment on Latin America. Juan Montalvo, the Ecuadorian writer of the nineteenth century, wrote from exile after García Moreno's assassination, that "my pen has killed him." José Martí, the Cuban patriot, spent more than fifteen years in the peripatetic school of exile, until finally his eloquence and energy ignited the flame of Cuban independence. Haya de la Torre has spent most of his life in exile and has written most of his *aprista* tracts away from Peru. Fidel Castro rose to his present position as *jefe máximo*, completing the circle of dissent possible in Latin America: the open dissenter who is imprisoned, granted an amnesty, escapes into exile in which he gathers hard and fast partisans, and returns as the rebel, ending as the absolute leader who, in his turn, cannot tolerate dissent.

The contrast between the Anglo-American system of politics and the Latin American should by now be fairly clear. In the former, dissent is tolerated and compromise promoted by tradition and institutions. In the latter, dissent has no real function and serves only as the road to exile and rebellion. We have cited the example of the dissenter as the wandering exile and his later return as the rebel. Now, we must see how dissent is impossible within these societies because of either a policy of government repression or the lack of viable institutional outlets.

Continuous criticism of a regime in power has no forums in which it can be expressed. The press, the radio and television, and journals and periodicals of all sorts are kept under the watchful eye of censorship, or their cooperation is obtained through bribery or coercion. The government tries, first of all, to establish a rapport with its would-be critics and keep its pressure unseen, effective, but always in the wings. Failing this, it uses more direct means of regulating opinion and criticism: The newspaper vendors' union will be an adjunct of the Labor Ministry; the government will have a monopoly on newsprint or will publish its own newspaper expressing the "official lines," that is, the safe, correct, and discreet pros and cons of any situation; or publishing and broadcasting licenses can be extended or terminated at the government's pleasure. In extreme cases, the government can arbitrarily declare a national emergency, impose a state of siege, and partially or totally suspend all constitutional guarantees. If the dissenter and his partisans persist and are clever, the government will resort to the use of open force: torture, incrimination, defamation, threats upon the lives of members of the family, and assassination. At any time the government can arouse apparent support for any or all of these steps by contriving a mass rally of 50,000 or 100,000 of its "loyal" followers. The mass of workers and party members gathers in the public square in the center of the city and with delirious cries reaffirms the words and actions of its leader. The effect is to drown out dissent and give the appearance of justice or the necessity of arbitrary measures. If the dissenter escapes into exile and represents an actual danger to the government, it can set in motion its international underground to kidnap or kill him. This was the fate of Jesús de Galíndez, whose book, *The Era of Trujillo*, was a scholarly exposé of the corruption and criminal excesses of that regime.[13]

Perhaps the most interesting illustration of a governmental policy repressing dissent is that which took place at the time of Perón's rule in Argentina. The consistent direction of his policy was to align all the powerful sectors of Argentine society behind his government, creating a monolithic structure with no real opposition. A primary target, naturally, was the free press and its docile acquiescence in all of the government's undertakings. *La Prensa*, venerable and internationally respected, sought to maintain its tradition as an independent critic of both Argentine society and government. The issue, therefore, between Perón's regime and the functioning of the free press came to a head in his struggle with *La Prensa*.

In 1949, the law of *desacato* (disrespect), passed in Congress on Perón's orders, made criticism of any public official tantamount to a penal offense. The government, naturally enough, was the sole judge of the point at which "constructive" criticism ended and vicious slander began. The policy of harassment continued until late 1950, when *La Prensa's* owner and editor, Alberto Gainza Paz, was indicted for "crimes against the safety of the state," and the paper was shut down for eight months. In March, 1951, publication of *La Prensa* was resumed, but this time under the vigilant censorship of the General Confederation of Labor and with Gainza Paz in exile. Until Perón's fall in 1955, there were no further instances of *desacato* by the "free" press.

If the dissenter is not forced into exile or killed, he may be branded as an apostate from official policy and imprisoned. The most recent instance of this form of repression is to be seen in Cuba in the "trial" of Major Huber Matos. Matos, one of the early supporters of Castro's revolution and military commander of the province of Camagüey, spoke out in 1959 against Communist influence in the rebel army, firmly stating his anti-Communist views and pleading with Fidel to put a stop to the Communist encroachment on the Twenty-sixth of July Party. Castro moved swiftly and with lethal cunning against Matos, whose statements he considered heretical. At Matos' trial in December, 1959, Castro, acting as the chief accuser—the chief inquisitor, if you will—branded Matos a traitor to the revolution and an enemy of the state. The court found, on the basis of Castro's "evidence," that Matos had, indeed, sold out to the antirevolutionaries and espoused imperialist doctrines. The court decision, based upon proof of treason, sentenced Matos to thirty years' imprisonment. In Castro's Cuba, where by late 1959 the press had been muzzled, there could be no criticism, let alone dissent. Matos, by his protest again Communist influence, showed his apostasy and his potential as a rebel. The wonder is that, being convicted of treason, he was not instantly executed.

There are notable exceptions, encouraging ones, where dissent is found and works its healing effect throughout society. Yet, even in these instances the dissenter's position as a free critic is not deeply rooted in traditional practice. He is not ensured by permanent institutions. Perhaps it is nearer the truth to say that in those countries there has been less repression than elsewhere.

Chile has what is generally considered a democratic way of life; dissent is allowed and, in its multiparty Congress, debate is not automatically ended when it becomes severe in its criticism of the government. But Chile is not without significant dictatorial experience in this century and the last. Diego Portales, in the 1830's, by his autocratic rule supported the traditional oligarchy of the army, the Church, the great landholders, and the emerging class of merchants and traders. He imposed stability, brought about conditions of prosperity mostly favorable to the classes of privilege, and consistently repressed the outcries of the *pipiolos*, his liberal, popular antagonists. Again, from 1925 to 1931, Chile felt the sway of autocratic rule under the regime of Carlos Ibáñez. Dissent was choked off by government policy, but the wave of prosperity of the 1920's sustained the entrenched oligarchy and lent some justification to Ibáñez' dictatorship of "order and progress." Portales and Ibáñez, even if exceptions to the rule of democracy in Chile, cannot be discounted as uncharacteristic of Chilean politics. Rather, they are symptomatic of what can and may happen. Debate exists in the Congress, but dissent is not ensured by daily practice and inviolable tradition.

There are other examples that could be used to demonstrate that a degree of dissent is allowed in other countries. There are some cases that would indicate an evolution toward a party system with similarities to the Anglo-American or European models. The dream of democracy is frustrated by the practice of tyranny. Compromise and political expedience—the trimmer's tools—are shunned as base or hypocritical. Democracy is depicted in the absolute terms of the Jacobin's lexicon. Liberty and freedom, he says, cannot be compromised. They must be total. The Latin American *homo politicus* lives in a world in which he must choose between one of two extreme alternatives. He must admit total allegiance to the leader and complete adherence to his system, or he must defy both and dedicate himself to their overthrow. His is a Hobson's choice. He will have to choose conspiracy and revolution to express his dissent. The channels of compromise have been blocked by institutional intransigence: The Latin American dissenter, inevitably, will be the apostate, the exile, or the rebel.

2

Crosscurrents in New World History

RICHARD M. MORSE

Anyone who follows currents of thought in Latin America cannot fail to notice the recent concern of many philosophers and historians with the search for an "ontology" of the Americas. By this term is intended not merely an equivalent for "national character" but a more cosmic notion of the historic destiny of the Americas in the Western or even the entire world. A Spanish and a Mexican writer have both observed that, after the eighteenth century, Spanish thought turned upon the past and inward upon itself in a search for the causes of Spanish decadence and for the still-vital elements of Spanish life. Spanish Americans, on the other hand, as soon as they had justified their newly won independence, were led to investigate what meaning "America" was to hold for them, not as a tradition, but as a future to be achieved. If elegy and criticism have characterized Spanish thought, planning and utopianism have characterized that of Spanish America.[1]

Another American nation, the United States, has been similarly preoccupied with its destiny. During the past century and a half this destiny has turned out to be largely a "manifest" one, running in vigorous phases from the winning of the Western Plains to the leading of the Western world. In contrast, Spanish America was mostly "won," it might be said, by the *conquistadores* in the sixteenth century. Since that time, there have been surprisingly few shifts in the geographic deployment of its people, if one excepts the mid-nineteenth-century surge of growth in the Platine region of Argentina and Uruguay. Since that time also, Spanish American history has offered slender nourishment for generous schemes of manifest destiny, such as Simón Bolívar's short-lived dream of a confederation of American states. Lacking the wherewithal for decisive political and economic projection in world affairs, Latin America has been forced to live out an "unmanifest destiny." It is this that turns its thinkers to contemplate destinies more subtle or more transcendental than are customarily present in the intellectual, and particularly the historiographical, tradition of the United States.

An exceptional instance of this concern is afforded by the book *Rendición de espíritu* by Juan Larrea, a Spaniard living in Mexico.[2] Larrea's thesis is shot through with a symbolism that verges, indeed trespasses, upon the mystical, and only a fragmentary recapitulation of it will be attempted here. The author defines an axis comprising three historic centers for religious pilgrimage: Jerusalem to the east, on the edge of Asia, representing the past and the origin of the Christian world; Rome in the center, mistress of Europe and the present; Santiago de Compostela to the west, looking toward America and the future. Each is built on a tomb—those of Christ, St. Peter, and St. James—and each harbors its own version of resurrection. Santiago is on Cape Finisterre, "end of the land," and Compostela can be read as Campo de la Estrella, "field of the star" —that is, the sky. Thus, Santiago, located on the westernmost headland of Europe, becomes the Holy Ghost in a trinitarian analogy that points toward a promised kingdom of God, a New World. The *non plus ultra* of the pillars of Hercules becomes the *plus ultra* on the blazon of the Spanish kings. The discoverer of America is one whose name, Cristoforo Colombo, means "bearer of the spirit of Christ" and whose saint's day is that of St. James the Apostle. In the New World of peace, the antinomies of the Old are resolved. And we learn that the letters of Roma, city of Caesar and a word meaning "force," spell "amor" when reversed, and that the Ebro, that eminently Spanish river, becomes in inversion the universal "orbe."

Only slightly less apocalyptic, but rather more accessible to orthodox historians, is the Mexican Edmundo O'Gorman.[3] O'Gorman's thesis is, quite simply, that America was not "discovered." It was "invented." For him, "discovery" implies the accidental stumbling upon something that is fully constituted and definable—something, in the Hegelian phrase, that is a "thing in itself." There was in 1492, however, no traditional knowledge and moral image of America as there was for the old continents of Europe, Asia, and Africa. For the moment, the only meaning to America was its newness and marginality. The sense of America was its lack of sense. Its only history was possibility. The *idea* of America had to be made up, a process that involved inventive accommodation, or continuing dialectic, between ancient notions of man and society and the unfolding experiences of the New World.

On the eve of the "discovery" of America (what else can we call it?), the mind-set of Europeans was provincial and Europocentric, although the culture they shared was, by virtue of its Christian and rationalist components, a universalistic one. On breathing its culture into the clay of America, Europe fulfilled its universalizing mission but, at the same time, touched off what O'Gorman calls its own "ontological disintegration." The "closed provincialism" of the mother continent could no longer "conceive of the universal as its private patrimony." The meaning of America, then, our writer concludes, is that it is "the instance which, in the heart of Western Culture, made possible the extension of the image of the world to the whole Earth and of the concept of universal history to all humanity."[4]

These two apocalyptic visions of New World history are cited here more for perspective than for content. That perspective is a view of the Americas as a totality. The modern Latin American intellectual is able—as many of his nineteenth-century predecessors were not—to apprehend a destiny common to the Americas, a destiny in which the share of the United States, its cultural and spiritual share, is relatively modest. This leads one to ask how many historians of the United States have perceived their country as one among a multiplicity of New World experiments to the extent that such a view informs the history they write. How many of them, in the last analysis, see the United States, or America as we immodestly call our country, as the big show, and the twenty other American nations as misguided endeavors that never took wing? In the field of European history, we are quick to criticize a theory of city growth or a theory of the Renaissance that is based upon a single national experience. Yet how many of our historians—in their studies of settlement and the frontier, of land systems and urban growth, of political leadership and economic interest groups, of cultural expression and intellectual trends—how many have drawn upon the rich comparative experience, perhaps the more varied and dramatic experience, of Latin America? The answer may be left to a political scientist who has written: "The truth is, the American historian at practically every stage has functioned quite inside the nation: he has tended to be an erudite reflection of the limited social perspectives of the average American himself."[5]

The apocalyptic vision shared by some contemporary Latin Americans is not without interest for our own historians, for it contains elements of the utopianism that, from the start, gave a distinctive cast to the settlement and history of the New World. The story of utopianism in the United States appears to have been well studied, particularly for the nineteenth century, as it is reflected in the schemes of crusaders, in collective-farming experiments, or in popular myths of the frontier. Most modern historians seem able to prove that every Brook Farm became an island of social disorder, and any given sector of the frontier the log-cabin Levittown of an unscrupulous real estate promoter. But many of these same scholars acquiesce in a more sanguine view of our country's achievement as a whole and harbor a cautious sympathy for the "great American dream." One even wonders if this journalistic toughness with detail and softness before the great vistas is a national culture trait that binds upon them.

There is one United States historian who should not be left out of account, for he attempted a bold, transnational view of frontier civilizations. Having studied our nation's westward march with understanding and zest, Walter P. Webb turned to a frontier far larger than the Great Plains that spans the two American continents, South Africa, Australia, and New Zealand. It was natural to expect that his perspectives would deepen and his conclusions become refined. One is therefore surprised to discover that scarcely more than one page of *The Great Frontier* is devoted to Latin America and even less to Canada, Africa, and Australia. The following sentences from the page on Latin America set forth boldly and without the usual camouflage a stereotype that inhibits

our historians from locating the modest British colonies within
the broad panorama of the settlement of America. Walter Webb
writes:

> The process of institutional disintegration which went on in the
> north until the individual remained in clear relief, free to rebuild his
> institutions from the beginning, did not take place to any such ex-
> tent in the southern continent and Mexico. . . . It is clear that if
> democracy . . . came to such a society, it would have to come in
> spite of the prevailing church and not because of it. . . . As it is,
> the dominant institution is an imported one, directed from without,
> one which the frontier with all of its abrasiveness would not wear
> out nor much alter. This rigidity and stability of the Catholic
> Church has done more to frustrate the atomizing influence of the
> frontier than any other single factor operating in the New World.[6]

Others who contemplate Latin America from afar might stress its
Iberian political and mercantilist heritage, rather than the ecclesiastical one, as the deterrent to "institutional disintegration" and
egalitarian democracy. But whichever the emphasis, it seems safe
to say that within much of United States historiography dwells the
tacit premise that Latin America is an archaic extension of southern Europe that has never booked passage on the great American
dreamboat. For the moment, this premise concerns us more than
the inaccurate institutional description in the passage cited.

Insofar as nations ever live out their dreams, the United States
has perhaps done so in achieving its "American way of life." But
those who achieve dreams are customarily impatient with the
dreams of others, whether larger dreams, smaller, or merely different. Most of all will they be impatient with those whose dreams
are unfulfilled. They congratulate results and no longer thrill to
aspiration. They scarcely see that their own fulfillment has meant
sacrifice because it has meant choice. Their gaze fixed on achievement, they become less sensitive to the quality of dreams and to
the sea changes of history, of institutions, and of the soul itself.

The two apocalyptic views from modern Latin America summarized above are latter-day versions of a Catholic millennialist
faith that supplied much of the impetus for the conquest of
America. This millennialism gushed forth from the Middle Ages,
and the thousand utopian schemes for which the New World was

a theater—even the later Protestant or socialist versions—stand clearly in its trajectory. The astounding conquest and settlement of Middle and South America within a few short decades can scarcely be understood without reference to the vision of the *plus ultra* of which Juan Larrea writes. John L. Phelan has shown that apocalyptic mysticism, tinged with a Joachimite spirit, was a powerful emphasis on Spanish politico-ecclesiastical theory, as were Roman and canon law and Aristotelian logic and Italian humanism. The apostolic calling of the Franciscan missionaries, the Mosaic role that their historian Mendieta ascribed to Cortés, the messianic dreams that animated Columbus himself, all instanced a millennial vision.[7]

Of special interest is the work of Don Vasco de Quiroga, sixteenth-century bishop of Michoacán, whose "hospitals" for the Indians of Mexico were closely modeled upon the rules set forth for his Utopia by Thomas More. Curiously enough, Don Vasco's communities answer more nearly to our modern notion of a utopia than did More's original version. As Jack Hexter has pointed out, the citizens of More's Utopia were "natural" men, but not "unfallen" ones. His point of departure was social criticism, not idealistic scheming. The sinful propensities of men were clearly present to him in his Old World wisdom. His imaginary society enjoyed no automatic mechanisms and had no eschatological significance.[8] For Don Vasco, however, the appeal of the Indians lies not merely in the opportunity they present for redesigning the anachronistic social institutions of Europe. For they are in themselves "people so gentle, so new, so smooth and of such soft wax that one can do with them what one wishes." "Not in vain," he continues, "but with much cause and reason is this called the New World, not because it was newly discovered, but because its people and nearly all else are as in that first and golden age."[9]

After a nineteenth-century interlude of positivism and Spencerian pessimism, many Latin American thinkers and historians have reaffirmed both the Christian and the Indianist components of their New World tradition. In a sense, of course, these two components cannot wholly be brought to terms. The archaeologist's difficulty in fitting the Mayan calendar to Western reckoning symbolizes all that was gratuitous in the impingement of Europe upon pre-Columbian America. There was no accommodation possible between the cyclical time of the Indian, sprung from the timelessness of the vast continents in which he lived, and the purposeful, unilinear time of the conqueror. This original incongruity is to the present day more profusely and tangibly manifested in the world of the Latin American historian than in our own. His imagination thus enjoys certain advantages once he discards the neat paradigms of national development that have flowed so easily from European pens, and gropes to define the native cast and destiny of his country. America was from the start a counterpoint between history and nonhistory, civilization and primitiveness, old wisdom and fresh experience—and it has always been difficult for the American mind-set to acquiesce in age-old processes of organic growth.

Millennialist history is congenial to a New World setting. It looks easily toward fulfillment of a destiny and conveys little of the toughness of historical process and dialectic. It embodies the sense that mere time has less efficacy here than in the Old World. By no means, however, does millennialism give a dominant cast to Latin American historiography. It is perhaps significant that of the two authors mentioned, one is a Mexican and the other wrote with special reference to Mexico. The high Mexican plateau has always been conducive to the apocalyptic vision, a circumstance, some would say, traceable to the days of the Aztecs, whose warlike but precarious political organization was reinforced by a fierce religious imagination. Modern observers as dissimilar as D. H. Lawrence and F. S. C. Northrop have been allured by the revelatory promise of Mexican life.

Another significant strain of Latin American history-writing turns us from a grand design of the Americas to the intimate view of society, habits, and attitudes as they develop and change within a New World setting. For such a view it is fitting that we turn to the historians of Brazil.

Brazil has had a more quiet history than Mexico and most of Spanish America. Its colonization was dispersive and "gangliated," and was left, in fact if not in theory, more largely to private initiative. Dominant urban centers of bureaucracy and ceremony were slow to develop. Partly from mercantilist design and partly for lack of resources, Portugal virtually denied to Brazil the elements of a citified, intellectual civilization. During much of the country's history, the primary ties of family and locality have overshadowed secondary ones of bureaucratic affiliation. The local institutions of Portuguese America developed a kind of pliant, vegetative strength. It has been said that "this society was the opposite of Spanish colonial society: more familialistic than stratified, more paternalistic than arrogant, more democratic than feudal."[10]

Millennialist dreams hover in the Brazilian, as in the Portuguese, soul, but often as a kind of brooding nostalgia. The classic form is *Sebastianismo*, the yearning for the return of the lost king, Dom Sebastião. The millennialist sects that flash into being like heat lightning in the arid Brazilian backlands one can attribute to transitory local pressures and to accidents of charismatic leadership.

Sérgio Buarque de Holanda, who has produced the most detailed and perceptive account of millennialism in Brazil, acknowledges in his *Vision of Paradise, the Edenic Motives in the Discovery and Conquest of Brazil* that

> . . . the whole legendary world born in the Spanish conquests which evokes El Dorados, amazons, mountains of silver, magic lakes, fountains of youth, tends to thin out, to lose color, or to grow dim as soon as it penetrates Portuguese America. Even the supernatural motives of pious origin, long established in the Peninsula, seem to die away in Brazil, and in any case they play a less important role in territorial conquest.[11]

Elsewhere, this same scholar advances the theory of the "cordial man" to explain certain aspects of Brazilian society and its historical development as a function of subtle psychological changes wrought in the New World environment. Brazilian "cordiality" is defined as the tendency to reduce institutions, ideas, and emotions to intimate and manageable terms. The Brazilian is averse to social ritual and to crusading religious zeal. It is no wonder that "our Republic was proclaimed by the positivists, and that our Independence was the work of freemasons."

> The intimate life of the Brazilian is neither coherent nor disciplined enough to involve and dominate his whole personality, integrating it, as a single unit, into the social structure. He is therefore free to

give himself up to the entire range of ideas, gestures and forms which he encounters, frequently assimilating them on the spot.[12]

If one were to pick a folk hero for Brazil, he would be a far cry from the apocalyptic god Quetzalcoatl, the great plumed serpent of Mexico. Most probably it would be Macunaíma, the amoral hero of a folk novel written a generation ago by Mário de Andrade, a composite creature of Brazil's three ethnic cultures (African, European, and Indian) who vagabonded through his vast country in a composite of historical time enjoying a composite of erotic adventures and who finally, bored with the suffering of the earth, went to wander, solitary, in an even vaster sky as one of its constellations of stars.

It is inevitable that a discussion of modern Brazilian historians center upon Gilberto Freyre, who has written a lengthy trilogy to present a socio-psychological history of Brazil from colonization to the early twentieth century. The series is called *Introduction to the History of Patriarchal Society in Brazil*. Each book bears a contrapuntal title. The first, *The Masters and the Slaves* (*Casa grande e senzala*),[13] deals with the formation of rural Brazilian society in the colonial period. The second, *The Mansions and the Shanties* (*Sobrados e mucambos*),[14] deals with the nineteenth century and with the ascendancy of what Freyre calls the semipatriarchalism of the city over the patriarchalism of the rural domain. The most recent book portrays the disintegration of both the rural and the urban patriarchy after the abolition of slavery and of the monarchy. Significantly, the title lacks the particularity of the other two. It is simply the positivist motto of the Brazilian republic, *Order and Progress*.

There is much in Freyre's work to suggest that his fascination with the themes of patriarchal authority and miscegenation carries intense personal meaning. Referring at one point to the oral testimony of some respondents born in the last century, he even speaks of the social scientist becoming a father confessor, as though the patriarchal past held for him some dark and enthralling secret.[15] Doubtless the psychoanalytic interpretation of Freyre's work will have a still broader base when he publishes his promised *Jazigos e covas rasas*, or *Fancy and Plain Graves*, a study of burial

practices in patriarchal Brazil.[16] Without pressing such an interpretation, we may say that, although Freyre's sensitivity to the details
and the texture of Brazilian life has developed at the expense of
theoretical precision and stylistic economy, he is today a foremost
historian of the Americas. Two aspects of his work are of special
interest here.

First, it is apparent that the master image in Freyre's history is
that of Brazil as a great manifold, or continuum, within which a
number of muted antagonisms are brought into a slowly evolving
balance. Some of these antagonisms are suggested by the contrapuntal titles of Freyre's books. But they would include a broad
range of tensions, some of them multiple ones, of the geographical,
ethnic, social, political, economic, and temporal orders. Brazil,
Freyre claims, is the only large-scale success of European colonization in the tropics. It is the most American of the American
countries, for it is the one in which the original cultural ingredients
—European, African, and Indian—have most fully achieved creative interaction. The intricate pluralism of Brazilian life and society, within a pervasive setting of plastic and rather passive unity,
makes of the nation a kind of "tropical China."

If this is the vision, what of the eye that sees it? As might be
expected, the strong point of Freyre's history is not causal explanation and systematic analysis of the growth and interplay of
institutions. He writes in the baroque, not the classical, manner.
In speaking of methodology, he stresses the importance of em-
pathy, the apprehension of the intimate thoughts and promptings
of a society. He writes what he and others have called a "Prous-
tian sociology," and criticizes the externality and alleged objectivity
of the Durkheimian tradition. He waits to catch the subject in un-
guarded moments, rather than attempting to endow what is more
readily apparent with order and structure.[17]

One of the most insistent themes in Freyre's writing is miscegenation in Brazil and the achievement of a society relatively free of
racial hostility. This vision of Luso-tropical democracy might seem
to have roots in millennialism. Perhaps, however, it has another
source (aside from a partly secure one in the facts themselves)—
namely, Freyre's close emotional identification with his society,
which leaves in his books many traces of personal introspection

and of the self-congratulatory attitude that is so frequently a by-product of self-analysis. The quest for self-identity through a quest for historical identity, and the quest for historical identity through self-identity, is a hallmark of New World historiography. It is a quest taken up as soon as the millennialist vision falters, as soon as it becomes clear that the American nations are not living out an Old World destiny that they have appropriated or that has been thrust upon them. At this point occurs the moment of historical introspection, the surveying of native grounds, and the alertness to what may be called—in both literal and figurative senses—the sea changes of New World life.

Although introspective historiography makes up for some of the omissions of the millennialist brand, there is one point at which it, too, is wanting. For the historian who, like Freyre, is concerned with habits and customs rather than institutions, with attitudes rather than ideas, with the tone and the feel of a society rather than with the mesh and the action of its parts—however legitimate and fascinating this concern may be—will, like the millennialist, fail to set forth the morphology of institutions or to convey the sense of irreversible historical dialectic. Freyre's long trilogy, for example, is less an examination of institutional change and innova-tion than the sensitive description of a set of psycho-social atti-tudes that are said to hover in Brazilian life long after the condi-tions that gave rise to them have been superseded. So important to Freyre are attitude and impression, and so collapsible is his time sense, that the chance observation of a French or an English visitor to Brazil a century ago has immediate relevance to his claims for the social achievements of modern Brazil.

If we turn for comparison to the literature on the role of the frontier in United States history, we observe that frequently its stress is not upon the morphology of institutions but upon identifi-cation of a frame of mind—experimental, optimistic, democratic—that frontier life is said to have produced, giving a dominant cast to the whole of our country's history. One refinement of this theory in effect brackets the question as to what the frontier was or did, and turns to examine the several shapes of the myth or image of the frontier in men's minds. It would not be surprising to learn that by now a graduate student is somewhere digging into such a topic as "Attitudes of American Historians Toward Attitudes of the American People Toward the American Frontier."

This phenomenon, which we might call attitudinal pyramidization, is characteristic of a New World culture in which the historian finds himself without clear grounds whereon to take a stance. In the face of a social structure either loosely or somewhat arbitrarily defined, and having no recourse to elaborated social philosophies of native inspiration, he will ever be on the alert for the chance attitude or impression that might be erected into an informed and stable vantage point. Hence, the frequency in New World historical literature of scissors-and-paste studies bearing such titles as "New England as Seen by Old Englanders," "The Old South as Seen by Northern Visitors," "Brazil as Seen by Englishmen," "Central America as Seen by Yankee Travelers." It is a literature of great interest to scholars who have learned to see *through* but not yet *with* the historical eye.

For the comparative history of the Americas, a thematic handling is perhaps more rewarding than a chronological one. This is because periodization appropriates too easily the ready-made categories for the history of the Western world, and the events and trends of the history of the Americas plop like billiard balls into the pockets of Enlightenment, Revolution, Romanticism, Nationalism, World War, World Depression, and so forth. What is distinctive about the New World, however, is precisely its divided response to the imperatives of that history on one hand and to those of two vast and empty continents on the other. While, for example, there is a history of urban, intellectual America that has more or less kept pace with Europe since the mid-sixteenth century, there is also a history of backlands America for which one must perhaps go to the twelfth-century Cistercians for a European parallel. No chronological strait jacket should be allowed to separate the winning of the North American West from the seventeenth-century saga of the *bandeiras* in Brazil and the sixteenth-century colonization of Mexico.

A more subtle aspect of comparative chronology is the fact that one senses a dark and deep development, which one might call a moral history of the Americas, underlying the textbook patchwork of events and periods. I refer to a trajectory of New World insti-

tutions that, whatever their immediate or eventual accommodation
to the American hemisphere, receive an initial moral impetus from
the communitarian, religious, and natural-law traditions of late
medieval Europe. Gradually, this impetus spends itself or, at least
by the nineteenth century, is scarcely distinguishable. The assumptions of a traditionally ordered society melt away in the fluidity
and improvisation characterizing American life—assumptions that,
it must be remembered, survived even the eras of *enrichissez-vous*
and Bismarck in Europe. The termination of this moral trajectory
can be thought of as marked by three quite different episodes: in
Spanish America by the Wars of Independence (1810–26), in the
United States by the Civil War, and in Brazil by the abolition of
monarchy in 1889. As long as these historical moments are studied
only in isolation, or are allowed to fall separately into such conventional Western categories as Romantic Nationalism, National
Unification, and Liberal Republicanism, we seal off three views of
a parabola of moral development that has a peculiar New World
shape to it.

To recapitulate, we have identified two native strains of New
World historiography. One, tinctured by millennial dreams, affords a glimpse of the freshness and freedom of the American
experience and celebrates a common destiny of the New World
nations. The second reflects the caution and skepticism of the
creole outlook, taking "creole" in the Latin American sense. It is
alive to the corrosive action to which Old World institutions,
habits, and attitudes were subjected in the New. It is wary of the
systems and stratifications and periodized dialectics that come
easily to European thought. Schematically, we may say that the
first strain catches the spirit of the conqueror and the missionary,
the second that of the settler, the creole, the *mestizo*, the Negro.
The first is biased toward *teleology*, the second toward *process*.
Both, therefore, exhibit a typically New World sense of time:
nimble, eclectic, often collapsible, rather than organic and se-
quentially patterned. If we wanted a view of the Americas that
was centered in *being*, or ontology, it might have to be that of the
Indian. But the voice of the Indian was stifled. It has been said
that the New World was, for the Indian, not *dis*covered, still less
invented, but *covered over*. In spite of the sophisticated attempts

of modern Mexican philosophers to re-create the Indian world view, it is probably beyond reconstruction, if not beyond influencing the expression of modern thoughts.

From the discipline and flexibility of mind that these historical outlooks impose, there are several escapes familiar to anyone who has dipped into writings on our own country. One is into the realm of biography. Another is into the realm of the purely descriptive, whether pedantry disguised as empirical research or the journalistic re-creation of events, personalities, and moods. Still another is "thesis" history, which, instead of offering a matrix of explanation for a set of facts, packages the facts and hurls them at our heads.

If we resist the temptation to employ such evasive tactics, what are some fields of study that might yield the sort of generalization that is being urged?

First and most obvious, there is the story of immigration. Oscar Handlin begins *The Uprooted* by saying: "Once I thought to write a history of the immigrants in America. Then I discovered that the immigrants *were* American history." This could be amended to read "the history of the Americas." We would except only the Indians, who, although immigrants for the prehistorian, had by the dawn of the historical era in the Americas absorbed a spirit of place such as no later immigrants have ever captured. "[The] history of immigration," Handlin continues, "is a history of alienation and its consequences."[18] Although he identifies the immigration of the nineteenth century as being a "more complex" experience than that of eighteenth-century Negroes or seventeenth-century Englishmen, his generalization can properly be extended to the earlier period and to the *conquistadores* themselves. One suspects that the solitude of the Argentine *pampas*, or of life among the taciturn Indians of the Andes, was once just as disquieting for social bonds and individual psychology as the turmoil of the immigrants' New York City.

The decision to come to America has always been a traumatic one. It is an act both of rebellion *against* one's society and of rejection *by* the society, insofar as that society fails to afford wished-for paths of fulfillment. Whatever the pitfalls of a clinical approach to history, there is a kernel of truth in the conclusion of a Norwegian psychiatrist that the "schizoid constitution alone (apart from any actually psychotic traits) will frequently lead to emigration—far more frequently than the syntonic [manic depressive] makeup."[19] The case of the involuntary emigrant—the African slave, the debtor, the deported criminal, perhaps even the wife who must follow her husband—is still one of traumatic, if nonrebellious, alienation.

Transatlantic migration, then, is a selective process that draws off an unrepresentative cross-section of the population of the mother continent. Whether we speak of the sixteenth or the nineteenth century, whether of Latin or North America, we find that emigration tends, however roughly, to select from displaced or marginal strata rather than from the peasantry and from vested aristocratic or bourgeois interests; that it selects more heavily for certain personality traits than for others; that it selects for and in fact kindles an attitude of rebellion toward the mother society. Rebelliousness, in turn, may be compensated for by a determination to return home, ostensibly in triumph, but also in the lurking desire for reconciliation. Such ambivalence of feeling imparts its tone to all New World societies.

Although colonization, the logical sequel to immigration, is too complex a theme for summary treatment, one schematic approach to it can be suggested. New World settlement patterns are conventionally classified as two disparate types: the "farm colonies" of British North America and the "exploitation colonies" of Ibero-America. Even the extremes of this exaggerated dichotomy, however, have common aspects of social organization. Carle Zimmerman has distinguished between "nominalist" and "realist" communities. The "realist" community is one with a settled, stable population; it has a single "personality" overarching the classes, groups, associations, and castes that may compose it. The "nominalist" community is characteristic of lands newly settled by persons uprooted from traditional communities and intermixed. Its binding force derives from mere geographical proximity in a threatening environment rather than from shared usage and funded experience. The reassembling of transplanted societies produces impromptu leadership and social gradations that seem arbitrary for being unsanctioned by precedent.[20] It is possible that a refined model of Zimmerman's paradigm (which in turn arises from a classic sociological polarity) would assist the cross-cultural analysis of New World ecology and institutions.

Certain facets of the social process are sometimes illuminated more sharply by cultural indexes than by the direct inspection of social institutions. If language, for example, in its inflection, imagery, and turns of expression is recognized as mirroring the history and leading concerns of a society, one may expect the study of European languages as they are spoken in the Americas to yield important clues to the processes of settlement.[21] Throughout the three principal New World language areas, English-, Spanish- and Portuguese-speaking, there occurs standardization of speech habits and a virtual elimination of dialects, a fact all the more striking in view of the much greater geographic extent of these areas in America than in Europe. The homogenization of language, one conjectures, comes from the continued intermingling of persons of diverse regional and social origin, which wore down dialectal differences to a common denominator. Frequently, a speech form that was a localized plebeian variant in the mother country became universalized in the new land. Such was the case in Spanish America of the *seseo*.[22]

In the Americas, language became an instrument for attack upon environment; its received meanings were forced into naming new things, situations, and processes. Connotation was sacrificed to denotation. Language became less important as a repository for inherited lore; it no longer preserved sharp distinctions of ceremony and etiquette. Using a European language, Indian and Negro women could not pass folk traditions in their fullness along to their masters' children or to their own children of mixed blood. In America, where communities were makeshift and social rank often arbitrary, language lost in specificity gained in evasiveness and ambiguity. Finally, as compensation for the thinning out and plebeianizing of language, we often find high-flown metropolitan rhetoric standing in striking counterpoint to the salty, planed-down idiom for which it is intended to make amends. These characteristics, familiar to those who know American English, can be amply illustrated in the Spanish and Portuguese of Latin America.

Another inviting theme for New World historians is the comparative history of the Indian and the Negro. Because of Mexico's presence at our doorstep, or perhaps because of Prescott's familiar and stirring narrative, United States historians tend to accept the subjugation of the Aztecs as the representative European experience with the Indians in Latin America. Since it is in many ways incommensurable with the English and the French experience, the comparison is passed off. Frequently overlooked are comparisons between the east coast of North America and the Brazil-Paraguay region, or between our own Great Plains and the Argentine *pampas*. In these cases, where Indian types were similar, the cultural backgrounds of the settlers themselves become a more manageable element of the historical complex.

The areas of the Aztec, Mayan, and Incan civilizations are not, however, without importance for the United States historian. For here alone are monuments of the pre-Columbian world preserved. Here alone—if we except the Amazon rain forests and scattered reservations elsewhere—do the faces, languages, customs, gods of the Indians linger on. The Indians north of the Rio Grande were eliminated, if not biologically at least historically. This left a vacuum at the center of our country's experience that could be filled only by the mists of legend. In Mexico or Peru or Bolivia, the presence of the Indian continues to objectify a prehistoric *genius loci*, while his long-silent temples and fortresses remain as hostages to the cyclical calendar of the Indian deities.

To one who visits the cave paintings of Altamira in Spain it might occur that the works of the Cro-Magnon, whom we can call the "Indian" of Spain, are buried underground; that the visible monuments, above ground, are within our familiar historical continuum. A cathedral 700 years old is still used for worship, and its successive architectural additions, embellishments, and renovations afford a line of visual continuity into the distant past. American history, however, is *dis*continuous, a fact that the regions of high Indian civilizations can still make present to the senses and to the imagination.

Several perspectives for the comparative study of the Negro in the Americas have been blocked out during the past quarter-century. Scholars like Melville Herskovits and Arthur Ramos have stressed contributions of the African heritage to our New World cultures. Their description of how a baseline common to the diverse West African cultures was transplanted to the Americas is similar to George M. Foster's account of how a common denominator of the regional cultures of Spain was factored out by the transatlantic migration. Other scholars, like M. G. Smith, argue that functional or situational analyses of Negro societies in the New World have more explanatory relevance than the identification of cultural vestiges. The debate appears to be restating in sophisticated terms the issues of a much earlier one that occurred in United States historiography between the "Germanic origins" and "frontier" schools of institutional analysis.

The nature of the Negro's experience as a slave in the several American cultures also arouses controversy. Eric Williams has treated slavery as a product of universal economic pressures. If at one time the institution appeared to bear more lightly upon the African in Cuba than in Jamaica, it is because at that moment Cuba was less advanced in its capitalistic development. Frank Tannenbaum challenges Williams, insisting that slave systems and race relations be viewed within the socio-legal traditions of the respective colonizing powers. Nor should slavery be regarded, he feels, exclusively as a massive saga of oppression and exploitation. As Tannenbaum puts it, the Negro has taken possession of an irregular half-circle of mainland and islands between Washington, D.C., and Rio de Janeiro, almost as if he, too, were descended from a breed of *conquistadores*. "These people of Africa have found a new habitat and it is theirs for all time to come, regardless of what men say, think, or do."[23] Within this area, several formal codes and many more unwritten ones governed the relations between master and slave, as well as between white man and freed Negro. In the nineteenth century, slavery was abolished, starting with Haiti in 1804, ending with Brazil in 1888. Sometimes emancipation came after bitter civil strife, sometimes in peaceful evolution; sometimes as a result of internal pressures, sometimes of international diplomatic ones. In all cases, abolition gave rise to a new set of relations between the races that were not always similar to those that had obtained between whites and freedmen in each locality before abolition.

This multiplicity of experiences should be of deep interest to historians of the United States. For the Negro is almost as unassimilable in our history-writing as he has been in our national life. Segregation extends even to historiography. Although there may be institutes or journals of Afro-Cuban or Afro-Brazilian studies in Latin America, there is probably no counterpart to that brave but implausible journal, *The Journal of Negro History.* "Afro-America" is a vast laboratory of differing racial situations, all of them more subtle, perhaps more complex, than our own precisely because they fall short of decisive polarization. Reasons commonly given for discriminatory attitudes in Latin America are similar to those advanced in our country: the stigma of slavery and poverty, sexual taboos for upper-class white women (stronger in Latin American countries than in our own), defense against economic competition from freed slaves, and so forth. Only comparative historical studies will isolate those variables that account for the emotional and psychological unassimilability of the Negro in United States life. They will also help our own historian to identify a "white" as well as a "Negro problem."

The last field for comparative inquiry to be mentioned, though by no means the last that might be mentioned, is intellectual history. Much has been written about the incommensurability of the mind-sets of the northern and southern Americas—the northern one stemming from English traditions of empiricism, utilitarianism, and Lockean rights; the southern from an Iberian, Catholic tradition said to emphasize spiritual and aesthetic values and to be less concerned with efficient rearrangements of the physical and social environment or with capital accrual for its own sake.

There was a period, from the mid-eighteenth century to the late nineteenth, when it appeared as if northern and southern America were coming to share common sources of European intellectual life. But the course of the nineteenth century proved two things: first, that the flower of Anglo-French constitutionalism was a delicate plant for the jungles and *pampas* of southern America; second, that *fin-de-siècle* evolutionism and materialism contained prophecies whose pessimism was all too credible for agrarian societies in which extensive mixing of the races had occurred. By 1900, therefore, Latin American thinkers were looking for salvation to the indwelling vitalities of the Bergsonian and Nietzschean worlds. Since then, they have found a Germano-Iberian axis of thought, which, philosophically as well as geographically, runs athwart the Vienna-England-United States axis. The principal European influences upon modern Latin American legal philosophy have been listed as Husserl, Scheler, Hartman, Dilthey, Heidegger, and Ortega y Gasset.[24] A measure of the paucity of exchange between the northern and southern intellectual worlds is the fact that, for some Latin American thinkers, two of the outstanding achievements of North American philosophy are the personalism of Borden Parker Bowne and the studies in phenomenology done at the University of Buffalo.

Even within this dichotomized situation, however, there are grounds for sensitive comparative inquiry. We have suggested, for example, that the time dimension of American history has its own shape. This leads us to ask whether American philosophers give, implicitly, their own definition to the category of time. North American instrumentalism tests its truths by actions and subsequent results. The existentialism that is popular in Latin America sees the process of decision as a springboard to subsequent choice. In both cases, time is a thrust into the future, not a record of sedimentation and accrual.

The way in which historical time is experienced in the New World is partly responsible for the fact that Marxist thought has taken only a weak hold in Latin America, as it has in our own country.[25] What makes Marxism unpalatable is not the ultimate vision, which is little different from hundreds of others that have been pursued on these shores, but the time-consuming dialectics and the requirement of a historically identifiable class structure. When the Peruvian Marxist José Carlos Mariátegui formulated his own brand of the theory in the 1920's, he cavalierly dropped from the blueprint the phase of bourgeois-proletariat struggle, in view of the slow emergence of these classes in his country. Then, in further defiance of a developmental viewpoint, he harked back to the Jesuit missions of Paraguay, and even to the old Incan empire, as inspiration for the socialist future.

The failure of a doctrinal socialist movement ever to achieve importance in the United States is customarily attributed to the absence of a militant sense of class identities; to the real or hoped-for opportunities for individual advancement; to the operation of demographic safety valves; and to a tacit national agreement upon political ground rules, enforced by the conformism of an egalitarian democracy. More broadly, one might say that these factors have weighed against the emergence in our country of any coherent, philosophically rooted body of political thought. In Latin America, however, one might gather that none of these factors is of any effect. That is, one would assume that Latin American societies are historically characterized by entrenched class systems and that they have never offered rich opportunities for self-advancement to the lowly born. One would further assume that the great land mass of Latin America has never furnished effective safety valves, either because of adverse geography or because of an unpromising distribution of natural resources or because of the weight of archaic social systems. Finally, a glance at the tumultuous political history of Latin America during the past century and a half would suggest that no political ground rules have ever received assent.

As historical generalizations go, these are somewhat but not wholly misleading ones. Logically, they should cause us to believe that programmatic socialism is on the march below the Rio Grande, ready to take over country after country at the least provocation. In fact, it should have taken over long ago, for the very factors that militate against programmatic political thought in the United States appear to be precisely reversed in Latin America. Yet, the truth is that Latin American political thought shows the same measure of derivativeness and eclecticism as our own; it is just as adrift philosophically; and much of it is tinctured with local equivalents for a bourgeois Jeffersonianism.

For the perspectives toward New World history that have been suggested above no originality is claimed. Many historians of the Americas, above all of the southern Americas, have for some time been concerned with these lines of speculation. The emphasis of this essay has, therefore, been more pedagogical than theoretical. Its only conceivable utility is as a partial survey of present points of departure, not as a setting out of advance posts.

3

No Panacea for Latin America

ARTURO USLAR-PIETRI

At the beginning of February, 1962, the University of Puerto Rico and the Weatherhead Foundation called together a group of people to discuss three lectures delivered by Arnold J. Toynbee on the principal economic, social, and political problems of Latin America.

In the growing, vigorous city of San Juan, during several tropical azure days, I was a part of that select group. A large, interested audience made up of professors, government officials, and students followed attentively the points of view that were presented on that complex, contradictory, and not very well-known world we call Latin America. The intense interest in the area responds mainly to political reasons and serves to reveal the enormous ignorance about this unique and changeable world and the total inadequacy of the quick generalizations with which one tries to define and categorize it.

One of the most exciting spectacles one can witness is that of a first-class mind struggling with an arduous problem. That, precisely, was what our group was privileged enough to watch during the Toynbee lectures in San Juan. We saw Toynbee enter, with the boldness of a hardened explorer, the *terra incognita* of Latin America, where certainty is slight, doubts are many, and contradictions glaring.

Professor Toynbee took a brief, over-all view in his lectures and did not restrict himself to the purely economic side of what we might call "the Latin American question." As a matter of fact, the economy is only a part of human activity, and the *homo faber* is as absurd an abstraction as the *homo sapiens* has been. What we can safely say is that economic activity is intertwined in the whole web of human behavior. We work and produce—both essential functions of life—but, as some wise man said long ago, "man does not live by bread alone." We must never forget the wisdom of this maxim. Along with our economic tasks is the great complex of culture, our understanding of the world, what we as human beings think and feel, want and fear—what, in large measure, decides our attitudes and vocations in everyday life.

Professor Toynbee is not an authority on the subject of Latin America and we may consider this most fortunate. Nor am I an expert. I have, I am quick to say, a certain droll distrust of that absurd being created by our contemporary culture called the "expert." If we had fewer experts and greater common sense, perhaps things would not be in such a sorry plight as they are today. Furthermore, I think it quite unlikely that there is anyone we might properly call an expert on Latin America. For my part, I am no more than a curious man who is concerned about his place in the world, amid his people, and in relation to his neighbors. This, more than anything else, has led me to study, observe, and read a bit more than is advisable for my own personal peace of mind. Of my own land, Venezuela, I know something; of the other lands in America, I know less—but what I know, I have learned well and at first hand. I think this experience is valid and will not be without some usefulness for the questions now before us.

The first question we should ask ourselves is: What is Latin America? I think, without any exaggeration, that seldom in world history has there been a civilization, a province, or even a branch of civilization such as Latin America, in which such dramatic importance is given to the constant question: "What are we?" Never before has a society had, to such a degree, this tragic obsession, which might be called "the ontologic anguish of the Latin American." The Latin American has always, somewhat like Hamlet, pondered his real nature, asking himself, "What am I: white, Negro, Indian, *mestizo*, European, something that partakes of all this, or something distinct?" And still the question has found no satisfactory answer. So unsatisfactory have been the answers thus far that even today we in Latin America have no collective name by which to identify ourselves. This is not a characteristic of ours alone, for our neighbors to the north, the United States, have not found one either. The difference is, however, that this lack doesn't bother them very much, while for us it means a deep, spiritual torment. We do not even know if we are Latin Americans; indeed, many mistrust this very word, for it appears to have been invented at one time by the French and then picked up and used by the North Americans. Others have suggested that we call ourselves Hispano-Americans, which is the most accepted and used appellation. Still others have offered "Iberoamerica," which sounds too much like anthropology, and even worse names like "Indoamerica" and, the worst of all, which I would never revive, "Eurindia."

The deep concern for knowing what we are, what I have called "the anguish of being," has existed since the Conquest and involves knowing where we can go and who will accompany us in our journey. Professor Toynbee said in his analysis that, before the nineteenth century, it would have been a utopian dream to think of extending civilization's wealth to all of mankind, while today it seems no longer in the realm of utopia because of technological means and our growing world wealth. I would like to recall here that the name Utopia was coined by Sir Thomas More to describe an ideal society, which, by a play upon the Greek word, could not really exist anywhere. And yet there was some place where people planned to settle and achieve this utopian dream and that place was precisely Latin America.

In Mexico, in the sixteenth century, Vasco de Quiroga decided to carry out More's Utopia in an indigenous community, fulfilling his plan by establishing charitable settlements in what is today the state of Michoacán. Later on, in the seventeenth and eighteenth centuries, the Jesuits in Paraguay effected one of the most extraordinary experiments in the social history of the world when they founded their well-known "reductions." In them, More's utopian vision of things was exactly realized: There was no private property, and among the rules the Jesuits imposed was that of erecting a kind of wall to keep Europe out. For Thomas More's idea of a corrupt Europe with a dissolute civilization led them to prohibit the entry of any European into the reductions and to prevent the Guaraní Indians from learning Spanish so as to avoid their contamination by European touch. For this reason they translated the

Catechism and the Bible into Guaraní. This also reveals the concern, which Vasco de Quiroga had stated in his dealings with Charles V of Spain, that America was to be a new world—new not in the common meaning of just having been discovered, but in the sense that society was to begin afresh and inherit none of the vices of European civilization. Thus, the Jesuits had the simple idea, no matter how gigantic and quixotic the undertaking, of beginning a new history of man upon American soil. This same intention has been a constant throughout Latin American history. There has never been in the world a people who along with this "anguish of being" have felt so intensely this kind of hope in the millennium, a quixotic urge to achieve in some fashion or another a golden age of justice and well-being. This has been a constant theme of the Latin American peoples in their historical development.

There is another generally ignored aspect of this struggle for justice in Latin America that we should remember. I refer to the famous Legislation of the Indies (*Legislación de Indias*). It antedated even the beginnings of all social legislation in Europe. From the end of the fifteenth century and specifically from 1512, with the promulgation of the Laws of Burgos, the Spanish Crown with its theologians and canonists created a system of laws that even today could be considered just, equitable, and advanced in any country. It proscribed slavery, prohibited forced labor, and set forth as its basic principle that all men were human beings and must be treated as brothers. It may be objected that these laws were never strictly enforced. I could reply by asking: What body of laws has ever been carried out to the letter? Is not the history of the law a history of the transgressions against it? Is it not better to make laws that are of themselves an ideal, a moral paradigm, condemning the mean human condition incapable of achieving them, instead of passing laws sanctioning crimes or tolerating acts repugnant to conscience and reason? Other peoples less idealistic and more practical have done so, but we need not emulate them.

The political ideals of the eighteenth century found fertile ground in the long struggle for justice that had Latin America as its stage. Even before Independence, Latin Americans had spilled their blood in the cause of equality and the strict enforcement of those ideals embodied in the Legislation of the Indies. The whole Spanish Conquest has a moral *leitmotiv*, a relentless concern about the justice of occupying those new lands. At the very start, the Hieronymites in Santo Domingo excommunicated the *encomenderos* because they did not treat the Indians as human beings. Bartolomé de las Casas convinced the Crown and its ecclesiastical councils that they should condemn outright the Aristotelian doctrine of racial inferiority and the natural slavery of the Indians. Francisco de Vitoria conceived the basis for what became modern international law by denying that Charles V was justified in his occupation of the Indian lands. Even the many revolts during the entire span of Spanish colonial history, led by Gonzalo Pizarro, Lope de Aguirre, Tupac Amaru, the *comuneros*, and Francisco de León, are mere portents ignited by this struggle for justice.

i

When we speak of Latin America, we take a risk and even commit a sin: We generalize. There is no doubt that there is a Latin America, that there are certain common characteristics, many of which Professor Toynbee has pointed out with great insight. No less important are the differences that distinguish the outlines of Latin America and make it a complex mosaic of people with differing degrees of problems and different approaches to life. It would be worth our while to review this mosaic, even if superficially.

Our first consideration must be the matter of geography. The old German geographer Ratzel said that history is a compound of land and humanity. By this he meant that man is formed partly by geography and not exclusively by his spirit.

There is a "*cordillera* America," a mountainous region where climatic and physical conditions are unique. The climate of the *puna*, the *altiplanicie*, and the highlands of Peru, Bolivia, Colombia, Ecuador, and Chile constitute a natural terrain totally different from other areas. Then, there is "jungle America," composed of the eastern Andean watershed, the Amazon basin, and the Chaco area. It is a region almost unpenetrated by man, a landscape of tropical jungle, of dense, untraversable stretches so ag-

gressive and luxuriant that human labor becomes difficult and precarious. It is here that some of the greatest rivers of the world have
their source. Obviously, in this setting there are traits and problems of life and work completely different from those found in
cordillera America.

There is also an America of the Atlantic coast and another of
the Pacific coast. They are remarkably dissimilar because their
geographic milieu dictated unique conditions and historical developments. Then we have an America of hot sun and hot lands—
"Caribbean America"—that arc of islands extending from the tip
of the Yucatán Peninsula to Trinidad and Tobago and dividing
the ocean waters into the Gulf of Mexico and the Caribbean Sea.
Here, of course, we discover a different kind of man and a distinct
pattern of life. Finally, there is an America of vast, flat ranges of
land, the *pampas* of Argentina and the *llanos* of Venezuela being
the two best examples. On these vast extents of land, conditions of
life and types of human existence are shaped by a treeless landscape of endless plains running without break to the great circle of
the horizon. This panorama of land is like the one viewed from a
ship upon the sea.

Not only is the geography varied, but the history of Latin
America has been equally uneven. If geography has given us a
tropical and subtropical continent, a land where there can be two
seasons or four as in Europe, with all that this means for crop
raising, food, housing, and clothing, then we should expect variations just as wide when we consider the region's history.

The history of the American Indians was not equal. When the
Spaniards reached America, they found not mere empty space, but
rather great indigenous civilizations in some areas. Although in
their final period of decline and decay, the Incas, the Mayans, and
the Aztecs were still great civilizations, each with its own social structure and system of labor. Consequently, it was relatively easy to
apply the traditional European pattern of conquest: that is, de-
capitate a society, convert the invaders into masters, and use the
whole existing framework of labor supply. This kind of conquest
was similar to the Spanish *reconquista*, which ended the same year
Columbus discovered the New World. In the Andean civilizations
and in the other high mountain civilizations, the Spaniards at-

tempted to employ the previous labor force and social organization without any great changes so that they could continue on as the substitute masters for the fallen lords. In the lowlands on the Atlantic coast and among the Caribbean islands, the situation was quite the opposite. Here the Indians lived on a primitive level and, therefore, there was no complex social structure or large labor force. This single fact explains the arrival of a great protagonist on the American scene, the Negro. The Negro was a stranger to the Americas, but the force of his presence in American history soon emerges. He came to the Latin American countries along the Atlantic coastline, the Antilles, to present-day Venezuela, Brazil, and Argentina because there was no indigenous civilization to do the Spaniard's work.

History has not been equal in its effect; therefore, the evolution of the various people has been distinct. There are places in which the Indian has predominated and where the most crucial problem has been that of absorbing and assimilating him into national cultures. There are countries where the Indian problem is non-existent, as, for example, in Puerto Rico, Cuba, or Venezuela, where there were no aboriginal foundations upon which to build. Thus, social structures vary according to their basic differences. We find countries where the white population is a majority, where the *mestizo* predominates, where racial mixture with the Negro has been the rule, or where the Indian influence is strong, giving accent and color to every form of life, appearing in literature, poetry, painting, and in the highest, most elaborate art forms of some American countries.

The historical development of these countries is also of the greatest importance. It was not a parallel evolution for all of them. Some countries were fashioned—that is, they assumed their distinctive outlines—in the seventeenth century. The nations whose character was essentially shaped in the seventeenth century are almost all located in the high mountains: Mexico, and the vice-regal sites along the back of the *cordillera*. Other countries were formed in the eighteenth century during the Bourbon rule when a pervading new spirit took hold of the Spanish monarchy, as was the case in Venezuela and Argentina. It is clear that, between a country that grew under the influence of the Hapsburgs in the sixteenth and seventeenth centuries and one that emerged under the French influence of the first Bourbon kings in Spain, there is a sea of difference.

Although there are not fewer differences in the area of economic activity, I will refer to these only in passing because they are the most commonly known.

We find countries or parts of countries that are in a primitive stage of agriculture and that have practically undergone no change from the seventeenth century to the present day: agriculture of the small plot of land, of the small Indian holding, of the large plantation, and of the great *hacienda*. There are others that have reached a more modern period in their development, such as Cuba and Puerto Rico or other lands where agriculture has been mechanized, industrialized, and now represents a branch of industry. There exist countries in which the predominant activity is mining or is of an extractive nature, as in my own country, Venezuela, where oil plays such an absolute role in the economy. Finally, we see countries where the emphasis has been placed upon the development of industrial capacity.

The trouble with all of this is that these several forms of development coexist in varying degree in every country. We can often say, with considerable justice, that within the official borders of one country there are several unofficial countries. Some branches of society and some regions of the country belong to the twentieth century because of their advanced state of industrial growth and social services. Other parts of the same country have yet to evolve out of the seventeenth century, and they are benighted by backwardness in farming techniques and general social and living conditions. This coexistence of disparate levels of development constitutes one of the most baffling internal problems of Latin America.

We must always bear in mind that we are considering some twenty independent countries that, over a century and a half of national history, have developed many individual traits and an ardent desire for autonomy. Each one believes it has a national mission, feels pride in its past and in its very own individuality, and possesses a concept of its own dignity that is sometimes almost suicidal. This particularism, this individualism, perhaps Hispanic in origin, is hardly an inconsequential factor in the whole Latin

American problem—if personality or individuality may be treated as a problem.

We must repeat that it is not a matter of some 200 million men and women of basic similarities contained within the same kind of land. Perhaps the most important characteristic of this area is its variety, the multiplicity of its ingredients, and the suggestiveness of nuance. They do not all speak the same language—nor, even if they do, do they pronounce it with the same accent and intonation. There is a Portuguese and a Spanish America and still others besides: French America, English America, Dutch America, and an America of half-breed tongues fetched out of the confluence of races and the crossroads of history: creole in Haiti or *papiamento*, a strange mélange of sounds spoken in Curaçao.

ii

One of the basic, yet least studied, phenomena of all in Latin America is *mestizaje*.

The Anglo-Saxons, generally, when they speak of *mestizaje* refer only to racial crossings and mixtures. They like to think of *mestizaje* as measurable in amounts of blood. In Latin America, the approach is quite different. With a happy combination of fortune and history, we have mixed the blood of the white man, the Indian, and the Negro, and this fact has obviated many serious problems in our societies. But, this crossing of the races is not, by far, the most significant aspect of *mestizaje*. It is, rather, the cultural *mestizaje* that has given Latin America the recognizable features it possesses today. We were born and made, as the weaver weaves many strands into one fabric, of different elements: the Hispanic culture, which we received from our first colonizers; the Indian tradition, which we have in one degree or another, depending upon the height attained by pre-Columbian civilizations, still alive today in many areas; and, finally, the Negro contribution to the process of *mestizaje*, which is strong, although it may seem less noticeable and obtrusive than the Indian's or the white man's simply because the Negro left no great monuments behind him in America.

Latin American history would be better understood if we studied

this side of its evolution with more care. For centuries the nurses
and governesses, the women charged with the early rearing of Latin
American leaders, were Negro women whose minds still throbbed
with vivid traditions of Africa and who transmitted to their wards
a world of images, traditions, and popular concepts that later became an active part of their souls. Simón Bolívar, the greatest figure of the Latin American world, was an orphan from birth and
raised by a Negress by the name of Hipólita. At the height of his
glory as *Libertador* and founder of free nations, he returned to
Caracas, to his family estate, dismounted from his horse, ran to
Hipólita, and embraced her then, as always, as his second mother.
What a curious speculation it is to think how many things in
Bolívar's thought, which we admire so greatly, came from the leg-
ends and stories he heard as a child at Hipólita's knee! And much
the same thing happens elsewhere in Latin American art, culture,
and architecture. Its infinite variety springs from its most characteristic trait, cultural *mestizaje*.

This is a most healthy sign, for otherwise we might be con-
demned as an appendix of European civilization or a second-class
Europe or a servile copy of an original pattern. If we did not contribute some testimony of our sensibilities to the world, even a
suggestion of our genius, we could not justify our right to occupy a
small corner of this planet. Fortunately, however, we do have a
sensibility, the same attitude of open mind that allows us to receive
so many influences and mix them in what might appear a helter-
skelter fashion. But this mixing of many components, I would
argue, is a fertile element of creation and is good evidence that
we are a young people ready to make history the world will remember.

This is the setting that makes it so difficult to speak of Latin
America in the convenient terms of generality as if it were a com-
pact unit. This is the background that makes it impossible to find
remedies and panaceas for ills we would like to overcome with the
simple application of a wonder drug and cure them all finally and
overnight. But, alas, there is no general remedy for Latin America.
There are regional and national problems that demand special
analysis and independent treatment. If we are to seriously examine

the "Latin American question," we will have to begin by making a real inventory of all the aspects of its problems. We fall too easily, and the experts fall too heavily, into the use of certain images that history has made too conspicuous. It is said, for example, that Latin America is a kind of Brahmin society that has lived statically outside the steady pace of history, divided into unbridgable classes separated abysmally from each other, without social mobility and without intercommunication. This is not entirely a true picture, or certainly it is a misrepresentation for many regions.

In the first place, we must remember two things: that Latin American colonial life was permeated by this problem of justice, by a desire to create a utopia, a better world than Europe, and that the War of Independence was a unique event and one not motivated by any material consideration. It was achieved because of the great force of an ideal that seemed absurd to many rational and thoughtful people. The most favored social classes lit the torch of a war that, at its roots, was a social war. It is quite remarkable to think that the leader of this great social movement, Simón Bolívar, belonged to the highest and wealthiest ranks of society. The outcome of the war could only be ruinous for him and his class; yet, he led the struggle against Spain over a large area of the American continent. There was an extraordinary idealism, a will to forge a new society and to create new conditions for man. There were no base purposes or considerations of material gain.

A quick glance at the history of the nineteenth century tells us that Latin America was profoundly shaken by social movements. In my country, as in Argentina and later in Mexico, the social struggle had the most far-reaching and unexpected consequences. After fifteen years of warfare, leaders had sprung up from the lower classes. The well-to-do oligarchs and landowners had disappeared as the ruling social class. The first president of Venezuela and one of the great heroes of the Independence, second only to Bolívar, was José Antonio Páez. Páez never learned to read with great care and never saw or used a table fork until he was made a brigadier general. When he worked as a *peón* on a *hacienda*, after finishing his chores he would return to the main house to wash the overseer's feet in the most servile manner imaginable. Born in these modest, unpretentious circumstances, he was ultimately to become the president of Venezuela, a position he filled three separate times. Páez is a national and international hero, who, after having lived more than twenty years in the United States, finished out his life composing music and writing his memoirs.

A parallel thing happened in Argentina's revolution. Under Rosas' influence, the movement he led was primarily of a social character. The struggle between the Federalists and the Unitarians was an openly social contest: a battle between the refinements of the city and the coarseness of the country, between the dandy (*el cajetilla*) and the cowhand (*el gaucho*). Rosas was the epitome of the *gaucho* who detested the men of the city. He especially hated the men of Buenos Aires, the arrogant *porteños*. And we find similar ingredients in the social struggle in Mexico which we call by the name of the Reform Movement.

It is superficial and, indeed, incorrect to picture Latin America as a caste society made sodden by years of complacent self-satisfaction where only recently has the clarion for social justice been sounded. In Venezuela, for example, as early as 1814, more than 20,000 soldiers followed the first *caudillo* (Páez) with a ringing cry of social portent and barbarism: "Death to the wealthy and the whites." They did not shout, "Kill the Spaniard," or, "Down with the bad government." Their shouts were clearly signs of a war between classes, of a war that was a struggle for greater social justice.

The long federalist war in Venezuela (1859–63) was a vast, bloody process in which people from the lowest social strata came to the national forefront. Similar processes were afoot elsewhere in Latin America. *Caudillismo*, the basic fact of political life in our nineteenth century, is best understood in the light of these egalitarian struggles. The *caudillos* were, for the most part, men of popular background who gained political power with the armed support of their people and represented a force of social leveling in all their actions. Rosas of Argentina, Melgarejo in Bolivia, and Flores in Ecuador, as well as the great civilian *caudillos* like Benito Juárez, the full-blooded Zapotec Indian president of Mexico in the Reform Movement period, were social levelers and embodied the struggle for greater justice in the example of their lives.

iii

The picture of a static Latin America divided into castes and cliques, impervious to the ideals of freedom and justice, unaware of the great changes that had taken place in the world until the emissaries of the Alliance for Progress proclaimed them, slowly awakening from its indifference or hypocrisy, has little to do with reality. The example and influence of Thomas More, the egalitarian struggles of the last century, the most liberal constitutions yet written in the world, even the extreme radicalism of its youth, attest this single characteristic of Latin America: its high sensitivity and receptivity to political idealism and its scorn of compromise and the *status quo.*

Only the sharp contrasts between ideals and reality, between productivity and programs, between principles and history, between human aspirations and the men who proclaim them, between social institutions and popular customs, between psychology and its doctrines—these contrasts, the factors that have created enormous difficulties, explain the dramatic and unstable development in the national life of almost all the countries of Latin America.

The Cuban Revolution is perhaps the most violent and dramatic example of the clash between the contrasts I have just mentioned. The source of this struggle comes from a clash between a pugnacious idealism and apparently insoluble contradictions. What distinguishes the Cuban Revolution from the general picture I have described for all of Latin America has been its rapid drift toward the Soviet bloc. Its special meaning is that it has transplanted the Cold War to America and has made hostile confrontations inevitable between the two great powers that divide mankind today. One would have to examine it dispassionately to see why it took this unexpected turn and also to see if it is possible, given the present circumstances of international politics and the Cold War, for the extreme left in Latin America to devise political programs of a truly national character.

The Cold War is one of the most difficult problems man faces today, and the great powers of the world are still stymied by it. We of Latin America would be, at the least, overambitious were we to think we could hit upon some workable formula when such

nations as the United States, England, France, and Italy have not
been able to deal with Russia and her neighbors behind the Iron
Curtain.

Another factor that is of overriding importance in our survey of
problems peculiar to Latin America is the presence of the United
States. By action or by omission, by sheer material expansiveness,
the presence in the same hemisphere of a great world power with
unpredictable economic capacity and with a past, a tradition, and
a moral and religious code sometimes antipathetic to the Latin
American way, has frequently been the source of disturbance and
rankling change. There are many Latin Americas, as we have already seen, and there have been many reactions, some favorable,
some unfriendly, to the different images and influences presented
by the United States. After all, the name "The United States of
America" is an entity that has meant many different things to us
in Latin America.

There is the United States with its liberal doctrines, admired
and emulated by our democratic leaders of the nineteenth century.
There is the United States of political expansion and military
might that has left unhappy memories in many lands. There is
the United States that, in many areas, has only the hard, aggressive face of great private-business enterprise. There is the
United States of a hardhearted, insensitive, and thundering foreign
policy that rides roughshod over the interests and feelings of many
countries in Latin America. And then there is the United States
whose thought and culture have always won the respectful applause
of Latin Americans. In most of these countries, Jefferson, Lincoln,
and Whitman are held in the highest regard, while Teddy Roosevelt's "big stick" and the brazenly cynical attitude of Foster Dulles
toward dictatorships are disdained and detested.

The United States, rich and powerful, yet inconsistent, has ap-
proached Latin America under many guises in the past century and
a half, and this inconsistency has naturally aroused confusion and
even suspicion about its real motives. No one knows with any certainty which of the faces that speak is the real face of the United
States, and this persisting uncertainty is one of the main causes of
misunderstanding between the two Americas.

The United States now seems to be sincerely concerned with

understanding and helping Latin America and also with preventing the further spread of the Cuban example. This is how its new policy, the Alliance for Progress, is best explained.

With all that can be said in favor of the new directions of this policy, we must be frank enough to say that until now it has been both ingenuous and couched in terms of extreme simplicity. Its policymakers seem to think that it is sufficient to preach the gospel of social justice, destroy the latifundia system of landholding, and disburse some $20 billion in a period of 10 years and thereby the problems that have been the torment of the best minds and bravest hearts in Latin America for well over 400 years will magically be resolved.

The undertaking will not be simple or quick. It is not a mere matter of money. Only Venezuela, because of its mineral riches, will have sufficient funds to contribute to the economic transformation of our continent. Nor is it a simple matter of distributing lands to the landless. Land that is distributed without organization, education, or technical direction has frequently led to a social and economic breakdown. Nor is it a clear-cut question of teaching everybody to read and write. The problem is vaster and more complex than all these. The productive capacity of most of Latin America has to be increased. Education must be channeled toward the virtues of work and the rewards of production. Formulas equidistant between the imperatives of social justice and the needs of economic productivity must be found. Governments must become more efficient and less theoretical. And none of these things can be accomplished overnight or by merely doling out dollars.

We are confronted by two contradictory demands, one for social justice and the other for economic efficiency. The maximum of economic efficiency is usually accompanied by a rather high degree of social injustice; and the utopian scheme of social justice, which would give everyone everything he wanted, always leads to high economic inefficiency. The free people of the world have to strike some kind of balance between these two extremes because, unfortunately, the Communists have a plausible solution to this problem. They say that to realize social justice within the next generation, this generation will have to submit to a coercive system of economic efficiency, sacrificing freedom and well-being for the greatest rates of production possible. And now, for the first time, Latin America has in its midst a regime, the Castro government, that forces its people to work and produce at a rhythm inconceivable in a free society. Naturally, the results of this system will be gained at a high price: the price of human sacrifice and the loss of happiness, peace, and freedom; but they may be similar to those won under the Red China regime of Mao Tse-tung. If we of the free societies of the world cannot coordinate the demands of economic progress with the spreading of liberty, justice, and well-being for all, our position in the world will be an untenable one. We will face the cruel efficiency of dictatorships that have appeared for the first time in Latin America, with such systematic rigor, in the bearded countenance of Fidel Castro—no matter whether he be labeled demon or messiah.

What we have said up to this point demonstrates my thesis that Latin America is not a homogeneous unit and that there is no miraculous panacea to bring a sudden cure for its maladies. For each country and for each region we must study the special conditions of the past and the opportunities of the present. We will have to seek the cooperation of all social groups, lay out concrete, realistic plans, and undertake them with stout heart and good will, without thinking that we are preaching the gospel to savages or that a magic formula has been found—a panacea that the best intellects in Latin America have not discovered in their 400-year struggle for justice and progress.

II

THE POLITICAL PUZZLE

4

Nationalism and Social Change in Latin America

ARTHUR P. WHITAKER

Latin America is no exception to the rule that, ever since the French Revolution, nationalism and social change and the interplay between them have been major factors in the historical development of the Western world. It is no mere coincidence that almost all Latin America began its national existence at the close of the period of the French Revolution and Napoleon. Opinions differ widely regarding the relative weight of various factors—French, English, North American, Iberian, and creole—in the early development of Latin American political and social thought at large; but there can be no question that in the particular area of this essay France took first place. During their first, formative years the new Latin American states came under the lasting influence of the French Revolutionary concepts of nationalism, as symbolized and popularized by the term *la patrie, la patria,* "my country," and of social change, as represented by the contradictory but fascinating and endlessly subversive slogan "Liberty, Equality, Fraternity."

Today, a century and a half later, nationalism and social change are not only still at work in Latin America; they are more important now than ever before. This is partly due to the combined and frustrating effect of two currently world-wide phenomena of which Latin America is a leading exponent, namely, the population explosion and the revolution of rising expectations. It is also due to further contagions from abroad, to which Latin Americans have always been highly susceptible.

These circumstances have rendered more complex and have invested with a new urgency the age-old, multifaceted Latin American problem of the relation between nationalism and social change. One way of approaching this problem is from the viewpoint of Latin America's own writers. No Latin American has perceived it more clearly than the Spanish-born Mexican, Víctor Alba, who has not only a keen eye for current issues but also a strong sense of history.

In his recent book, *Las ideas sociales contemporáneas en México* (1960), Alba makes two points that are particularly relevant to the question before us. First, he complains of the universal Latin American habit of *politización*, that is, of "politicizing" ideas and problems of all kinds, including even those of an obviously social character, such as *latifundismo* and the appallingly unequal distribution of wealth. The result of looking for solutions in the wrong place, he observes, has been frustration, mounting protests and indignation, and the development of highly explosive situations.

Alba's second point relates particularly to Mexico, but, as I shall show later on, the essence of his proposition is even more applicable to other Latin American countries than to Mexico at the present time. This point is that Mexican nationalists are split into two rival schools of thought, one of which insists that development programs must be sound, gradual, and beneficial to all classes; whereas the other school gives top priority to immediate social reform for the exclusive benefit of the Mexican masses. The importance of this point is great, for similar rifts—and bitter ones—exist in the other principal Latin American countries as well, notably in Argentina and Brazil, not to mention some of the smaller countries; the Castro regime in Cuba represents the victory of the second school. But even more important for our purposes is the fact that the rifts in question are not between nationalists and anti- or nonnationalists but between different groups or factions of nationalists.

This fact has an even broader significance, namely, that there have always been different schools or sectors of nationalist thought at any given time in any given country. Since these change with the passage of time, the diversity of nationalist types increases as the space-time span is broadened. This diversity is an elementary fact, and yet it needs to be stressed because it is so often overlooked in discussions of nationalism, many of which treat the phenomenon as something monolithic and static. The chief authorities on nationalism, however, know better than this and hence define it in broad, flexible terms. To Hans Kohn, nationalism is at bottom a modern version of the feeling of belonging to an "in group," and to Carlton Hayes it is a religion.

Perhaps the best clue to the particular character that nationalism assumes in any given situation is the function it performs. As Crane Brinton has pointed out, in early nineteenth-century Europe, nationalism provided the cohesive force needed to fill the gap left by the overthrow of the old regime. It did likewise in the United States and Latin America after the destruction of bonds of unity and authority formerly provided by the European mother country.

In other words, nationalism has sometimes been introvert rather than extrovert, in the sense that its orientation has been domestic rather than foreign and its function has been to promote or secure internal unity rather than to aggrandize the nation in relation to its neighbors. This was its main function in both the United States and Latin America during most of the nineteenth century.

Also, let us remember that, while nationalism in all its forms is ultimately political, there are nevertheless times when its primary expression is concerned with other themes—cultural or economic or social. Thus, in his first works, about 1910, that leading Argentine nationalist and man of letters, Ricardo Rojas, was mainly concerned with fomenting cultural nationalism. But from the start, this had political and economic implications, and later he increased the stress on economic nationalism, as did many other Latin Americans.

One last comment by way of definition: Let us maintain the necessary distinctions between patriotism and nationalism, and between nationalism and chauvinism. If asked for a brief differentiation of the three phenomena, I would suggest that nationalism is patriotism with a program, and chauvinism is nationalism with a punch. What the program and the punch will be in any given case depends on the circumstances; and, being a historian, I would insist that each group of patriots or nationalists or chauvinists constitutes a special case, and that the circumstances of every case vary as the historical process unfolds.

Rise of Nationalism in Latin America

The most salient historical features of Latin American nationalism must be noted here, however briefly, for such a background is essential to an understanding of the relation of nationalism to social change in that area.

To begin with, the development of nationalism in Latin America is marked by the same combination of diversity and unity that characterizes every aspect of Latin American history. Stated in the baldest possible terms, nationalism was the birthright of all the Latin American countries in the early nineteenth century, and it flourishes in every one of them today; but in the intervening century and a half there have been wide discrepancies in its rate and direction of growth from one country to another.

Because Argentina and Bolivia are neighboring countries, they illustrate this discrepancy most vividly. In Argentina, nationalism flourished from the start, though there was much debate and conflict over the questions: What kind of nationalism and for whose benefit? In Bolivia, on the other hand, the contemporary nationalist movement dates only from the 1920's; so, at any rate, says the historian of Bolivian thought in the twentieth century, Guillermo Francovich. I suspect that further investigation of nineteenth-century Bolivian thought may show this hiatus of a hundred years to have been more apparent than real; but, even so, there seems no reason to doubt that Bolivia lagged far behind Argentina in the development of nationalist thought.

It was stated above that nationalism existed in all the Latin American countries from the beginning of their independence in the early nineteenth century. The continentalism of Simón Bolívar and other leaders of that generation might seem to contradict this statement, but in fact validates it. Bolívar's continentalism was not a denial but an affirmation of nationalism. The issue he raised was not whether or not the former Iberian colonies should be turned into nation-states, but simply how many such states there should be.

As everyone knows, it took time to work out the answer to this question in certain areas, notably the Plata basin, northern South America, and Central America. In each of these areas, a decade or more passed before planned unity gave way to what we may call succession states, with a consequent delay in the definition of the national spirit. Ecuador, for example, formed part of Gran Colombia until the disintegration of the latter in 1830 and did not develop a specifically Ecuadorean nationalism until about 1845. Then, for the first time, Ecuadoreans treated as foreigners the people of Colombia and Venezuela, who had formerly been their fellow citizens in Gran Colombia. It is worth noting that this new Ecuadorean nationalism of the mid-1840's was antimilitaristic and liberal. It was also romantic: The Inca Atahualpa, Pizarro's victim, was hailed as the "father of Ecuadorean nationality"—a notion that has parallels in the early nationalist thought of Mexico, Peru, and other Spanish American countries, including even Argentina.

When the new states of Latin America won their independence, modern nationalism had already assumed its classic modern form as the result of contributions first from England, then from the United States, and finally and most of all from Revolutionary France. It was from these three countries that the Latin Americans drew most of their political ideas in that era.

The nature of this source helps to explain the two most enduring features of Latin American nationalism in the nineteenth century. One was its relatively liberal and benign character; the other was its introverted, domestically oriented character. The latter feature was also a consequence of the fact that the political map of independent Spanish America reflected particularisms that had developed behind the false façade of unity of the Spanish imperial period. Once particularism had been unchained by independence, a strong counterforce was needed to hold it in check—witness the disintegration of Gran Colombia, already alluded to, and similar schisms in Central America and the Río de la Plata area in the first generation of independence. Such a counterforce was provided mainly by nationalism, which thus performed in Latin America the same integrating function that it had already begun to perform in the United States after the American Revolution and in Europe after the French Revolution.

Until the close of the nineteenth century, the operation of nationalism in Latin America was obscured by a number of factors: by what Henríquez-Ureña called the alternating anarchy and despotism of the first generation of independence, by a widespread but superficial conversion to the economically antinationalist doctrine of *laissez-faire*, and by the prevalence of *caudillismo*. Yet, during these years, nationalism was only in eclipse. The will was there even if ways to express it could not be found. In a perverted way, it was expressed even by the *caudillos*, for they represented as close an approximation to the paternalistic nation-state idea as was feasible in those tumultuous times. And some of these *caudillos* made their appeal to nationalism explicit and won a big and enthusiastic following by doing so; Rosas of Argentina, one of the most famous of all *caudillos*, is a prime example of this type.

Since the turn of the century, Latin America's original fund of nationalism has grown greatly. Domestically, it received a strong stimulus from the centennial celebrations of independence in and after 1910. First in point of time among the external factors in its growth were the real or fancied threats posed successively by Europe's new imperialism and then by "Yankee" imperialism. Other factors were World Wars I and II, the great economic depression of the 1930's, and various contagions from foreign doctrines. Notable among these in the past generation have been fascism and Communism, both of which combine a universalist with a national appeal.

Among the various aspects of nationalism, the economic has increasingly been the most highly advertised in Latin America during this period, especially since national planning for economic recovery and development acquired a great vogue during the depression decade of the 1930's. Yet the other aspects of nationalism as well have been highly developed. Political nationalism is eminently represented by Latin America's matchless devotion to the rule of nonintervention in its most extreme form—most extreme in the double sense that it is absolute and that it is interpreted by Latin Americans to cover practically every kind of activity by a foreign nation that they find objectionable.

Cultural nationalism, too, is very strong among them; and the term "cultural" is used here in its broad, anthropological sense, as equivalent to the loose but handy phrase "way of life." To be sure, the strength of this traditionalist sentiment puts the Latin Americans in a dilemma, for it conflicts with the equally strong national-

ist urge for economic and social development through modernization, which requires foreign aid and cooperation. How they can
have their cake and eat it is, as always, a problem.

One final aspect of nationalism in present-day Latin America
needs to be noted. This is the recent widespread revival of continental nationalism à la Bolívar. "Continental nationalism" seems a
contradiction in terms, but the contradiction is more apparent than
real, for, as in Bolívar's time, advocacy of this idea implies, not the
rejection of the nationalist principle, but, on the contrary, its application to an enlarged geographical area; it is simply extended nationalism. Whether or not it is practicable is another question.

The point to be stressed here, however, is that, whether in its
conventional sense or in the extended, continental sense, nationalism is a basic assumption of present-day Latin American thought
about public affairs, and that it is an assumption that has formed an
essential element in the Latin Americans' emotional and intellectual attitudes from the beginning of their independence. Among
them, as among every other people in Western civilization (to go
no further), nationalism has faced the problem of either absorbing
or competing in a kind of sibling rivalry with other group concepts
and interests that are either much broader or much narrower, such
as the universalism of Christianity or Communism and the particularism of family, trade union, or professional guild. But the same
is true, perhaps in even higher degree, of Western Europe and the
United States. Indeed, it is one of the chief stigmata we have in
mind when we speak of the societies of Western Europe and the
United States as characteristically plural; and surely their pluralism
has been no bar to the existence of a vigorous and powerful nationalism among them. Where, after all, was modern nationalism born
but in Western Europe?

A more profitable line of approach is the one proposed by Karl
Deutsch, who relates the range and effectiveness of "nationality"
(as he calls it) to the ability of the various sectors of a given society to communicate with one another. Communications (in this
sense) are being rapidly enlarged in Latin America these days, and
their enlargement is obviously germane to the theme of social
change, to which we now turn.

Nationalism as a Factor in Social Change

What part nationalism plays in social change, and vice versa, varies from one situation to another and in any given situation depends upon many variables. Among these are the kind of nationalism involved, its purposes, and the character and influence of its advocates.

If we simplify (and admittedly oversimplify) the question by approaching it on the basis of the familiar social groupings of right (upper class), center (middle class), and left (working class), we come up with such generalizations as these: Right-wingers use nationalism as a brake on social change and as a means of maintaining the *status quo* for the benefit of the privileged classes. That is what they did in Argentina and Mexico in the late nineteenth century. The middle sectors, on the other hand, are selectively hospitable to social change, which may benefit them; but being relatively well placed and hence relatively patient, they generally prefer long-range, gradual improvements. In present-day Mexico and Argentina, for example, they give economic development the priority over quick and sweeping social reform. Left-wingers, by contrast, give the primacy to social reform for themselves; they want the good life—and they want it *now*.

This left-wing drive is the essence of the "revolution of rising expectations" south of the border. Almost everybody in Latin America has rising expectations, but the other classes could settle for a more gradual rise with some equanimity, and it is the pressure of the impatient masses that makes it revolutionary. Bolivia since 1952 is one example: Even the left-wing Paz Estenssoro regime espoused agrarian revolution only when forced to do so by a peasant revolt. Castro's Cuba appears to be another example, though with a different formula: Brought to power by the middle class, Castro instigated an agrarian revolution for the benefit of the lower class in order to keep himself in power. This was a revolution from above, but if we may judge by the Cuban peasants' enthusiasm for it, it responded to a latent demand on their part.

As already noted, this schematic arrangement is an oversimplification. Class lines in Latin America are in fact much less clearly drawn at any given time than it seems to imply; they change from time to time; and in no two countries is the situation exactly alike. As for Latin America's middle class, it provides leaders for the right wing as well as the left; and the great bulk of its members, who remain middle class, lack cohesion, discipline, and even class consciousness. As for the Latin American oligarchies, which constitute the core of the right wing, they are far from monolithic. In Argentina, the traditionalists among the oligarchs were hostile to the recent Frondizi administration because it was changing Argentina in ways they detest, whereas industrialists and even *estancieros* supported Frondizi (though some of them held their noses while doing so) because they thought his sound economic policies would be good for business—their businesses—in the long run. And in 1961, Brazil presented a curious spectacle: In a national political crisis fraught with connotations of social revolt, the Brazilian left wing had as its leader the wealthy "Jango" Goulart, just back from a pilgrimage to Red China and an *abrazo* by Mao Tse-tung; and this millionaire pink was supported at the risk of civil war by a large part of Brazil's armed forces, traditional pillar of entrenched privilege in that country.

Yet there is one thread that runs through all these permutations and combinations: Almost without exception, every group at whatever social level seeks justification and support by draping itself in the national flag. Illustrations abound in the whole history of Latin America, beginning with Argentina in the age of the tyrant Rosas: Both Rosas and his enemies claimed to be fighting each other in defense of the true Argentina; they merely happened to represent irreconcilably different conceptions of what constituted the true Argentina. The brand of nationalism that triumphed then was one that, according to recent Argentine "revisionists," benefited the entrenched classes, principally those in Buenos Aires.

Nationalism of the Left

One of these revisionists, Ezequiel Martínez Estrada, describes the whole "patristic canon" of Argentina's nineteenth-century nationalism as the work of men who were members of the bourgeoisie, bureaucrats, and *porteños*. Theirs was a liberal, cosmopolitan, and almost wholly political nationalism, as befitted a country

ruled under democratic forms by an *estanciero*-mercantile aristocracy. They stoutly maintained its political independence but, according to twentieth-century nationalists, opened it to cultural conquest by France and to economic conquest by British and other
foreign capital. Paradoxically, this view found clear expression both
in the University Reform movement of 1918 and in Peronism. The
paradox lies in the fact that, when Peronism emerged in the 1940's,
it was stoutly opposed by those leaders of the University Reform
who were still alive and active—Ricardo Rojas, Gabriel del Mazo,
Alfredo Palacios. Yet, despite important differences, these movements were alike in making nationalism integral and in linking it
with social change for the benefit of the masses and at the expense
of Argentina's oligarchy. Where the two differed most was in
Perón's greater stress on xenophobia and class conflict and his use
of authoritarian rather than democratic methods.

"University Reform" sounds narrowly academic, but the movement under that name that spread from Córdoba to other parts of
Argentina in 1918–19, and then to other Latin American countries,
had broad implications for almost every aspect of national life, political and economic and social as well as cultural. These combined
with its ardent nationalism to arouse widespread enthusiasm for it
both at home and abroad. Unrest was already rife in several Latin
American countries over their "colonial subjection" to foreigners
leagued with local oligarchs. Resentment on this score was strong
among the rising middle class, and in none of these countries was
the middle class stronger than in Argentina. There, in 1916, it had
won a political victory in the election of a radical president, Hipólito Irigoyen. The University Reform, launched two years later,
was designed to extend the conquest to a much broader field. Perhaps in order to improve its chances of success, however, it was
presented not as a middle-class but as a national movement, designed for the benefit of all but the privileged few—the oligarchy
through whom the hated foreign domination was maintained.

To Gabriel del Mazo, who championed it from the beginning,
first as a student leader and later as vice-rector of the University of
La Plata, and who became its chief historian and interpreter, University Reform was nothing less than a resumption of the uncom-
pleted independence movement of the early nineteenth century.

Foreign domination of Argentina's whole educational system, he said, had stunted the growth of "national organization" in all its aspects. The key institutions, the universities, were isolated from the mass of the nation, drilled un-Argentine and even anti-Argentine ideas into the students, and, instead of educating them, only trained them for professional careers in the service of the oligarchy and its foreign masters. Hence the reform had to be total. "Our first cultural struggle," wrote Del Mazo, "is the political and social struggle to free ourselves from everything that hampers the development of our native culture."

Thus viewed, University Reform meant not only "nationalization" of the universities, their democratization through student participation in their governing bodies, and their integration with Argentine society at large. With the passage of time it came to mean also, and even more, a change in the country's whole social and power structure in the interest of social justice to the disinherited Argentine masses. By 1938, Del Mazo was writing that "the cultural problem is only one phase of the social problem" and was presenting the social problem in such phrases as "the poor proletarian child, the world's orphan, undernourished and destitute." Thus, a University Reform movement that at the outset in 1918 was primarily an expression of cultural and political nationalism had, at least in Del Mazo's view, shifted its emphasis to social reform.

Also by 1938, Del Mazo was projecting this broad movement on a world-wide scale, saying that "University Reform is one of the names for an ample transformation which responds to a general crisis in the world and to a particular crisis in national development . . . [and] which rises out of the entrails of our country and our America. . . ." Whether under the label "our America" (*nuestra América*) or some other term, the idea of Latin American solidarity in this movement crops up again and again in Del Mazo's writings. To him, Latin America at large was, in his words, *la Patria grande*, "the great Fatherland."

The trend toward left-wing nationalism was carried much further under the regime of Juan Perón, which began to take shape in 1943 and lasted until 1955. Of the regime's three watchwords, two —"Political Sovereignty" and "Economic Independence"—were nationalistic, and the third—"Social Justice"—fixed the particular meaning of this nationalism by assigning first place to "justice" to the *descamisados*, the "shirtless" workers of Argentina. Perón also gave his nationalist regime an authoritarian, quasi-totalitarian character. This affronted nationalist social reformers of Del Mazo's democratic type, but it won the lasting devotion of most Argentine workers. As a result, they remained loyal to Perón after his overthrow in 1955.

For a time thereafter, it looked as if the leader of the left-wing Intransigent Radical Party, Arturo Frondizi, might succeed in weaning many of them away from Perón with promises of sweeping social reforms, coupled with inflexible nationalism, under a free, democratic system. After his election to the presidency in 1958 with the Peronists' aid, however, Frondizi soon alienated them by adopting a conservative plan of financial stabilization and economic development with the backing of the International Monetary Fund and the United States government. The failure of the plan, capped by a Peronist victory at the polls in March, 1962, provoked a military intervention that ousted Frondizi after canceling the Peronists' victory. Thereupon, the bulk of them—about one-third of the politically active population of Argentina—moved even further to the left and adopted a program that was both socially revolutionary and ultranationalistic. The eclipse of Frondizi and his Intransigent Radicals left the Peronists as the principal group exponent of nationalism in Argentina.

In short, Argentine nationalism is identified no longer primarily with the middle class, as it was in most of the Western world until a generation ago, but rather with the working class. The same kind of change has taken place in other Latin American countries. In the largest of all, Brazil, the leftward shift of nationalism was pronounced even during the brief interval between 1940 and 1960, that is, between the heyday of Getúlio Vargas and the rise of his political heir, João Goulart. In Mexico, there has apparently been no such shift since the Cárdenas administration in the 1930's, but on the other hand it may only have been concealed behind the façade of one-party rule. In any event, present-day Mexico is an exception to the general Latin American rule in this respect. To be sure, the vogue of nationalism was never greater than now among all kinds and conditions of Latin Americans, but today its most dynamic and aggressive expression comes not from the middle class, but from the workers and their spokesmen. To the latter, as John Johnson justly observes, "Modern-integrated nationalism represents the collective demand of frustrated people for direct action by the State." And, thanks to the population explosion, Latin America is teeming with frustrated people.

Social Change and the Military

This brings us back to the point that nationalism has no fixed meaning except in a given context and is not the monopoly of the middle class or of any particular class or group. Its lack of a fixed meaning or social habitat does not, however, lessen, but rather augments, its significance for the historian, by the evidence it gives of the universality of the appeal of nationalism in the climate of opinion of the modern age. In recognition of this fact, the Communists today are skillfully exploiting Latin American nationalist sentiment at all social levels, despite the fact that it is logically irreconcilable with their own brand of universalism. It will be difficult for the United States to combat them without showing a similar flexibility.

To what has already been said about social change as a factor in the development of nationalism, three points need to be added. The first is that, contrary to a common assumption, the growth of the middle class in Latin America cannot be counted on to produce the safe-and-sane kind of nationalism preferred by the United States, for at times that class has produced some of Latin America's wildest-eyed nationalists, both of the extreme left and of the extreme right. This occurs with such frequency that I am tempted to proclaim it as "Whitaker's Law" that the only sure thing about the more enterprising members of the Latin American middle class is that they will not stay in the middle.

In the second place, we need much more help, such as sociologists and social psychologists might give us, in analyzing the behavior of previously submerged groups when they become full-fledged, active participants in the public life of their respective countries. Those who are emerging in this way—and the Alliance for Progress is designed to speed their emergence—are virtually certain to become nationalists of one kind or another: What kind may we expect them to become? Argentina provides us with a test case, and a warning, from its recent history. The Argentine masses, who owe their political elevation to Juan Perón, are still behaving like the ultranationalist *descamisados* of a decade ago. Most of those who are no longer Peronists or neo-Peronists are apparently transferring their allegiance to Castroism or Communism; in short, they seem to prefer almost any other type of nationalism to the benign and reasonable and democratic one that we in the United States would like them to choose.

What lessons can be drawn from this Argentine case as regards Latin American nationalism? One lesson is that promoting the proletariat is no more a panacea than strengthening the middle class. Another is that the United States stores up long-range trouble for itself when it uses foreign aid to buy the short-range benefit of the cooperation of a fundamentally alien regime, as it did in the case of the Perón regime in its later years.

The third and last point regarding social change as a factor in the development of nationalism relates to the armed forces of Latin America. I do not intend to broach the general problem of their important role in public affairs, but only to raise a question about the social basis for the assumption, widely held in the United States, that the Latin American armed forces are "good" nationalists and a major bulwark of the anti-Communist, pro-democratic forces in their respective countries.

This assumption seems to be based mainly on two further assumptions. The first is the rather involved one that most Latin American officers come from the middle class, that this class is soundly anti-Communist and pro-democratic, and that the officers retain the imprint of their social origin. The second is the belief that professionalization has made the military an even stronger bulwark for this purpose than the middle class, partly by insulating them from contamination and partly by increasing their efficiency for decisive action in a national crisis through greater *esprit de corps* as well as better training and weapons.

Such reasoning is too generalized to fit the diversity of Latin America. Also, I am doubtful of its validity even with respect to those countries to which, superficially, it might seem most applicable. How can we have faith in its validity after what has happened to Cuba, which was such a country up to three years ago? On the Latin American scale, Cuba had a large middle class, a high standard of living, a high rate of literacy, and a large army, which had for several years received substantial aid from the United States in both matériel and training; and yet this Cuba fell an easy prey to Castro-Communism.

But let us consider the reasoning on broader grounds. There is no warranty for it in the middle-class origin of the Latin American officers. Many of them come from other classes; the Latin American middle classes suffer from many weaknesses, as suggested above; and, as I said in a book about Argentina several years ago, officers of middle-class origin are often what might be called refugees from that class—instead of reflecting middle-class views and ways, they react against them, and the reaction often takes them either far to the right or far to the left.

Again, it remains to be proved that professionalization insulates the Latin American armed forces from the rest of society. On the contrary, in those countries in which they have been most highly professionalized, they seem to have become even more closely linked with the rest of society than formerly. Nor is it at all clear that *esprit de corps* has given the armed forces unity. It has certainly failed to do so in either Argentina or Brazil. In the national crisis of 1961, discussed above, Brazil's armed forces split down the middle, although social issues were deeply involved. In 1962, they did likewise in Argentina, where rival factions of the military have come to the point of armed conflict with each other over the question of what to do about the large, intractable Peronist minority.

Conclusions

To sum up: In Latin America, as in the rest of the Western world, nationalism has been a major force in public life ever since the early nineteenth century; at least in Latin America, it is now at its apogee. Its meanings and purposes have varied widely, in Latin America as elsewhere. in the past century and a half. With equal plausibility and success it has been exploited in widely differing contexts and for widely different purposes by forces of right, center, and left. The unanimity with which it is invoked by public leaders of all kinds testifies to the strength and universality of its appeal: Whether or not patriotism is, as Dr. Samuel Johnson affirmed, the last refuge of a scoundrel, nationalism is certainly the first reliance of every politician. But, except that it exalts the nation-state, nationalism has no specific meaning, for either policy or action, that runs through all situations. Nationalism resembles science in that it gives us tools but does not tell us how to use them. In some ways it also resembles religion, as Carlton Hayes has shown in greatest detail; perhaps it reminds us most of Olympus with its many strangely assorted gods.

For these and other reasons, quantitative studies of nationalism by the social sciences, while deserving all encouragement for the light they shed when data are available, are of very limited value for unstatistical nineteenth-century Latin America, and their value is limited even for the present situation. Today, nationalist movements in Latin America aim at coping with the revolution of rising expectations in one way or another, but are frustrated in all by the population explosion. Frustration favors the employment of utopian short cuts, among which Fidel Castro's effort to promote Cuba's national interests by tying himself to the Communist bloc is perhaps the most utopian. And utopias are hard to quantify.

5

The Emergence of Modern
Political Parties in
Latin America

ROBERT J. ALEXANDER

Latin America is growing up politically. One of the indications of
this maturity is the emergence of modern political parties. The
traditional *caudillismo* of the region is declining. Politics is becoming increasingly a clash of interests, programs, and ideas and less a
mere struggle for power among conflicting charismatic leaders.

At least in part, the emergence of modern political parties in
Latin America is a reflection of the basic economic and social
changes that have taken place during the last two generations.
With the development of important middle groups in society,
politics is no longer, as it was during the first century of independence, merely a game played among rival cliques of a small ruling
class.

Today, Latin America is characterized by increasing industrialization, urbanization, and population. The old social molds, built in
an era when all wealth, education, and political power were the monopoly of a small landed and commercial aristocracy, are cracking
or, in a few countries, have been swept away already.

As a result of these changes, the organized urban workers, rapidly
growing professional classes, students (who come more and more
from the middle ranges of society), the new industrialists, and, in
some countries, even the peasantry are now playing a part in
political life. Each of these groups has concrete objectives that it is

seeking to obtain through political activity. Each seeks to mold the process of change in its own way. At the same time, conservative elements remain strong. They seek to resist the process of change altogether or to cede before it as little as possible. Finally, the whole process of social and economic transformation of Latin America has created fertile ground for political ideas and philosophies from abroad.

The political parties mirror these changes. They show the influence of various interest groups, reflect the clashes of political philosophies, and take a wide variety of points of view concerning the basic issues of social and economic change. There has emerged a type of party that is itself an integral part of this change.

The Traditional Party Pattern

Latin America has had political parties, at least in name, since the early days of independence. Almost every country had its Conservatives and its Liberals. The former generally stood for ultramontanism, opposition to free trade, and a highly centralized form of government; the latter faithfully reflected the liberalism of Europe in being both anticlerical and Manchesterian, and in addition often favored some form of federalism, at least in theory.

These parties held the stage until World War I. They fought out the great issue of nineteenth-century Latin America, the struggle over the secular power of the Church. In most cases, the Liberals won at least a qualified victory. However, it is a commentary on the politics of the time that if the great masses of the people had been consulted on this issue, it would in all likelihood have been decided in favor of the Church.

In the main, the Conservative and Liberal parties of the nineteenth and early twentieth centuries were political organizations of a special sort. They involved only a minute fraction of the population, they engaged in little day-to-day activity, and generally the party was a great deal less important than the man. Within the parties of both types there arose *caudillos*—more often than not, military men or civilians-turned-soldiers. They were the real binding force around which politics ebbed and flowed. Often there would develop a group within one of the parties, a subdivision spe-

cifically devoted to the interests of a particular *caudillo*. Sometimes
such a personalist group would develop entirely outside the structure of the traditional party.

The armed forces played a crucial role in this process. The *coup
d'état* (*golpe de estado*) and even civil war were more or less normal extensions of everyday political activity. The armed forces
themselves were usually organized around particular military-politi-
cal leaders. Frequently, they were a kind of federation of armed
bands of regional *caudillos*, united for a longer or shorter time
around a single national chieftain. The military training of such
armies was low, their personal devotion to a particular leader high.

In Argentina, Brazil, and Chile, there were variations of this
general pattern. These countries were characterized by a degree of
political stability unusual for the area, and the rule of the landed
and commercial aristocracy as a group was more important than the
individual. The game of personal rivalries was generally channeled
within bounds that most politicians agreed to and understood. As a
result, the resort to force in these countries was much less frequent.
Nevertheless, in the ABC countries, too, politics remained the monopoly of a small group belonging to or associated with the dominant economic and social oligarchy.

The Nature of the Modern Parties

The kind of political party that has evolved in Latin America
since World War I differs fundamentally from the parties of the
first century of independence. It is an organization with reasonably
well-defined programs and ideologies. The various parties represent
the widest spectrum of political philosophy. Often they are organizations representing or seeking to represent the interests of particular groups within the evolving society. It is upon the basis of their
ideologies, platforms, and programs, and their appeals to special interest groups, rather than on the grounds of allegiance to a particular political leader, that they recruit their membership.

The new political party in Latin America also has a much more intensive internal life than did the older kind. It has local organizations throughout the country conducting activities of their own
most of the year and not merely on the eve of an election or in the

morning after a *coup d'état*. They hold periodic membership meetings. They gather for regular local, regional, and national conventions, and they do so even when no election or other change in government is in the offing.

These parties involve relatively large numbers of citizens drawn from various classes. They often carry on organized activities within the ranks of labor unions, professional associations, and other non-political groups. Many support a variety of periodicals and publish pamphlets and even books. Some have organized groups within them to carry on a continuous study of the economic and social problems of their countries—regardless of whether they are, at the moment, in the government or in the opposition. These studies may form the basis for policy and be published. Sometimes, though by no means always, the parties collect dues from their members and issue membership cards or other means of identifying those who belong.

Finally, the new parties are *civilista*. Although they have certainly not completely eschewed political cooperation with groups among the military (including participation in *coups d'état*), such contacts tend to be circumstantial and temporary, and their attention is centered on political action in the civilian field. Generally they seek, at least in principle, to keep the military out of politics.

Typology of Parties

There are many possible ways of analyzing the types of organizations that we have included under the heading of "new" or "modern" political parties in Latin America. We shall divide them here into three basic groups, each with its own subgroupings.

There are, first of all, the old traditional parties, which have been able to adapt themselves and their programs to the changing circumstances, the Conservatives and the Liberals.

Secondly, there are the parties of more recent origin following or seeking to follow European models. They include the Radicals, Socialists, Christian Democrats, Fascists, and the Communists and their splinters.

Finally, there are what may be called the indigenous parties of change, which have developed in recent decades. This type may be subdivided into what we shall call the national revolutionary parties and the personalist revolutionary parties.

Obviously, any attempt to put into nice categories all of the important political parties of Latin America is beset with serious difficulties. One may quarrel with the categories themselves, or one may doubt the validity of assigning a specific label to a particular party. Nevertheless, we feel that, for purposes of analysis, there is something to be gained by establishing some sort of system in what at first glance appears to be a confusing conglomeration of organizations with peculiar and often meaningless names. We believe that there is some discernible rhyme and reason to the political parties of Latin America and that they are among the most important phenomena in the process of revolutionary change in the area.

The Traditional Parties

In most of Latin America, the traditional parties of the nineteenth century have ceased to be a major factor in political life or have disappeared altogether. In Mexico, El Salvador, Costa Rica, Venezuela, Peru, and the Dominican Republic, the Liberals and Conservatives no longer exist. In Guatemala, Cuba, Bolivia, and Brazil, their political weight is slight. In Haiti, they may be said never to have existed at all, since, until recent years, politics in that country has defied all description except in terms of rivalries among competing *caudillos* played against a background of permanent tensions between mulattoes and full-blooded Negroes.

Only in Honduras, Nicaragua, Colombia, and Uruguay are the traditional parties still the dominant competitors for power, and even in these nations, as we shall see, the Liberals and Conservatives have greatly changed in character. In Panama, Ecuador, Chile, Argentina, and Paraguay, they still have an important role in national politics, but they share the stage with more recent parties.

In countries where the traditional parties have maintained a foothold in the political arena, they have done so at the cost of a radical change in outlook. They have adapted themselves to changing circumstances by appealing to particular interest groups and by modifying their programs and methods of action.

THE CONSERVATIVES. Where the Conservatives continue to be a factor of importance, they are, in most cases, the party of the large landowning class engaged in a rear-guard struggle to maintain its privileges, or, as the Partido Blanco in Uruguay, the spokesmen of the rural areas against the encroaching power of the cities. Their voting strength in Ecuador and Chile comes largely from the ability of landlords to march their tenants and agricultural workers off to the polls to vote for Conservative Party candidates.

However, even in the Conservative parties, the "winds of change" have not failed to leave things untouched. Generally, the Conservatives are no longer distinguished principally as supporters of the secular power of the Church. Dissident groups have arisen under the banner of Social Catholicism, in direct and sometimes bitter opposition to the Conservative Party, as in Chile, or in co-operation with the old guard, as in Ecuador. In Argentina, the Conservatives have been profoundly shaken by the Peronista experience, with some of their leaders attempting to appear as more fervent advocates of social reform than Perón himself.

In Colombia, Paraguay, and Uruguay, the Conservatives probably owe their strength to the traditional appeal of party labels to their followers. In these countries, the active membership in the Conservative parties tends to cut more generally across class lines than in most of the other nations.

In Nicaragua, the Conservatives have, in recent years, played a unique role as the principal legal opposition to the dictatorship of the Somoza family. As a result, they have tended to attract many people of advanced ideas more anxious to fight the tyranny than concerned with problems of political tradition or ideology.

THE LIBERALS. With the exception of Chile and Nicaragua, the Liberal parties have become the spokesmen for important new segments of the population that have arisen in the wake of the economic and social revolution in Latin America. Thus the Liberal parties of Colombia, Honduras, and Ecuador are the principal political vehicle for the urban workers employed in factories and modern transportation, public utility, and agricultural enterprises. In Colombia and Honduras especially, the influence of the Liberal politicians is extensive within the organized labor movement itself.

The Argentine Radical Party (Unión Cívica Radical), which, in spite of its name, holds the same position in Argentina as the Liberal parties in other Latin American countries, has from the beginning differed from its counterparts in other nations. From the 1890's on, it has been the principal representative of the urban and rural middle classes, drawing much of its voting strength from the city workers. However, there has always existed within the Radical Party an element from the landowning aristocracy. The struggle for pre-eminence between this element and the more middle-class leadership had been partly responsible for the first major split within the Radical ranks in the 1920's between the so-called personalistas, led by Hipólito Irigoyen, and the antipersonalistas, led by Marcelo T. de Alvear. During the 1930's, the antipersonalistas shared control of the government with the Conservatives in a thinly veiled dictatorship backed by the military.

Since the advent of the Peronista phenomenon, the Radical Party is more clearly a middle-class party. The majority of both the urban and the rural working classes has come to regard the Peronistas as its chief defender and spokesman. Consequently, there has been a sharp division of opinion among the Unión Cívica Radical leaders as to what approach should be taken to the Peronistas, a division that in part led to the split of the party late in 1956 into the UCR Intransigente (more inclined to work with the Peronistas) and the UCR del Pueblo (more definitely anti-Peronista). However, even the Intransigente Radicals have been unable to exert any real influence in the organized labor movement.

Although recent years have been marked by much confusion in Argentine politics in general, and Radical affairs in particular, rough lines of political loyalty of various classes are fairly clear. Taken together, the Radicals may be said to represent the great bulk of middle-class folk, the Peronistas to speak for the majority of the wage workers; while the many smaller parties have minority followings among these two major classes and among the old aristocracy.

One of the most remarkable examples of adaptation to a modern environment by a traditional Liberal Party has been that of the Partido Colorado of Uruguay. Early in this century, under the leadership of José Batlle y Ordóñez, the party became the principal vehicle for social, political, and economic change in that small republic. Not only did it carry out the nineteenth-century program of separation of Church and state, but it also established some of the country's first social security and labor protective legislation. Under its leadership, Uruguay was the first Latin American country to establish a policy of economic nationalism as a means of achieving economic development and diversification. Finally, the Colorados sponsored the experiment in a multiple executive that has been one of the few serious attempts to deal with the Latin American tendency of converting a strong executive into a dictatorship.

The Chilean and Nicaraguan Liberal parties are exceptions to the general picture. In Chile, the Liberals have continued to represent a fraction of the traditional ruling class, and if anything have become more conservative than the Conservatives. They have joined with the Conservatives in the battle against agrarian reform and more equitable distribution of wealth. In Nicaragua, their survival is due partly to the fact that they have been the chosen political instrument of the Somoza family, which has run the country's affairs for more than a quarter of a century. The fate of the Liberal Party, once this clan has been ousted from power, is difficult to predict. Even under the Somozas, the Liberal Party has had support among some segments of the urban working class. This element may eventually assert control over the party in the post-Somoza period. Or the Liberals may, by that time, have become so discredited by their long association with the dictatorship that they will disappear.

European-Patterned Parties

Many of the newer-style political parties which during the last two generations have challenged the Conservatives and Liberals were patterned after European models. These include at least one Radical Party roughly similar to the Parti Radical Socialiste of France, various Socialist parties, the Christian Democrats, the Fascists, and the Communists of various shades.

The emergence of European-patterned groups reflects the impact of Old World ideas on Latin America. In not a few cases, immigrants from Europe sought to establish in their new countries the kind of political organizations with which they had been familiar at home. As was perhaps inevitable, most parties took on their own characteristics. At times they moved far from the original European pattern.

THE RADICALS. The oldest of these European-oriented parties is undoubtedly the Partido Radical of Chile. It was established in the last decades of the nineteenth century as a left-wing offshoot of the Liberals. Like its counterpart in France, the Radical Party of Chile has been the typical expression of the middle class. At first a favorite among artisans and small shopkeepers, it subsequently became the party of the white-collar class, particularly the government bureaucracy.

Like the French Radicals, too, the Chilean party has oscillated violently in political philosophy and orientation. At times proclaiming themselves as socialists, they have at other times participated in Conservative government coalitions. Although they consider themselves to be of the left, they have more truly been the fulcrum of national politics, determining at any given instant whether the left or the right was to have the majority in Congress and even in public opinion.

For all their oscillations, the Radicals have played an important role in the modernization of Chile. They participated in the early 1920's in the government of President Arturo Alessandri, which was largely responsible for enacting the country's basic labor and social laws a decade before such legislation became popular in most other Latin American countries. In the early 1940's, Radical presidents headed governments that encouraged the almost universal unionization of urban workers and developed a program of economic development, making Chile one of the four most industrialized nations of Latin America.

The Radicals may well play a decisive role in determining whether Chile launches once again a program of democratic reform in the 1960's or falls into the arms of totalitarians. A great deal depends upon their willingness to form a center coalition with the Christian Democrats and other groups for the 1964 election. Their willingness or lack of it will probably determine whether changes of vital importance, like agrarian reform, can be carried out democratically, or whether the totalitarians will be faced with a divided opposition, permitting them to convert Chile into the first Latin American nation voluntarily to adopt the Communist path to social change and economic development.

THE SOCIALISTS. The Socialists were among the first political groups on the Latin American scene to advocate a fundamental transformation of their economies and societies. During the 1860's, 1870's, and 1880's, numerous immigrants who had been active in the First International and the first European Socialist parties found their way to America. They established small groups, and some of them sought affiliation with the International. Although most of them remained relatively isolated from the political life of the Latin American countries, a few became nuclei around which Socialist parties were organized.

The claim to be the oldest Socialist Party in Latin America is disputed between the Chilean Democratic Party, which appeared in the 1880's but subsequently gave up all pretense of belonging in the Socialist camp, and the Argentine Socialist Party, founded in 1896. During the decades before World War I, Socialist parties appeared also in Uruguay, Brazil, Mexico, and Cuba. In this period, they generally disputed control of the organized labor movements with the anarcho-syndicalists. In most cases, the parties were organized by immigrants from Europe. Although they quickly gained local adherents and even leaders, they regarded themselves as American counterparts of the Social Democratic parties in the Old World. In philosophy they were Marxist.

The Brazilian, Mexican, and Cuban parties disappeared during or soon after World War I. The Chilean Socialist Labor Party and the Uruguayan Socialist Party joined the Communist International. In Chile, a new Socialist Party did not appear until 1933. In Uruguay, Emilio Frugoni, the party founder, withdrew from the Communist ranks and re-established the Socialist Party in 1922.

In the 1930's and 1940's, a number of new Socialist parties were organized in Peru, Bolivia, Panama, Brazil, and Ecuador. In the 1950's an attempt was made by the Socialist International to associate all of these in the International. A Latin American Secretariat of the International, with which most of the parties did become associated, was established in Montevideo. The only actual members of the International, however, were the parties of Argentina and Uruguay, and the Uruguayan party withdrew in 1960.

Unfortunately, most of the Socialist parties of Latin America have abandoned the camp of Democratic Socialism. In some cases, they have been heavily infiltrated or influenced by the local Communist parties. In most instances, they have adopted xenophobic nationalist positions that have made them violently anti-United States and pro-Soviet. Only the Argentine Social Democratic Party and the Ecuadorean Socialist Party have remained more or less loyal to the ideas they originally espoused.

THE CHRISTIAN DEMOCRATS. The Christian Democrats are a relatively new type of party in Latin America. They reflect the emergence of a more socially conscious wing of the Roman Catholic Church, a phenomenon produced largely since World War II. Although the Uruguayan Unión Cívica and the Chilean Falange Nacional antedate the war, all of the others have emerged subsequently.

The Christian Democrats find their philosophical inspiration in the principal papal encyclicals on social problems: *Rerum Novarum, Quadregesimo Anno,* and *Mater et Magistra.* Although their main constituency is found among the middle class, they have in a number of instances successfully sought to gain influence in the organized labor and peasant movements. They are strong advocates of basic social and economic change. The quality of their leadership is generally high. They include among their ranks some of the outstanding intellectuals of the region, particularly those of the younger generation.

The three most important Christian Democratic parties are those of Uruguay, Chile, and Venezuela. The first of these was formed between the two world wars. It is unlikely to become one of the major Uruguayan parties, but it has an assured place in that country's political spectrum. It has mainly a middle-class following.

The Falange Nacional of Chile was established in the 1930's in the wake of a revolt of the Young Conservatives against their party. Although in the beginning its democratic orientation was the subject of some conjecture, the party evolved into one of the strongest supporters of the democratic traditions of Chile. Very early it began to seek support in the labor movement, and it has had considerable success in that direction. In the August, 1962, congress of the nation's principal central labor body, the Central Única de Trabajadores de Chile, the Christian Democrats had about 35 per cent of the delegates. They represent the principal challenge to Communist control of the country's trade unions.

In the late 1950's, the Falange Nacional merged with a number of smaller groups of more or less the same orientation to form the present Christian Democratic Party. It is one of the six major parties of Chile and has a fair chance of electing one of its members president in 1964.

The Venezuelan Christian Democratic Party, known as the Partido Social Cristiano (Copei), was established in 1946. It brought together a group of young intellectuals under the leadership of Rafael Caldera. Between 1946 and 1948 it was the country's second largest party. During the dictatorship of General Marcos Pérez Jiménez from November, 1948, to January, 1958, the party lost most of its more conservative elements because of its opposition to the regime. In 1958, it emerged as a strong advocate of basic social reform.

With the inauguration of President Rómulo Betancourt in 1959, the Copei entered the government along with Betancourt's Acción Democrática and the Unión Republicana Democrática (URD). The Copei remained after the URD withdrew in November, 1960. With the Acción Democrática, it bore the responsibility for carrying out a program of rapid industrialization, agrarian reform, educational expansion, and general transformation of Venezuelan economic and social life.

Although the Copei emerged from the Pérez Jiménez dictatorship proportionately smaller than it had been in 1948, it made slow but steady progress after 1958. It has achieved some influence in organized labor, and considerably more in the peasant movement. Its strength is still concentrated (as it was in the 1946–48 period) in the three mountain states of Táchira, Mérida, and Trujillo, but it has succeeded in broadening its base both geographically and socially.

In addition to these three parties, Christian Democratic groups have appeared since World War II in Argentina, Peru, Bolivia, Paraguay, Brazil, Cuba, the Dominican Republic, Haiti, Puerto

Rico, Nicaragua, Guatemala, and El Salvador. Generally, they are on the moderate left, although their exact position in national politics has varied with the general alignment of forces in a particular country.

The Latin American Christian Democrats regard themselves as counterparts of the European parties of the same name. They all belong to the Christian Democratic International. In a congress of the International in Santiago de Chile in August, 1961, the Venezuelan and Chilean parties sponsored a successful resolution urging a general alliance between Christian Democrats and other parties of the democratic left in Latin America.

THE FASCISTS. The European totalitarians have had counterparts in Latin America as well. There were Fascist parties in a number of Latin American countries, particularly in the 1930's and 1940's, when fascism was at its apogee internationally. In Brazil and Chile, the Fascists, known respectively as Integralistas and Nacistas, were for some years parties of considerable consequence. They had all the trappings of their European brethren, including uniformed storm troopers and anti-Semitism. With the international defeat of fascism, the Chilean Partido Nacista disappeared, but the Brazilian Integralistas transformed themselves into the Partido de Representação Popular, which in its new form has tried to eschew its Fascist past.

The most alive member of the Fascist International in Latin America is the Falange Socialista Boliviana. Formed in the late 1930's on the model of the Spanish Falange, the FSB remained a small group until 1952. Then, because it had not been discredited by participation in the regimes that preceded the national revolution of the year, the Falange became the principal focus of the forces opposed to the revolution. In the presidential elections of 1956 and 1960 and the congressional elections of 1958 and 1962, it received most of the opposition votes, and elected several members to Congress. For a while, a splinter of the government party known as the Partido Revolucionario Auténtico threatened to displace the Falange as the principal opposition group, but an alliance between the two was formed in the middle of 1962.

There have been Fascist parties in Argentina, Mexico, Peru, and perhaps one or two other countries, without, however, any significant role in the political life of these nations.

THE COMMUNISTS AND THEIR SPLINTERS. Among the European-patterned parties there are, finally, the Communists. There is now a Communist Party in every Latin American country. Some of them date from the early years of the Comintern, others arose in the 1940's and 1950's. Generally, the Latin American Communist parties follow the pattern of such organizations in other parts of the world. Over the years they have had two basic objectives: to serve the purposes of the Soviet Union and to establish the when and where of possible dictatorships of their own parties. They have followed faithfully the zigs and zags of the international Communist line.

The nature of the Communist appeal has varied from time to time. Generally, they have sought to picture themselves as the only real advocates of social change in Latin America and as the only true defenders of the working class. They have consistently pointed to the Soviet Union and other Communist countries as models that the Latin American nations should follow, first in terms of social revolution and more recently in terms of rapid economic development. In recent decades, they have sought to make the utmost use of nationalism and to turn it especially against the United States.

Until the advent of the Castro regime in Cuba, the Communists in most Latin American countries were little more than nuisance groups. Since 1959, however, they have achieved new importance. Their support of Castro has opened wider fields of contact with other political groups and has removed them from their almost complete isolation of the 1950's. The Castro phenomenon has also made the Communists more willing to use methods of violent insurrection and guerrilla war than they had been during most of their history. Moreover, the Cuban Revolution has sharpened the issue of social and economic revolution in Latin America. Thus, it has created a wider audience for the Communists' propaganda that only their particular totalitarian way would provide the kind of rapid change that the situation demanded.

The Communists have since acquired new allies in the Fidelista parties and groups in various countries. These Fidelistas have not formally joined the international Communist movement, but they have been willing to work openly with the Communists. They have been more anxious than the Communists themselves to engage in what the latter have called "putschism," that is, armed conflict with the supporters of the *status quo* or the advocates of peaceful change.

Although the Communists and Fidelistas have become allies, it is by no means certain that they will always remain so. Should the conflicts between Soviet and Chinese Communists come more clearly into the open and the various national affiliates of the international Communist movement be forced to align themselves with one or the other, it seems likely that most of the Communist parties will side with the Russians, while the Fidelistas might throw in their lot with the Chinese.

Previous splits in the international Communist movement have not found much echo in Latin America. The only exception has been the Trotskyites. At one time or another, there have been Trotskyite parties in Mexico, Peru, Bolivia, Chile, Argentina, Uruguay, Brazil, and Cuba.

The only member of this group to achieve any real significance in national political life has been the Trotskyite party of Bolivia, the Partido Obrero Revolucionario (POR). For a few years in the late 1940's and early 1950's, the members of the POR achieved considerable power in the trade union movement, and for a few months after the beginning of the Bolivian National Revolution in 1952 it controlled the Central Obrera Boliviana. However, their insistence that President Víctor Paz Estenssoro was going to play the role of Kerensky as against their own Lenin in the Bolivian Revolution incurred the enmity of the Movimiento Nacionalista Revolucionario, which was leading the revolution. It also caused disillusionment among most POR trade union leaders, with the result that the POR quickly lost its influence. Today it is reduced to two small groups of little significance.

The Indigenous Parties of Change

In addition to the parties that derived their ideological and programmatic inspiration from Europe, there are two groups of parties that have grown out of the changing situation in Latin America itself: the national revolutionary parties and the personalist revolutionary parties.

THE NATIONAL REVOLUTIONARY PARTIES. The single most important group of democratic political parties in Latin America are the national revolutionaries. They have grown out of the particular circumstances of their countries. Because of the similarity of problems in various Latin American nations, however, they have tended to adopt broadly similar ideologies and programs. They include the Acción Democrática of Venezuela, the APRA Party of Peru, the Liberación Nacional of Costa Rica, the Movimiento Nacionalista Revolucionario of Bolivia, the Febrerista Party of Paraguay, the Partido Revolucionario Dominicano, and the Partido Popular Democrático of Puerto Rico. The Partido Revolucionario Institucional of Mexico might also be placed in this category.

These parties present in their platforms a program for the democratic transformation of their particular countries and of Latin America as a whole. They advocate an agrarian reform adapted to the specific needs of their respective nations. They favor extensive social and labor legislation and the development of strong trade union and peasant movements under democratic leadership. They are nationalist without being xenophobic. They seek to bring the key elements of their countries' national economies into the hands of local citizens or the national government. While not rejecting foreign investment, they seek to establish conditions for its entry that will not compromise their national sovereignty. They favor mixed economies, with the government performing the key function of stimulating and directing rapid economic development. Above all, they stand for the firm establishment of political democracy.

In recent years the national revolutionary parties have borne the responsibility of government in Mexico, Bolivia, Venezuela, Puerto Rico, the Dominican Republic, and Costa Rica. To be sure, conditions have varied considerably in each case. In general, however, these nations have been in the vanguard in Latin America because of their insistence on effecting basic social revolution through democratic means. Whether or not Latin America can achieve a solid basis for democracy depends to a very considerable degree on the ability of the national revolutionary parties to carry forward with sufficient rapidity the social transformation and economic development essential for making democracy the rule rather than the exception.

The Mexican Partido Revolucionario Institucional has been in charge of the conduct of the Mexican Revolution for a quarter of a century, and it has almost become synonymous with it. Unlike its kindred parties, the PRI came into being after, rather than before, the country was well started on the revolutionary path. It was established some eighteen years after the beginning of the Mexican Revolution. Through the PRI, a pacific method has been evolved for solving the perennial problem of the presidential succession, with Mexico enjoying an unusual degree of political stability. The PRI has also shown remarkable ability to adapt the pace and direction of the revolution to changing circumstances. Although other parties do function legally in Mexico, with considerable freedom of speech and the press, the machinery of government is fully in the hands of the PRI.

The Movimiento Nacionalista Revolucionario of Bolivia has led a revolution with many similarities to Mexico's PRI. It has attempted to incorporate the Indians into the nation by granting them land, the vote, and arms and by trying to bring as rapidly as possible education, medical care, and other social services to the Indian areas. It has at the same time pushed a program of economic development that is at last beginning to bear some fruit. It has sought to strengthen the nation's control over its own economy, principally through expropriation of the three largest tin-mining enterprises. The momentum of the revolution and the popular support of the government have given the country the most stable regime in its history.

For almost a quarter of a century the Venezuelan Acción Democrática has likewise been urging a fundamental revolution in the country's economic, social, and political affairs. When it was first in power between 1945 and 1948, it sought to obtain the largest possible return for the nation from the exploitation of its main export industry, petroleum, by foreign companies. And it tried to invest this return in the diversification of the economy, the development of education, and the improvement of living standards for large parts of the population.

Since 1959, the Acción Democrática has again been principally responsible for the conduct of government under President Rómulo Betancourt. Its regime started an agrarian reform that, by the time Betancourt went out of office early in 1964, provided 100,000 peasant families with land. It has doubled the number of students in school. It has sought to bring basic public services such as electricity, sewage, and water supply to virtually every town and village in the country. It has energetically pushed a program of agricultural and industrial development in which both government and private enterprise have played essential roles.

But the Acción Democrática regime since 1959 has had to face a degree of opposition from the extreme right and the extreme left unequaled in any other Latin American country. Remnants of the military clique that traditionally ran the country have been relentless in their efforts to overthrow the Betancourt government. At the same time, Betancourt has been the chief target of the Communists and the Castro government of Cuba, who are fully aware that his regime represents a clear negation of their claim that rapid economic development and drastic social reform are possible only under totalitarian tyranny.

The Puerto Rican government of the Popular Democratic Party under Governor Luis Muñoz Marín has operated under very different circumstances. But like the governments in Mexico, Bolivia, and Venezuela, it has pushed a land redistribution effort, a vast program for agricultural diversification, and industrialization under government inspiration and orientation, albeit largely through private firms. It has also succeeded in putting virtually every child of primary-school age into the classroom, and it has carried out public-health measures that have given the island one of the world's lowest death rates.

The Partido Revolucionario Dominicano was organized in exile, under the leadership of Juan Bosch, a distinguished literary figure. When dictator Rafael Trujillo was assassinated in May, 1961, PRD leaders returned home to establish grass-roots units of the party. It won the presidential election in December, 1962, putting Juan Bosch in the chief executive post; since taking office in February,

1963, the PRD government has launched a program of social reform and economic development—now again in jeopardy since the overthrow of the Bosch government in the fall of 1963.

In Costa Rica, the Liberación Nacional governments of Presidents José Figueres and Francisco Orlich have had perhaps the easiest task of any of the national revolutionary regimes. Social problems in Costa Rica have been less critical than elsewhere. But the Liberación Nacional governments have successfully initiated programs of industrialization and electrification of rural areas. They have encouraged the class of small landowners and assured it of adequate markets and credit facilities. At the same time, they stimulated the rise in urban living standards and the passage of sound, progressive labor and social legislation. In Costa Rica, too, the government has sought to increase the nation's return as a catalyst for economic development and social reform.

The national revolutionary parties of Peru, Paraguay, and the Dominican Republic have not as yet had an opportunity to show what they can do in government. However, the APRA Party, the first of the national revolutionary parties to come into existence, has contributed very considerably to developing a body of ideas shared by all of them. Several times it was kept out of control of Peru by force (the latest instance was in 1962).

All the national revolutionary parties recognize a kinship among themselves. On several occasions they have held international conferences. They have joined with some of the more advanced liberal parties to establish an Institute of Political Education in Costa Rica for the training of second-rank leaders, and they have lent moral support to one another in moments of great crisis.

PERSONALIST REVOLUTIONARY PARTIES. The second category of indigenous parties consists of two organizations, the Partido Peronista of Argentina and the Partido Trabalhista Brasileiro (PTB). These two parties are similar in origin and are likely to evolve in somewhat similar directions in the years immediately ahead.

Both were organized by socially minded dictators, Juan Perón and Getúlio Vargas. In both instances, they were designed as vehicles for organizing working-class support for the dictators and their tenure in power.

Since the disappearance of their founders—Perón is in exile and

Vargas committed suicide—the parties have seemingly taken different directions. Yet, there is good reason to believe that they may both end up in the camp of the national revolutionary parties.

During the 1950's, the Partido Trabalhista Brasileiro was the refuge for a large number of opportunistic politicians, who tried to use it as a means for sinecures and nepotism. It had been founded ten years earlier by trade union leaders and Ministry of Labor officials loyal to Vargas. But by the mid-1950's, the PTB had no important trade union figure in its top leadership. True, the urban workers continued largely to look upon the Partido Trabalhista as "their" party, but it had no identifiable philosophy or program. This state of confusion allowed pro-Communist elements to infiltrate the ranks of the PTB in several states.

When President Jânio Quadros resigned in August, 1961, the head of the PTB, Vice President João Goulart, became President of Brazil. However, this had relatively little effect upon the PTB as a party. The important currents at work within it were far removed from the national capital of Brasília.

In recent years, new forces within the PTB have come to the forefront in a number of states. They seek to clean out the more blatantly opportunistic elements and forge a program similar to that of the other national revolutionary parties, favoring planned economic development, agrarian reform, and vigilance against party subversion by corruption and Communism. The renovators have indeed seized leadership of the party in the states of Bania and Paraná. In Rio Grande do Sul, a similar movement under the leadership of Fernando Ferrari has sought to take control of the party from "orthodox" elements.

To be sure, the PTB is still a very heterogeneous grouping. In the city of Rio de Janeiro, it is led by pro-Communist xenophobic nationalists. In some other states, the opportunists are still dominant. However, if the grass-roots movement for cleansing and rebuilding the party on the basis of a genuine program of the democratic left gains national momentum, it is likely to convert the PTB into an ideologically consistent national revolutionary party.

The problem within the Peronista Party is of a somewhat different order. When Perón left the country, the work of reorganizing the party fell largely to its trade union members. They looked upon the party as a vehicle for the political expression of the organized labor movement. In general, they did not seek a return to Perón's kind of dictatorial regime. The ex-dictator himself, however, has made no secret of his desire to return to absolute power. In that case, he has assured the nation, "heads will roll." Most Peronista leaders have remained personally loyal to Perón, and as long as he is alive, there remains the constant danger that the Partido Peronista may be used as a vehicle for re-establishing his particular type of dictatorship. Without Perón, the political movement he began may well be incorporated into the democratic life of Argentina as a group of the moderate left, supporting a program not unlike that of the national revolutionary parties elsewhere.

The Decline of Personalism

This review of the complex network of political parties in Latin America has indicated the key role they play in civic affairs. Among the many effects they have had on the traditional political structure and behavior, one of the most important has been that of diminishing the influence of "personalism" in Latin American politics.

Traditionally, Latin American politics have been viewed only in terms of the conflicting ambitions of rival leaders. During much of the nineteenth and early twentieth centuries, there was considerable justification for such a viewpoint. However, the emergence of political parties of the various types we have noted has been a principal factor in converting politics into something a good deal more complex than a game between personal rivals.

It would be foolish to maintain that leadership is a matter of no importance in the present parties. Particular individuals have played exceedingly important parts in determining the orientation of the older parties and bringing into existence the newer ones. Thus, the influence of José Batlle, who put his stamp on the Uruguayan Colorado Party, is still alive today, thirty-five years after his death. Similarly, it would be hard to think of the Aprista Party without reference to Haya de la Torre, or of the Acción Democrática without pointing to Rómulo Betancourt. The fact remains, however, that the purpose of these parties is not to advance the fortunes of these men, nor will the parties disappear if they pass from the scene. The parties we have discussed were organized by groups of individuals, not by a single leader, and they were established to advocate and carry out a program.

It is noteworthy that the great majority of party leaders themselves have sought to avoid *caudillismo*. Thus, the very purpose of organizing the Liberación Nacional in Costa Rica was to break with the national tradition of leadership by *caudillos*. In 1962, the party showed that it could elect a candidate even if he was not the man who had first led it.

Another indication of the nonpersonalist nature of most Latin American parties today is the fact that when their leaders reach office, they do not engage in the age-old Latin American practice of altering the constitution to keep the president in power indefinitely. As presidents, both José Figueres and Rómulo Betancourt supported amendments to the constitution to make it impossible for them to be chief executives again until after two terms had passed. The Mexican PRI has been scrupulously loyal to the absolute prohibition of re-electing anyone who has ever been president. In Colombia, the Liberal and Conservative parties sponsored a constitutional amendment to require rotation not only of individuals but of parties in the presidency.

One factor that further diminishes the chances of personalism in the modern political parties is the fact that they must appeal to increasingly well-organized and vocal interest groups. Thus, a leader who had ridden to power on promises made to a particular group, e.g., organized labor, would find that personal mystique was not enough to maintain the loyalty of that group if he failed to fulfill his promises. Arturo Frondizi, who came to power as the undisputed leader of Unión Cívica Radical Intransigente in 1958, discovered that he quickly lost popular support when as president he adopted a program markedly different from the one he had advocated as candidate.

Even the Peronista Party and the PTB, which had been frankly personalist, turned out to be a good deal more than vehicles for their founders. The PTB, which has gone on for more than eight years after the death of Getúlio Vargas, virtually ceased to be a Getulista party and has become in the eyes of most workers a real labor party. It seems certain that the Partido Peronista will also outlive its founder.

The Parties and the Military

In Latin American politics, personalism and military participation have, historically, been closely linked. Most of the great *caudillos* of the first century of independence were military men or were put in power by the armed forces. The organization of modern political parties provides a strong counterweight not only to personalism but to militarism as well.

In theory, virtually all of the modern parties are opposed to military intervention in politics. True, this has not prevented many of them from conspiring with the military. The Acción Democrática made a revolution in alliance with younger army leaders in 1945. The Radicals and others conspired against Perón with dissident military chiefs. And since 1955, the Peronistas have done the same. Both Conservatives and Liberals have worked with elements of the Colombian Army.

Nevertheless, present-day political parties represent a challenge to the traditional role of the military as the ultimate arbiter in national affairs. They have been able to arouse and to organize popular civilian opposition to military tyrannies. If they control the organized labor movement, they are able through the general strike either to thwart attempts by the military to seize power or to overthrow them once it has done so.

In recent decades, the political parties have displayed a healthy vigor in the face of persecution by dictatorships. The rank and file have remained loyal, and tens of thousands have risked death, jail, or exile to struggle against dictatorial oppression.

The Problem of Losing Elections

The future of democracy in Latin America depends on the resilience of the modern political parties. Many of the parties still have much to learn about how to make democracy work, and a fundamental lesson for them to learn is how to lose an election gracefully.

Although all of the Latin American parties, except the totalitarians, are formally committed to democracy, many of them have not learned that an election can be lost honestly and that opposition to an elected regime must be conducted by democratic means.

In Colombia, the refusal of the Conservatives to accept a minority-party status led to nine years of virtual civil war (1948–57) and, finally, to a system of compromise whereby they and the Liberals must constitutionally alternate in power for two decades. The tendency of all opposition parties in present-day Venezuela is to turn to conspiracy instead of legal opposition to the regime in power. In Argentina, several parties loudly professing their belief in democracy became so conspiratorial under Perón that they have found it difficult to engage in purely legal opposition ever since.

The Parties and the Latin American Revolution

The democratic parties of Latin America must not only learn how to lose an election; they must also succeed in bringing about the social revolution and rapid economic development that Latin America requires—or else the task will be taken from them by the totalitarians. At the present time, the great majority of the workers, peasants, and middle class of Latin America are still loyal to the democratic parties. If these organizations cannot fulfill their promises, the Latin American masses will opt for some other alternative.

The often-cited "revolution of rising expectations" has had a tremendous impact upon the people of Latin America. They are fully aware that poverty is not supernaturally created; and they know that the landlord class has no God-given right to keep the great mass of the rural population landless. They have become convinced that if living standards are to be raised, the land must be redistributed and the economies diversified and industrialized.

Nationalism is virtually universal in Latin America. The same masses that seek social change and economic development also want to see the control of their national economies in the hands of their own citizens, and they are demanding this from those who control their governments.

The democratic parties of Latin America are committed to a

program of social reform, economic development, and nationalism. Only the future can tell whether or not these parties will be able to carry out such a program on the basis of political democracy. This is today the great problem in Latin American politics. And the fate of the hemisphere rests upon its solution.

6

The Mexican Left

DANIEL COSÍO VILLEGAS

The idea of "Left," "Center," or "Right" is by its very nature a relative one: One is to the left of someone or something. Even though it takes a Mao to push Nikita to the right, in Guatemala an ordinary citizen who advocates better maintenance of public parks may be considered a wild radical and be tried and punished for his radicalism. In this essay our point of reference is the Mexican government and its general or particular stance in regard to a given issue. This will be the best standard of measurement and also the best approach, for the federal government is the strongest political force in Mexico and therefore it sets the political tone for the entire nation.

i

There is a very special circumstance that makes the Left's position in Mexico a difficult one—bearing in mind always that the concept of the Left covers ideas or plans as well as action undertaken by individuals, groups, and parties. Today's Mexico, indeed, apart from being a completely new society, has within itself the ingredients of a dynamic society that is transformed each day not only in outward appearance but to its very core. Contemporary Mexico is not a petrified or stratified society where change must be wrought by dynamite or the pickax.

Mexico's "very special circumstance" can be better understood if it is contrasted with the Guatemalan and Peruvian societies. For almost a century, since García Granados and Barrios led the "lib-

126

erals" to victory, there has been no significant and enduring change
in Guatemala. In Peru there are still vast areas where today's society is exactly the same as it was during the Spanish domination.
The best way of understanding this difference, of course, is to recall
facts that Mexicans themselves tend to forget or have already totally forgotten.

The Mexican Revolution was a true revolution in the sense that
it was a profound change effected in a relatively brief span of time.
In the years from November, 1910, to December, 1920, it destroyed
Porfirian society and from 1920 to 1940, let us say, it created all
that it was to create during its first great impulse. But Mexico has
forgotten, and the rest of the world has never known, to what extent
the country was laid waste by the revolution. It wiped out the governing echelons and the official bureaucracy, on the national level
as well as in the states and municipalities; it did away with the
army and the federal police, the famous *rurales*; it completely abolished the old landholding class and especially the latifundista, the
nucleus of its political and economic power; none of the periodical
publications, particularly the newspapers, managed to survive; only
two banks out of the old credit system are in existence today; such
public services as railroads, tramways, the telegraph and telephone
systems, and water, light, and electric power were so badly dis-
rupted that they had to be rebuilt from their foundations. Even
more significantly, the first postrevolutionary census revealed that,
for the first time in its history as an independent nation, Mexico
suffered a net loss in population as a result of war, hunger, and
epidemics. In truth, it can be said that by 1920 absolutely nothing
was left of the *ancien régime*.

As it destroyed the old society, the Mexican Revolution was creating a new one, particularly after 1920, when its military and political victory became complete. Besides entirely new political groups,
the revolution fashioned a popular army commanded by rough and
ready generals who were to attain great military and political
power. The peasant and the worker, political forces undreamed of
in the *ancien régime*, were exalted by the revolution, and their welfare was declared to be the principal and sole purpose of the whole
movement. An oligarchy of tradesmen, bankers, and industrialists
gradually emerged and prospered. It had, to be sure, its counter-

part during the rule of Porfirio Díaz, but it was very different in its composition and far more powerful and aggressive than its forerunner.

The Mexican Revolution, however, while forging an entirely new society, endowed it, so to speak, with the necessary energy to continually renew itself. The factional struggle within the revolution itself was the initial instrument of a savage renovation that prevented the new ruling class from perpetuating itself in its entirety. Madero's triumph in 1911 removed the Flores Magón group; Victoriano Huerta's treachery practically did away with *maderismo*, which, in any case, had not attracted the southern revolutionaries. Once the revolution regained momentum with the *constitucionalista* movement, another big split occurred—first between Venustiano Carranza and Pancho Villa and later between Carranza and the Constitutional Convention. As a result, the Villa group and the supporters of the Convention disappeared from the political scene. The Constitutional Convention gave rise to a new ideological contest between Carranza and Obregón, which exploded three years later on the occasion of choosing Carranza's successor. By 1920, with Carranza's assassination, *carrancismo* had ceased as a political force. Four years later, again at the time of presidential elections, there was another fissure in the revolution that literally divided it into two halves, with the De la Huerta faction finally being expelled. The process, first of internal fissure and division and then its subsequent spark of renewal, was for all practical purposes completed at this point, even though less important political groups were from time to time eliminated, as was the case with the partisans of General Serrano and General Cedillo.

All through these bloody conflicts, Álvaro Obregón was the only figure in the revolutionary circle whose power and fame grew until they surpassed everyone else's. After all, he had earned recognition by his military victories over Villa, the Convention, Carranza, and Adolfo de la Huerta. Besides, the harsh lessons of experience had greatly refined his innate political acumen. In these circumstances, Obregón thought he could and ought to reassert the power he had won, and to this end he initiated a constitutional reform allowing him to return to the presidency. After overcoming great opposition,

particularly stanch within the "revolutionary family," the constitution was amended. But, before he could reassume the presidency,
Obregón was assassinated. Since then it has been generally accepted
that the attempt at re-election created a favorable climate for Obregón's murder.

Thus, the principle of no re-election, another great instrument of
renovation in the new society of Mexico, was almost upset. It had
been established by Francisco I. Madero, a man always taken for a
good, simple-minded fellow by those blind Mexicans who think he
only saw the "political" aspect of the revolution he himself began.
Plutarco Elías Calles, who added Obregón's power to his own,
never dared to take advantage of the constitutional reform allowing re-election. Instead, to retain and increase his political power,
he created the system and title of *Líder Máximo de la Revolución*
(Supreme Leader of the Revolution). This system failed when
Lázaro Cárdenas became president and soon shook off Calles' over-
bearing patronage. For the past thirty years, the governing group
has been renewed each six years, regardless of what is said abroad
and even in spite of what Mexicans themselves may think. It is obvious that a president is designated rather than elected and that,
since this choice is largely dictated by the outgoing president, the
latter's influence necessarily continues beyond his appointed term
of office. It is clear that the law of political survival will force the
new president to remove this influence quickly and thoroughly. To
round out our picture of the political scene, it ought to be remembered that the sexennial process of change and renewal is not limited
to the president's office but reaches down to the federal and local
legislative bodies, the governors of the states, and all governmental
leaders, high and low, national and local. Naturally, I do not at all
wish to imply here that Mexico has become a model democracy or
that she is even now at the stage of development where she could
and should be.

These forces of renewal and change are at work not only in the
very important but limited political sector but can be seen in society and the economy as well. Agricultural production for the export and domestic markets, even though based on the old Porfirian
foundations, has been vitally stimulated, creating in the northeast

and the northwest a new kind of farmer closely resembling the North American. These forces can be most clearly seen in industry, where within the last twenty or twenty-five years new entrepreneurs, managers, technicians, and skilled workers with much better training have come to prominence. To be sure, the first period, the "easy stage" of industrial growth, is past and it will be difficult to overcome the obstacles to the second and more authentic "modern" stage of development. However, unless there is a total breakdown, the process of renewal and change will continue, although its effects will certainly not be as general or penetrating as before.

The progress in communications and transportation begun in 1929 and carried forward unstintingly for almost forty years has given Mexico for the first time in history a real circulatory system in which there are not only three main arteries as before, but many secondary ones, many tiny arteries and veins that spread out and cluster together just as they do in the human body. The result of this is the free flow or circulation of ideas, people, and goods from one end of the country to the other. As a parallel development of great importance, there is an increasingly rapid trend toward a heavy urban concentration of people. The Indians or the impoverished *mestizos* abandon their traditional agricultural pursuits, leave their familiar, routine way of life, and rush to the great cities to make their living. Once in the city, they try one job today and attempt another tomorrow, thereby creating social instability, harmful in many aspects but nonetheless a source of renovation, as are all social ferments.

The task of education in the last forty years, despite all its regrettable ups and downs, its lack of direction and imagination, is a tremendous force for change and renewal because of its variety and because of the number of people it has reached. For example, as late as 1922, a young Mexican had only three possible alternatives in higher education—the law, medicine, and civil engineering—while there was only one agricultural school in the whole country.

All this has given Mexican society an entirely new social mobility, endowing it with a social capillarity previously lacking. The flow of people who easily reach the middle class is downright torrential and, indeed, they do not tarry there but immediately try to become members of its upper levels.

ii

The position of the Left is difficult in Mexico because the society in which it operates is both new and receptive to the pressures of change. The Left cannot resort to the hackneyed method of destroying society with a stick of dynamite, as it might do in the petrified class systems of many Latin American countries. Unless he is a Communist, the Mexican leftist must necessarily offer remedies or progressive cures, and is forced to renounce the use of demagogic techniques, perhaps effective elsewhere, or he is obliged, if he intends to present a plan for progressive change, to show just how to implement it.

There is still another circumstance—as "special" as the foregoing one—that undercuts his position. The Mexican Revolution, in spite of all that it destroyed and in spite of how much it has created, is an unfinished work: Like Schubert's Unfinished Symphony, it has only two movements and needs at least one more to be completed. If the word "revolution" means, as already indicated, a rapid and profound transformation, it is scarcely a matter of debate that Mexico has not lived at a revolutionary tempo from 1940, let us say, until today. This does not mean, however, that in 1940 everything "the Revolution" proposed to do was accomplished; nor does it mean that the revolutionary word and gesture have completely disappeared from the political scene. On the contrary, many of the things that were to be done were left half finished when the initial, really revolutionary energy was exhausted and replaced by a cautious evolutionary approach to change. The governing group refuses to admit that this is the state of affairs and maintains that the third movement of the Unfinished Symphony still has to be written.

An examination of agrarian reform will cast some light on this curious development. Clearly, the Mexican Revolution realized certain important objectives through the agrarian reform. Most of the arable land changed hands and, of primary importance, the attitude of the slave or serf disappeared. The servile mien was erased from the face of the Mexican peasant (*campesino*), as can be seen when he is compared with today's Bolivian or Peruvian Indian. The peasant, more precisely the *ejidatario*, the farm worker on *ejido* lands, is both the pampered child of the revolution and a political force of the first order—although to a large extent a negative one and a parasite, as it were, completely dependent on the government. But the objective of decisively raising his standard of living has been accomplished only in those regions of the country where soil and climate make agriculture profitable, as is true in parts of the south and especially in the northwest. In the two great high plateaus, the central and the northern, the economic condition of the *ejidatario* has scarcely changed. It may even be said to have grown worse, if his lot is compared with that of other sectors of the population. One might wonder whether education and sanitary improvements, for example, not to mention better living quarters, recreational facilities, and social services, have benefited him notably and whether they have met the avowed aim of making the peasant the first and foremost beneficiary of the revolutionary program.

The leaders of the Mexican government are entirely right when they say that there still remains a great deal to be done in the whole area of agrarian reform. Yet, they are not so right when they conclude that, "therefore," the Mexican Revolution is as vibrant today as it was in 1915, the year in which the first agrarian law was promulgated. They are not so right because, even assuming that new governmental efforts were to recover the lost revolutionary *élan*, it is no longer a clear-cut matter of solving problems by sheer determination alone. There are natural obstacles in the path of all progress, and there are adversities that require years of hard effort to overcome: The fight is against early or late frosts, barren soil and mountainous terrain, and insufficient and capricious rainfall. And these conditions cannot be easily remedied by artificial irrigation, because there are almost no rivers with regular courses and an abundant supply of water.

As we have already said, the position of the Left is a difficult one because the Mexican Revolution is an unfinished undertaking. It is difficult because the final movement of this unfinished symphony still has to be composed or orchestrated and the government still has in its hands the bright red flag of change, transformation, and progress and not the black flag of retreat or regression or the gray conservative banner of the *status quo*. In short, the government merely waves its progressive banner and occupies a position on the left. This gives the government an invaluable advantage over the Left in the daily political skirmishing. Since advancing the work of the Mexican Revolution only vaguely indicates its direction, but by no means reveals definite goals and, much less, a precise measure of the distance that must be covered each day to reach them, the government can vary its position, taking occasional and discreet steps toward the left. It can do so by enacting some progressive measure or by simply announcing its intention of doing so. Thus, the government pushes to its right people or groups that before thought they were, or actually were, to its left.

iii

Nevertheless, not everything in Mexico is adverse to the Left. The "unfinished symphony" character of the revolution favors it and enables it to exert influence disproportionate to its actual political representation. Thus, if the government goes for long without taking those occasional and discreet steps toward the left, the Left will insist that they be taken, and will even demand that the revolutionary march be interrupted no longer. And a government that calls itself revolutionary cannot indefinitely refuse to take these steps. Another circumstance, not often taken into account, also favors the Left. Since independence, the whole history of the country may be characterized as a long series of episodes in which regression has been exceptional and the *status quo* practically unknown. Strictly speaking, the only stable period was under Porfirio Díaz and not all of it was stable, since, in its beginnings, it was not without a revolutionary sense of change. Mexico, then, has the habit of living precariously, of changing and moving. Therefore, the Left frightens Mexico much less than it might with a different historical experience. And we should add that the Left is further emboldened by its string of victories over the opposing camps since independence.

Another circumstance favorable to the Left is that in Mexico it is much more profitable to be a leftist than a reactionary or simply a conservative. This has enormous importance because, not counting the Marxist multimillionaires we will mention later, the great majority of Mexican leftists live from public or semipublic employment. Their political posture, or activities, does not pose a problem of hunger or privation for them. Since only in very exceptional cases are they the object of vigilance, persecution, and still less of punishment, their personal safety is assured. Without doubt, in Mexico it is more popular to be a rebel than a conformist, a leftist than a rightist, and this occurs above all among the young generation.

iv

What has been said up to this point suffices to give a general idea of the present setting in which the Mexican Left operates. To clarify it more exactly, one would have to distinguish between its main groups and its principal tendencies. If any great rigor were demanded in this task, it would have to be abandoned, because, among a thousand other reasons, much of Mexican politics is done not publicly but privately and even intimately. It is not expressed in shouts in the public square but is carried on in subdued and informal tones in the café or in the office corridors. Rarely is Mexican politics articulated in books, folders, or periodical publications. Instead, it emerges mainly out of private conversation, gossip, and even a joke. Furthermore, the Left is an amorphous group, the largest segment of which is made up of people who have never tried to define their ideas and feelings about the principal problems of the country and its leading public men. They simply feel or guess that things are going badly or that things ought to be better, that their government officials are inept or dishonest or that they lack the necessary training or the indispensable scruples of true public servants. In short, it must be remembered that governmental leaders in Mexico, the men whose public functions should put them in the limelight (deputies, senators, cabinet members, governors of states), have regulated their political behavior by two rules or principles: The first can be expressed in the popular saying "Silence is golden," and the second is that the role of the oracle is the exclusive right and property of the president.

The part of the Left least difficult to identify is the one to the extreme left, the Communist Party. Its program and ideas are those of any national Communist party, except that in Mexico it is singularly poor, both in party registration (the generally accepted figure is between 5,000 and 10,000) and in the intelligence and aggressiveness of its leaders. On the other hand, it has the advantages of discipline and loyalty and a clearer idea of what the Party is and does and what it can ask of its members. However, since it has not been able to meet the requirements of the electoral law, especially the one about a minimum number of party members, the Communist Party in Mexico does not act as a political party. For this reason, the Popular Socialist Party (Partido Socialista Popular) has taken its place. Founded and directed since its birth by the well-known intellectual and labor leader Vicente Lombardo Toledano, it is not without some ideas. Yet, without a sustained and energetic drive to proselytize, the party languishes during the six years between one presidential election and the next. Its participation in local elections, notably on the municipal level, is weak and sporadic, and certainly its political activities have never been developed on a nationwide scale. What is more, the few deputies the PSP has managed to get into the federal legislature are hardly outstanding. Some have brazenly turned their back on their party, and others soon lose the intense aggressiveness with which they entered the parliamentary lists. And, finally, PSP prospects are limited by its well-known Communist ideology and the slightly paradoxical character of its leader.

After the Communist and Socialist parties come the Marxists, who, actually, have never tried to join together, much less act, either as a party or as a group. There are not a few multimillionaires and many professors and intellectuals in their midst, but they speak infrequently outside of the university and they write still less. It can now be predicted with reasonable assurance that they will never produce a great theorist or even an intelligible writer. Nevertheless, they have a noticeable influence among the young university students, who, anxious to have a few ideas to give them some direction, see an appealing posture of rebellion in their professors and are impressed with a few truisms they can repeat and even defend against their fellow students.

The largest group that at first appears to have the best leverage in the game of politics is the one recognized by the label of *carden-*

ismo. This group is inspired, or presumes to be inspired, by the achievements and the personality of former President Lázaro Cárdenas. This group actually does not exist as a political party or as an inventor and paladin of an ideology or political program. General Cárdenas often publicly stated that after he left the presidency he would no longer take an active hand in politics. I think almost everyone would agree that he completely upheld his promise in the first fifteen years after he stepped down, but in the last eight years the story has been somewhat different. A fifteen-year absence of its leader from politics would dishearten any political group. The only way that followers of a man or a party can be held together is by an eventual victory or return to power.

General Cárdenas' recent participation in politics has been infrequent and sporadic and, still worse, usually prompted by foreign affairs, as at certain points during the Cuban Revolution. It was, therefore, literally impossible to keep a *cardenista* political movement alive; still, we can ask whether its continued existence would have been worth while. Would Mexico and the Left have gained anything from its activity? It is doubtful, especially when one considers that the group of advisers who surrounded Cárdenas as president were possibly the worst any revolutionary president has had. Moreover, there is reason to suspect that Cárdenas himself would doubt that giving them power again would benefit him or the country. The tragedy of the Mexican Left is that Cárdenas did not choose to give it direction, because he, better than any other man, could have provided it with real substance. Indeed, he enjoys great prestige and authority, is endowed with an undeniable popular charisma, and possesses a natural instinct for discovering the real interests of the Mexican people.

With precisely this urge somehow to galvanize the Left, another leftist faction, the so-called "Movement for National Liberation" (Movimiento de Liberación Nacional), was recently created. Its very name testifies to the barren imagination and pseudo-originality of its founders. Not only did they slavishly copy it from other models, but it has no relation whatever to the real problems of the country, since Mexico does not have to free itself from any foreign yoke.

v

Do these disparate factions of the Mexican Left share any common ideological ground? There are, in fact, some areas of agreement. Viewed from the negative side of things, they are anti-clerical, anti-imperialist, and above all anti-Yankee; on the positive side, they are fervently nationalistic and outspoken advocates of statism, particularly in the control of economic affairs. They have other common traits, although not specifically ideological. They do not believe that there has been any real progress or general advancement of the country. For example, although they do not deny the clear statistic that Mexico today has thousands of kilometers of highway she never had before, they complain that the time, money, and effort needed for their construction ought to have been expended on something else. They are skeptical about the ability of today's or tomorrow's leaders to guide Mexico along the path they would like it to follow. The curious but actual meaning of this is that their general attitude, the little they do, say, or write, is based not on the way things happen in Mexico, but on the way they happen in foreign countries they rarely know and do not even attempt to study. The answers given by the Mexican leftists are so plainly remote, unreal, and crude that they do not really impress anyone.

vi

We cannot end this brief discussion without raising an important question: Does contemporary Mexico need a Left? Perhaps this question may be better phrased by asking whether or not Mexico's present development demands a progressive orientation that may come partly from the government and partly from a leftist opposition. Fully aware that personal opinion accounts for very little in such serious matters and also that one's opinion is really about the only thing one can fairly accurately express, I would not hesitate for one second in saying that today's Mexico certainly needs a Left and that a great deal of its future progress will depend upon it.

Regardless of its many shortcomings, mostly unnecessary, irritating, or simply ridiculous, the Mexican Left has exerted a good influence, although unwittingly so. Naturally, the essence of democracy is diversity and opposition of opinions, and the health of a social organism depends upon its nonconformist, nonorthodox, and rebellious youth. In Mexico, the undeniable progress, and the merciless publicity given to it by the government, creates an easy atmosphere of unjustified and unjustifiable complacency that the Left healthily denies or dispels. It is both consoling and reassuring to see the dissenter's boldness, even if, as we have seen, it is modest and risk-free, and to see a government that is tolerant and even generous. In sum, today's imperfect version of the Left may be the forerunner or seed of a more effective Left in the future.

Further, we must add a word or two about the reason why Mexico's progress needs a progressive or leftist opposition. In the first place, because everything in the modern world changes, moves, and is not stable or static. And in the second, because it is perfectly obvious that only he who has something can keep or hoard it. Mexico cannot do this, for it has not achieved enough and still has a long way to go. How right was the first person who remarked that it is a sign of prudence to lock a golden coin in a closed fist and an act of madness to do the same with an empty palm.

vii

Now we can consider what elements would go into making a better Mexican Left. The first condition, I think, is intelligence, which certainly until now has been lacking—not so much because there is no keen mind in the ranks of the Left but because the few intelligent men it has have not used their wits to formulate their ideas and organize a party. One of its weaknesses—indeed, the one that has emasculated today's Mexican Left—is its irrational, capricious, and superficial reaction to national problems. The second prerequisite is of a moral order. It would be foolish to ask every member of a political faction or party to be a martyr, ready to sacrifice his life and his family's for his political convictions. Still, it is high time to admit that it is contradictory and repugnant to call for the salvation of the oppressed and the destitute when the "crusader" owns a sumptuous mansion and two automobiles and makes a mistress out of every secretary.

The third condition is intellectual and moral and can be expressed in a brief motto: Avoid appearing the seer in the streets and the blind man at home; study and think first, and then, and only then, speak and get to work. The Mexican Left will never be regenerated as long as it preaches that Castro, Mao, or Nikita will solve Mexico's problems. Mexico might sink with all of them, but surely none of them will save Mexico.

The fourth stipulation would be for the Left to limit for the moment its role, to concentrate its attention and activity upon a single but far-reaching problem, for example, economic and social development. If it could devise a first, though necessarily rough, outline, subject to later revisions, in which both immediate and future goals are stated as clearly as possible, the new Left would almost overnight take on an authority it does not have, and will not have in any other way. In such a tentative outline, the Left ought to clarify the great question of the role of private enterprise in Mexico's march toward greater progress.

7

Mexico: The Preferred Revolution

STANLEY ROBERT ROSS

On his arrival in Mexico City on June 30, 1962, President John F. Kennedy appropriately chose to stress the revolutionary origins of the current Mexican regime and to applaud the revolutionary spirit that has influenced United States as well as Mexican history. He noted that Mexico and the United States "are both children of revolution" with a "common passion for social justice."[1] It has become almost routine during the past few years for United States journalists, politicians, and statesmen to laud the Mexican Revolution and to suggest that the Mexican experience afforded a preferred solution for the hemispheric problem of change and development.

The attitude of Mexico's northern neighbor has not always been characterized by such enthusiasm for her twentieth-century upheaval. Preoccupied with a global Cold War, the United States finds itself confronted by a hemisphere in ferment with irresistible demands for change and the Cuban "Leninist-Marxist"–oriented revolution offering a visible and unpalatable means of achieving that change. By contrast, revolution Mexican-style seems preferable. In an editorial prompted by the Kennedy visit to Mexico, the *Denver Post* supported this view:

> It [the Mexican Revolution] has proved to the distressed and restless people of the hemisphere that economic and social reform can move forward effectively in an atmosphere of political stability and individual liberty.
>
> Under the impetus of the Mexican Revolution, our neighbor to the South has expanded its industry, diversified its economy and raised the standard of living of its people. . . .

. . . the Mexican Revolution—*minus the violence that brought it about*—is the symbol of the kind of development that the United States would like to see among the nations of the Western Hemisphere.

Our whole Alliance for Progress is built around the idea that the hope for the hemisphere lies in the path of non-Communist social reform, that path that Mexico has been following since 1910. . . .

Reform on the Mexican model offers the most feasible alternative for the hemisphere and President Kennedy has made it clear that the United States supports that kind of reform.[2]

It should be noted that the editorial writer would like other nations of the hemisphere to emulate the peaceful, evolutionary development of Mexico during the past two decades, precluding the violent and more dramatic, earlier phases of the movement. It is only since Mexico achieved political stability, welcomed back foreign investors—albeit with supposedly built-in protective devices—and shifted emphasis from agrarian reform to industrial development that United States opposition and intolerance were replaced by enthusiasm and approval. Whether or not agrarian and tax reforms, economic diversification, and social change can be achieved effectively and rapidly enough by peaceful, evolutionary means is a question that remains to be answered. Available illustrations of far-reaching changes brought about by agrarian reforms— Mexico, Bolivia, and Cuba—all have been initiated by a period of revolutionary violence.

Knowingly or unwittingly, those proclaiming the Mexican Revolution as the "preferred revolution" are suggesting that Mexico serve in the future, as Professor Frank Tannenbaum perceptively conceived of it having served in the past, as the "anvil of American foreign policy":

. . . for the United States the experience with Mexico during those fateful years proved both a test and a challenge. Its policy toward Mexico could not be divorced from its actions in other parts of Latin America, and its behavior toward Latin America was of necessity but a part of its broader policy in the world at large. The conflict with Mexico had to be resolved in the light of world-wide commitments and responsibilities, not merely political and material, but also spiritual and moral. . . .[3]

There are good reasons for preferring the Mexican Revolution. Valuable lessons for the formulation of hemispheric policy can be learned by the United States from the experience with revolutionary Mexico. However, both the reasons and the lessons must be based on an understanding of the history of the Mexican Revolution and the record of North American reactions to it. Without it, the avowed preference becomes a desperate grasping for an alternative to Communism or a futile equating of contemporary Mexico, stable, mature, evolving, and developing, with earlier revolutionary Mexico.

Not only was the Mexican Revolution the first of the twentieth-century revolutions, but the evils it fought to destroy and the problems it sought to resolve foreshadowed many of the conditions provoking ferment today throughout the hemisphere. Mexico, at the turn of the century, groaned under a political dictatorship that intensified the burden of an institutional heritage dating back to the Spanish Empire. It further aggravated the problems of the country by superimposing an exploitative foreign capitalism. Neglect and suppression of the masses and disdain for the Indian population were rationalized by foreign ideologies. The regime's policies perpetuated a colonial-like social structure and intensified an externally dependent economy in a nation that theoretically had achieved independence when it severed its connection with Spain during the War of Independence.

Beginning as a political upheaval aimed at toppling a dictatorial regime and establishing a more democratic system, the Mexican movement evolved during its fighting decade into a full-bloom social and economic revolution aimed at destroying or weakening the role in society of the existing military establishment, the Church, and the foreign capitalist. Most important of all, it sought to abolish a caste system based on land ownership, to destroy the hacienda, and to carry out a far-reaching agrarian reform. For three decades, the Mexican Revolution was in essence an agrarian upheaval.

Viewed from another perspective, the revolution sought to mold and bind the disparate elements of the population into a unified nation, a nation that would be economically as well as politically independent and would be directed by Mexicans for the benefit of

Mexicans. The basic goals of a better life and social justice for the Mexican people persisted through changes in leadership, philosophy, and policies. When it appeared that agrarian reform in itself would not provide the answer, emphasis shifted to making the land more productive and to industrializing the economy.

Perhaps the most striking aspect of the Mexican Revolution is the absence of a monolithic character. The revolution was not born in full bloom nor did it evolve in a single direction. It was a tentative, experimental, and pragmatic movement. It was local and regional before it became national. It grew piecemeal, with many a step backward and many an oscillation to right and left. A key element in the explanation of this movement lies in the fact that it lacked, in large measure, a prior or even accompanying ideology.[4]

With the bulk of the intellectuals, products of an urban, cosmopolitan environment, committed to the dictatorship, it is not surprising that prior to the inception of the movement and for many years of its development, the intellectuals had little effect on its character. Their principal, and largely unsuccessful, effort had been to introduce foreign ideologies. It is true that the precursory movement of the Flores Magón brothers was strongly colored by the anarcho-syndicalist philosophy that persisted on the fringe of the mainstream of the revolution; that Marxist ideas similarly existed on the fringe during the 1920's, experiencing some application in the creation of collective *ejidos* during the Cárdenas period; that Madero was imbued with ideas of Anglo-Saxon democracy and French egalitarianism; and that the Mexican constitutional labor article and subsequent national code represented extensive borrowing from abroad. The fact remains that the Mexican Revolution was a nationalistic upheaval that emerged from a Mexican situation and was met essentially by methods derived from the Mexican experience. This predominantly indigenous character is a major element in the potential attractiveness of the Mexican Revolution for other nations in the hemisphere.

The Mexican Revolution's doctrine is noteworthy for its complex, even contradictory, character. Having found that traditional liberalism did not achieve the desired well-being of the masses of the people, not to mention its failure to prevent the creation of a dictatorship, the Mexican revolutionaries at the Querétaro Constitutional Convention, establishing the judicial framework for the Mexican Revolution, rejected or modified traditional liberalism. Departure from traditional liberalism is the hallmark of the key revolutionary constitutional provisions: Articles 3, 27, 123, and 130. While retaining individual liberties, the *constituyentes* made the interests of the state and of society as a whole prevail in the event of conflict over those of individuals or groups. The state was tremendously strengthened as rival institutions were weakened and restricted.

The state was given direct dominion over the nation's subsoil resources, the power to carry out agrarian reform, the means to nurture and control the labor movement, the direction of the nation's educational pogram, and the means to restrict the Catholic Church as an economic and political institution. The makers of the Constitution retained the tripartite governmental structure as well as the federal form. In effect, however, a firm presidential structure was created, with legislative, judicial, and provincial organs clearly subordinate to presidential control.

Maintaining the form while allowing for internal change is characteristic of Mexico's party structure. Although minority parties do exist, the political reality has been a one-party government. The official revolutionary party was created in 1929 to assure political stability and to provide a means for reconciling the ambitions of factions of the revolutionary family. By the introduction of the functional sector system, the official party achieved a potential for representation of major social group interests and for being responsive to popular needs. However, the efficacy of the Mexican political system continues to depend on the quality of the individual occupying the presidency.

The exercise of the president's legal powers within the framework of Mexican revolutionary philosophy not only results in a strikingly presidentialist regime but also is characterized by a strong flavor of nationalism and statism. Here, one might mention the legislation favoring Mexican nationals over foreigners in matters of landholding and exploitation of natural resources, nationalization of the railroads and other public utilities, expropriation and governmental exploitation of petroleum. As regards economic development, considerable economic planning and financing has

been done by Nacional Financiera, a governmental development
agency, along with banking establishments and laws favoring
Mexican majority control in the private-investment field. Quite
often, noneconomic considerations, social, psychological, and political, have strongly influenced Mexican decisions, policies, and
programs. This is true of some aspects of the agrarian program as
well as the initial dozen years of the operation of Pemex, the government petroleum monopoly.

These characteristics of the Mexican experience are, indeed,
noteworthy; yet caution should be exercised in assessing certain
aspects of Mexico's development during the last two decades. On
the one hand, Mexico seems to be a showcase of political stability
or, at least, political regularity, as seen in its national self-confi-
dence, educational advances, social changes including the rise of a
significant middle class, and economic development and progress.
However, there are shortcomings revealed at every turn. Much of
the forced economic development has come at the expense of the
workers and peasants, particularly the latter. The newly created
wealth has not been equitably distributed, making possible the appearance of a new oligarchy of wealth associated with industrial
and financial operations. Population growth has limited the degree
and extent of social advance. Least satisfactory of all has been the
political situation, with its strong personalist element and the absence of free play of political interests. The political milieu has
been clouded by corruption and by the gap between the continued
and loud reaffirmation of revolutionary ideals and the deeds of
government officials in successive administrations.

That the Mexican Revolution should reach its *Thermidor* was,
perhaps, inevitable. The philosophy of a new generation of Mexican leaders and their decision to industrialize the nation helped
determine the turn to the right. A perceptive Mexican scholar,
Daniel Cosío Villegas, adds this significant comment on the revolution and the way it developed:

It is a generally accepted observation that a revolution always produces a corresponding reaction; but in our case there is a particular
circumstance to be considered. The drive and energy of the Revolution were consumed much more in destroying the past than in con-
structing the future. As a result, the past certainly disappeared, but

the new present came into being and began to develop haphazardly, so that, for lack of another image to imitate, it finally ended by becoming equal to the destroyed past. From this standpoint the reaction won a complete victory over the Revolution, since it has succeeded in taking the country back to the exact point where it was when the Revolution broke out. I mean "the exact point" where Mexico was before the Revolution, in the sense of the general mental outlook prevailing now in the country, but not in the sense that the country itself is like the Mexico of 1910, and much less in the sense of what Mexico will be like in ten or twenty years.[5]

The Mexican Revolution has had an impact on other reform movements in the hemisphere. Latin American leaders have adopted its goals and studied its methods. However, Mexico has not become the acknowledged leader of a hemisphere in ferment. Dr. Cosío unhappily comes to this conclusion:

Mexico, which for many years led the other countries not only of Latin America but of the world in its reformation of economic, social and political structure, shaking off the lethargy of an economic progress that was undeniable but not general; Mexico, the intrepid leader of so many good causes, has failed in this hour crucial for Latin America. For some time the United States has persisted in presenting Mexico as a model to its brother Americas. This—says the United States—is a country that, after a revolution to get rid of its useless and cumbersome past, has put its house in order. It lives in peace and has achieved political stability; a civilian government has succeeded a military; it has made spectacular economic progress, and the lower classes are entering the middle class in ever increasing numbers and with considerable ease. All this is true and nonetheless we Mexicans believe that Mexico could have done more, very much more, than it has; and that by not doing so, it has lost the initiative in Latin America in basic and just social reform.[6]

The Mexican Revolution was a nationalistic movement colored by a strong strain of antiforeignism, striving for economic independence and, in no small measure, against the exploitation by foreign interests. Therefore, it was inevitable that foreign-policy principles should loom large in the revolutionary scale of values. Some of these principles are deeply rooted in the Mexican historical experience. They were all tempered during the revolution and received systematic expression from the revolutionary leadership.

The key principles[7] of Mexican foreign policy are: national sovereignty, juridical equality of all nations, national self-determination, nonintervention, peaceful settlement of international disputes, the right of political asylum, and a recognition policy[8] that precludes judgment of the regime involved. Implicit is a rejection of colonialism and imperialism, priority for the large and powerful over the small and weak, and any interference in the internal affairs of another nation, whether by military, economic, or diplomatic means. On these principles Mexico's revolutionary leadership, beginning with Carranza, was impressively intransigent. Some leaders might, and did, bend, but none would yield on the essentials.

The United States was the most immediate major nation whose interests were directly affected by the course of the revolution. Many of Mexico's prohibitions against outsiders grew out of experiences with, and were directed against, its northern neighbor. From the experience gained in reacting to the Mexican Revolution there are valuable lessons to be learned for the formulation of United States policy in a continent in ferment for change.

During the fighting years of the Mexican Revolution, the United States was preoccupied with the threat to American lives and property, border raids, questions of neutrality, arms embargo, and recognition. After the Constitution of 1917 and the implementation of its revolutionary provisions, the resulting threat to established and presumed American economic interests became the principal bone of contention.

During the initial decade of the revolution, there were occasions when troops were mobilized along the border and war vessels dispatched to patrol both the Gulf and Pacific coasts; in two instances —the Veracruz landing and the Punitive Expedition—American military personnel did tread on Mexican soil. In neither case of major armed intervention did the use of force accomplish the desired objective and, although directed against Huerta and Villa respectively, these actions were resented deeply by revolutionary and popular elements.[9]

The Mexicans are convinced that armed intervention was a real possibility during 1926–27 and was forestalled only by Calles' adroit use of purloined documents. While Ambassador Sheffield does not appear to have been averse to more forceful measures, it soon became evident that the Coolidge Administration could not and would not act in this manner. This was implicit in the recall of Sheffield and his replacement by Dwight Morrow. Once again, in 1938, when Cárdenas expropriated foreign petroleum holdings, the voices of affected interests advocated retaliation in the form of armed intervention. However, a fortuitous combination of circumstances and key personalities enabled the recently initiated Good Neighbor Policy to weather this most severe test.[10]

Diplomatic pressure, including the withholding of recognition and support, also played an important role in United States relations with revolutionary Mexico. Woodrow Wilson withheld recognition from Huerta on constitutional and moral grounds, while the Harding Administration refused to recognize Obregón's government for three years without a prior guarantee that vested American interests would be exempted from constitutional provisions.[11] In 1925, Secretary of State Kellogg implied that United States support of Mexico's government would continue only so long as adequate guarantees were provided for American interests.

However, neither armed intervention nor diplomatic blackmail could change the course of the Mexican Revolution. The relative effectiveness of diplomatic representation also is revealing. Henry Lane Wilson and James R. Sheffield left a heritage of resentment and bitterness. Both lacked sympathy for the Mexican upheaval, both associated themselves with the interests of the American colony and investors, and both assumed exceedingly narrow, legalistic positions. In contrast, Morrow and Daniels sought to associate with the Mexicans and to understand and appreciate what they were trying to do, and, most significantly, both placed the interests of improved relations between the two nations ahead of vested private interests.

An informed and sympathetic public opinion at times had a salutary effect on the relations between the two countries. In this regard, popular sympathy for the Madero movement, revulsion at the assassination of the first revolutionary president and Huerta's usurpation, and insistence on peaceful solution of differences between the two nations in 1926–27 might be listed as examples.

A truly popular upheaval cannot be stopped effectively by external pressures, nor should it be forced into a mold that is not derived from that country's heritage and experiences. Sympathy, knowledge, and understanding rather than threats, pressure, and force are the keys to diplomatic success and popular support. Relations between the two peoples must take precedence over the vested interests of the few. The United States had to concede another nation's right to legislate within its jurisdiction, including the right to expropriate in the public interest. There was maintained, in accordance with international law and practice, the insistence on prompt, adequate, and effective compensation. However, both the extent and form of meeting this condition may be the subject of considerable disagreement in specific cases.

Professor Frank Tannenbaum perceived how both nations evolved ideals and policies that were to fuse with great significance for the Inter-American movement:

> If Mexico developed a foreign policy fitting to her needs as a weak neighbor in conflict with a powerful one, it also stimulated the United States government to enunciate a doctrine consistent with American tradition and belief, befitting a great nation devoted to the ideals of individual liberty, representative government, and the equality of states within the nation. These divergent streams of policy and theory fused to become the foundation upon which the Inter-American system was ultimately to be constructed under the aegis of the Good Neighbor Policy. . . .[12]

By 1938, in the name of the Good Neighbor Policy under the guidance of Roosevelt and Daniels and impelled by the gathering clouds of World War II, the United States had learned to sympathize with Mexican goals and to tolerate divergences in means.

Of all the subjects for investigation and analysis in Latin American history, the Mexican Revolution has enjoyed a prominent place in the writings by historians of both contemporary world colossi. The dean of Soviet Latin Americanists, M. S. Al'perovich, has charged that the real reasons for increased United States interest in the Mexican Revolution derived from "the aggressive plans of United States imperialism in Mexico and the role of American monopoly and its enormous capital in that country."[13]

The basic importance of the Mexican Revolution as a historical phenomenon and the sympathy for the Mexican Revolution and its objectives revealed in the writings of the majority of scholarly contributions by North Americans to the historiography of the Mexican Revolution[14] would seem to effectively dispose of Professor Al'perovich's allegation.

Soviet preoccupation with the Mexican Revolution similarly can be attributed to selfish motivation as the principles of scholarship bow to the exigencies of political and methodological considerations. Soviet presentations are directed toward demonstrating the villainy of United States imperialism and toward forcing Mexican developments to conform to Marxist preconceptions. Professor Juan A. Ortega y Medina of the Mexican National University, in his historiographical survey of Russian literature on Latin America, offered the following judgment of four essays on the Mexican Revolution by Soviet scholars:

> . . . Soviet historiography presents a straight-forward style: If you have read one author, you have read them all. The tone is the same, monotonous, dry. . . . The language is for the mass reading audience; it is plain, political, and at times crude.[15]

Soviet writings on the Mexican Revolution reveal another underlying motivation. The Mexicans have succeeded in carrying out a revolution that has transformed their society without becoming Communist. Professor Ortega, in his analysis of the two principal Soviet volumes treating the Mexican Revolution,[16] notes that the insistent message of Soviet historiography is that "the Mexican example is not useful for Hispanic America."[17]

The Mexican historiographer feels that a great debate has begun in which both North American and Soviet historians seek to discredit the Mexican Revolution, the former in defense of capitalism and the latter in behalf of Communism. In true Mexican nationalistic revolutionary spirit, he urges Mexicans to understand the situation and to assume their proper role in the controversy:

> The two colossi, which today face each other, attack and defend the crucial themes of our . . . history in their own ideological interest. This situation is doubtless flattering. But we ought to remain alert to the inevitable external and internal repercussions which this dra-

matic historical colloquium produces and in which, even without wishing it, we are gambling with our historical being. It is obvious that those most interested in investigating and writing about our history should be ourselves; this inescapable and imperative task is the only one which can free us from the foreign intellectual colonialism threatening us. . . . We are on the verge of a tremendously active Russo-American dialogue; it is imperative that we understand it, follow it, and interrupt it—making ourselves heard—when it goes astray. We also have the obligation of knowing the opposed points of view in order to avoid, on the one hand, being converted into noxious instruments of imperialist reaction or, on the other hand, into noxious instruments nourishing pseudo-revolutionary demagoguery; in sum, we must prevent the ideas that are at stake from falling into ingenuous, wicked, stupid, or ignorant hands.[18]

The great debate is indeed upon us. It is to be hoped that the Mexican scholar has misjudged the role of the North American historian. There is little evidence of a predilection to attack the Mexican Revolution in defense of capitalism. However, it must be added that neither can the revolution be considered as a defense of the capitalist system, since this would involve a distortion of the essential character of the movement. Hopefully, North Americans in general, and their historians in particular, will realize that there is much to be learned from the Mexican Revolution. Most particularly we must recognize what the Russians already appreciate—namely, that the Mexican Revolution, by its achievement of social progress while maintaining freedom, offers a meaningful alternative to revolution Communist-style. Then, and only then, will it be possible to regard the Mexican upheaval as the preferred revolution.

III

THE BRAZILIAN VARIANT

8

The Patriarchal Basis of Brazilian Society

GILBERTO FREYRE

For some years I have suggested to students of Brazilian history an approach I believe more appropriate than the more conventional standards for a clear sociological analysis of the Brazilian past. Anyone studying a people's past from the sociological point of view will find that the historical constants are more significant than the ostensibly heroic episodes that sparkle independently on the pages of history books. He will further discover that what happened within the family and the intimate walls of its dwelling place is far more important than the well-known, often-cited events—those recorded in official chronicles about what happened in the salons of regal palaces or in presidential mansions, in parliaments, ministries, and large factories, in the high schools, in public squares mobbed by angry rioters, and, finally, on the battlefields themselves. On these points there is little doubt or controversy today. What is still discussed is just how far the analyst can or should go in his investigation of the make-up of the intimate past of a social group.

In Brazil, I was something of a pioneer in the development of this kind of "intimate history," so useful for the anthropologist, the sociologist, and for social psychology in general. As it developed and took special shape, it seemed even scandalous to the rigidly conventional historians, whether Brazilian or foreign, who first heard of it. There was some justifiable criticism to the effect that it followed the trend of some social history—or sociological introduction to historical studies—considered more sexual history than real social history. For them it was sexual history with almost no clinical interest at all, and certainly with no sociological or historical relevance.

It was necessary to consider sexual behavior in the Brazilian male as a member of a patriarchal family, polygamous in practice, yet thoroughly Christian in its beliefs. After my first and still rather bold essay on this subject, "Social Life in Brazil in the Middle of the Nineteenth Century," I began to explore, from a sociological standpoint and with full academic rigor, the intimate sexual behavior and domestic manners of Brazilians during the middle of the past century. I wrote this essay as a very young man at Columbia University, when it was the source of many revolutionary pressures in the academic universe: the theories of the "New History," anthropological science as introduced by Franz Boas, and the social philosophy of John Dewey. This method, which peered into the intimate ways of people, was generally abjured by both historians and sociologists. I always thought it was going to the heart of the matter, since in this way a man of my time could understand the era of his grandparents. Becoming a philosopher for a moment, I would suggest that the public image of an age does not reveal its private substance. Rather, it is the private or "intimate" history that makes us see the true meaning of public history.

Furthermore, we can say that history in depth, which ferrets into the past recesses of a people, cannot be written without the aid of anthropology. It then becomes not social history alone, but sociological history. We will understand the man we see garbed in daily, genteel dress much better when we have surprised him, unpretentious, and in slippers, in the intimacy of his home.

Since the domestic life of a social being in large part conditions his public life and political activities, we must know what he is and does at home. Only in this way will we really be able to judge him for what he is and does out-of-doors. The public man is wont to deceive the historian and escape the sociologist. The private man rarely is capable of such deception. His intimate life, his habits of hygiene, sleep, and dress, how he loves, what he eats, how he plays, define and characterize the roots of his culture and the very ethos of his age. The way he lives with his mother and father, his grandparents, his wife and children, and with servants reveals more about him than what he does and how he behaves with other people, the people of his public life: fellow citizens, businessmen, inferiors or superiors, encountered everywhere, in the street, in the public square, in the army, in the office, in factories, and at school.

Thus, we see the importance of that sociology or history of life and living which goes on every day in the circle and shadow of the family. The French sociologist Georges Balandier has said that this sociological history or historical sociology was really born in the attempt to plumb the depths of the Brazilian conscience. This innovating approach to the study of Brazil has become a necessary area of specialization for modern historians, anthropologists, and sociologists. Men like Georges Gurvitch, Balandier, Roland Barthes, and Roger Caillois in France, Ortega y Gasset and Américo Castro in Spain, Juan Antonio Portuondo in Latin America, and Frank Tannenbaum in the United States, in commenting on my work on Brazil, have agreed with me on the need for a sociology of the intimate and everyday life of the family.

Both Tannenbaum and Balandier have caught the essence of these new studies and view them as significant contributions in the fields of history and sociology. Both believe that this kind of "intimate investigation" of a people's past can and should be used in the analysis of other societies.

We might summarize what we have outlined to this point by saying that the reinterpretation of the Brazilian past and its ethos by a sociological history in depth no longer recognizes the state and the Church as the principal influences in the psycho-social and cultural formation of Brazil. To the contrary, it places the major, really the maximum, importance upon the family, its patriarchal structure, and this familial arrangement as a special economic system. The individual's role in Brazil's early make-up has often received too much attention from scholars. No doubt the individual, the European who came to Brazil to live and die, has left deep marks upon both soil and character, but his singular action has not been the decisive one for Brazil.

The colorful and the picturesque were dominant notes in Brazilian history from the very beginning. Its dyewoods brought adventurers and avid merchants in quest of profits. Brazil's name comes from the trees that filled its coastline and hinterland, the brazilwood, rather than from a liturgic name like Santa Cruz and Vera Cruz. Men came to Brazil in search of precious animal hides and other tropical curiosities, which then began to attract considerable attention in the commercial and trading sectors of Europe. The French came to Brazil precisely because of this commercial stimulus, settling on lands later used solely for sugar cultivation, and mixing with and marrying native women. Their offspring, the blond *mestizo*, surprised some of the early Portuguese settlers, who had come to Brazil less as individuals without lord or law or unchecked libertines than as somewhat serious men seeking a patriarchal, solid way of life. The Portuguese wanted to sink their roots deep into the new land, rear families, and build great mansions as their abodes.

The European and Christian imprint came to Brazil, as I have often written elsewhere, with the sugar cane and the industrial activities related to it. The *engehno de açucar*, the sugar mill, became the basis of the economy and a continuous historical prototype for an extensive system of organizing the economy, the family, the society, and culture. From a sociological standpoint, what is important to emphasize here is that this model of organization—life around the sugar mill—spread to other areas and activities as the dynamic basis for unity where the Portuguese, along with the Amerindian and the African, particularly developed a new type of civilization. The ecological, economic, ethnic, and even cultural elements of its make-up varied according to the differences of time and space from those sugar mills established in the main in the rich sugar-growing lands of the Brazilian northeast. But the social forms used in other regions still had as their model those that were first developed in the northeast around the sugar cane and the sugar mill: a system of relations of men with nature and with each other, characterized by the predominance of patriarchal organization in the family, the society, and the economy, whose system of labor revolved around the productiveness of the slave.

I have tried to give a schematic view of my theory of Brazil's social formation, a theory that is at the heart of most modern interpretations of Brazilian society. We could employ two sets of symbols to clarify this new sociological interpretation. The first is that which I have written about before, "the big house and the slave hut"; the other is a common enough sociological symbol, the "rural triangle," referring to the sugar mill, the big house, and the chapel. These symbols describe a system of social forms that, with some variations in the agrarian northeast where sugar, the Portuguese, the African slave, the Indian half-breed, and the horse and the ox were dominant from the sixteenth until the nineteenth century, was to re-extend to other regions, thus giving a fundamental unity to Brazil's interregional complexity.

Each region had its own special traits, although never at great variance with the original pattern. In one area there was cocoa, the Portuguese, the Amerindian, and the slave or the quasi-slave; in another, there was coffee, the Portuguese, the African slave transported from the extreme north and principally the northeast to the south, and the Italian settler; in an almost adjacent region, gold, the Portuguese, and the African slave existed side by side; in still another, cattle, the Portuguese, and the *mestizo* or Amerindian peasant; elsewhere, cotton, the Portuguese, and the mulatto peasant; and, finally, in another part, rubber, and the Brazilian of principally Portuguese origin derived from either the Amerindian or the mulatto.

This Pan-Brazilian social system reached out to many other areas with greater or lesser force, molding the family, the economy, and the culture after its own image. Its first and decisive growth—decisive for Portuguese America—took place in the *massapê*, the sugar-bearing lands of the northeast. Here, nature brought forth crops of sugar in luxurious harvests, while the region itself exported this product as a "staple commodity" to the rest of the world. Sugar was king and brought wealth to a vast region of Brazil.

It was sugar that excited Dutch greed and brought the Dutch to northern Brazil in the seventeenth century. At that time, Brazil was populated not only by whites, Amerindians, and Africans but by many *mestizos* as well whose culture was as hybrid as they were, even though the cultural mainstream was Luso-Catholic. The expulsion of the Dutch from Brazil's sugar-producing territory can be explained by two events. The first was a war—not a conventional war fought according to European rules—but rather a series of guerrilla encounters and surprise attacks by a motley corps of soldiers made up of Amerindians, Africans, and the *mestizos*—all conspiring with the tropics to defeat the Dutch interlopers. Secondly, it was a pseudo-social event in which the whites, browns, blacks, and reds joined forces and expelled the invader, who was uniformly white and European. This momentary unity in face of the Dutch invaders reflects the ethno-cultural interpenetration that had already gone on among them.

With the Protestant Dutch defeated by a combination of Portuguese, Spaniards, and primarily Brazilians (who now became aware of sharp differences between themselves and the Europeans, and even between themselves and their European brothers, the Portuguese), there arose in Brazil a paranational feeling identified with the Catholic religion. The Catholic religion, naturally, had undergone a certain metamorphosis or contamination in the Brazilian setting, never completely propitious for orthodox European faith or costumes. Priests of lax morality, for example, would wink their eyes or tolerate the open polygamy practiced under the patriarchal shadow of the sugar mill. The result of this was the already mentioned *mestizo* population dominated by feudal and capitalistic forms of production and society.

Officially, the cultivation of sugar cane in Brazil began when Martim Afonso de Sousa brought sugar cane from the Madeira Islands to São Vicente (now São Paulo) in 1532. There he founded a sugar mill known as Senhor Governador, later called Engenho de São Jorge dos Erasmos because it had been purchased from him by two German brothers, Erasmus and Júlio Esquert. In reality, cane had been planted and sugar produced as early as 1520, when Cristóvão Jaques, according to reliable evidence, built mills in Iguarassu or Igaraçu in Pernambuco. By 1526, the Customs House in Lisbon recorded the entrance of Brazilian sugar, probably from Pernambuco, into Portugal. In 1549, Bahia had its first sugar mill. In 1559, all mill owners, *senhores de engenho*, received permission to import 100 slaves from Africa in addition to those they already possessed. By this time it was evident that the prosperity of the sugar-growing areas rested mostly upon slave labor.

The sugar prosperity was not confined to São Vicente alone, where by 1548 there were six mills in full operation. Pernambuco, too, came alive with the sound of the mill's rolling wheels. There, in 1583, sixty-six mills flourished as against thirty-six in Bahia, while São Vicente's six had fallen to just one in 1587. The *engenho* began to make its appearance in other parts: in Paraíba, Sergipe, Ilhéus, Espírito Santo, and Rio de Janeiro. The Brazilian littoral offered the best combination of land and climate for sugar cultivation, with Pernambuco (Nova Lusitânia), Bahia, and Rio de Janeiro in the vanguard of production. Pyrard de Laval, a widely traveled Frenchman who had seen both the Orient and Brazil at the beginning of the seventeenth century, tells us that the *senhores de engenho* he met surpassed viceroys, governors, and bishops in wealth and opulence. They surpassed them not only in riches but also in real forms of power and influence in a society whose center was, in the sugar lands and later in those areas where another product was to take sugar's place, the patriarchal family. The patriarch was lord, master, and virtually a temporal god in his family and within the reach of the *engenho's* attraction. He was father, husband, master of women and sons, primary overseer of tenants and slaves, and absolute leader for a diverse retinue of followers. Few Egyptian pharaohs exceeded the untrammeled power and authority of these *senhores de engenho* in the sixteenth, seventeenth, eighteenth centuries, and even into the nineteenth century. Even the power of great kings pales beside their total fiat.

The Christian and patriarchal organization of the family, going back to the early Portuguese colonization, originates most clearly in those groups made up primarily of agrarian families emigrating from the mother country. Its source is not with the adventurous-hearted individuals who came to the New World to roam and get rich and perhaps finally to settle. The same thing happened elsewhere in Nova Lusitânia, where similar family groups were sociologically decisive in Brazil's formation, always overshadowing the acts and influence of the wandering "lone wolves."

These family groups belie the generally accepted myth that Brazil was colonized only by adventurers, outcasts, criminals, and *cristãos novos* (converts to Christianity), unaccompanied by families or wives. This myth presents a sharp contrast between the

Brazilian and the North American colonial experience with its exclusive emphasis in favor of North America and its puritan families, the well-known Pilgrim Fathers, eager to find the religious liberty denied them in Europe. As North America was not without her adventuring pioneers in its period of colonization, so Brazil in the sixteenth, seventeenth, and eighteenth centuries was not without her colonizing nuclei of solid and even virtuous families, like that of Duarte Coelho. These families had rural residences as their permanent dwellings, with adjacent chapels where Mass, baptism, weddings, and the Christian burial rites were solemnly celebrated. These rites and the Christian precepts behind them ultimately became an integral part of the patriarchal family system.

What is certain is that the almost completely Christian orientation of the family was not rigidly determined by monogamy or other ethical considerations of life and family formulated by the Church and sometimes urged upon a parish faithful by a zealously orthodox clergy. Just the contrary was true. There was a degree of coexistence between the religious orthodoxy of the Church and the patent polygamy in many families which some observers have traced back to the Muslim influence on the sexual habits of the Portuguese. This influence was perhaps increased by the freer kind of life made possible in the new environment of the New World. Liberty was often carried to an extreme and became license, where men would take unfair advantage of women, freely satiating their lust and passion.

Polygamy occurred principally because of the slave-labor system and the presence of the white European or his descendants in an ethnic group less advanced than his own. The women of the backward cultures seem to have abandoned themselves to their masters as if being white and foreign were sufficient patents of superiority. They hoped by sexual intercourse with the foreigners to acquire greater prestige in the new social structure imposed by the newcomers. A large *mestizo* population was the result of the sexual encounters between native and newcomer. Their descendants could be wild and reckless, as those of João Ramalho in São Paulo, or Christian and European in outlook, as was the case in the north, where families grew up around patriarchal plantations and imitated the lordly ways practiced in the master's "big house." A good example of these polygamous ways and their tacit tolerance by the Church is the large *mestizo* offspring of one Jerônimo de Albuquerque, an outstanding early colonist in Brazil, who acknowledged them as his own in his last will and testament along with his legitimate heirs born by a white Portuguese lady chosen for him by the Queen of Portugal herself.

The *mestizo* descendants from the union of Jerônimo with the daughter of an Indian cacique were raised in such a Christian manner that they soon became men of valor and women of virtue, progenitors, in their turn, of honorable and respected families. The men, once established as great lords in their own right, had the freedom to beget children with women other than their actual wives. With this marital liberty went, almost invariably, the responsibility of recognizing those children born out of wedlock and educating them at times in the same schools as their legitimate children.

This kind of polygamy was characteristic of Brazil not only in the sixteenth century but in the entire era of splendor of the patriarchal family, first as a catalyst of unity in the period of colonization, and then as a center of prenational and finally national society. It may be called the "other Albuquerque method." The first "Albuquerque method" referred to the mixed marriages encouraged by Alfonso de Albuquerque in India as soon as that part of the Orient was occupied by the Portuguese. At that time they were generally lone wolves, that is, unaccompanied by European wives. Many of them, however, were nobles or relatives of nobles, as was the case in Brazil. The "other Albuquerque method" was obviously useful in Brazil. It spread Portuguese blood and mores among the natives, diffused Christian beliefs and practices, and increased the culturally Luso-Christian population—an increase caused by the polygamous activities of the Portuguese Christians and their offspring. Thus, on the one hand, the Portuguese and their descendants distorted the monogamous character of the Christian family, while, on the other, they contributed to the creation of an essentially Luso-Christian family in America.

The sixteenth century marked the first consolidation of this kind of family developing in the shadow of a patriarchal economy and society both in the north and the south, although the sugar-growing areas were first in attaining familial stability and a solid economic basis of living. In the south, with the *bandeirismo* of the *paulistas* (that adventurous, enterprising, expansive spirit of the Brazilian roughly equivalent to the North American pioneer), conditions were influenced by the intensely fruitful mobility of the frontiersmen who extended the limits of Portuguese-speaking America with every bold step they took. From the sixteenth century onward, the *paulistas* contributed to the growth of Brazil by uniting Europeans and their descendants with Amerindian women. From this union were derived large, vigorous, hybridlike families, predominantly European and Christian in outlook but always retaining a cultural substratum of Indian ways and values, whether evidenced in the foods eaten, the remedies used to cure maladies, or in the ingenious hammock for rest and sleep.

In the north as well, there was a considerable assimilation of Amerindian values and techniques. Here, however, the African influence was felt along with that of the Amerindian. The majority of Africans had been imported as slaves since the sixteenth century for work on the sugar plantations and in the sugar mills. On these plantations and their *engenhos*—in the sixteenth century more productive and prosperous in the north than in the south—a type of patriarchal family evolved with feudal and aristocratic traits in its organization and its forms of domination over tenant farmers and slaves. These characteristics were emphasized in the same century with the division of Brazil into hereditary captaincies and with land grants that could not help favoring large landholdings and conferring a prestigious status upon the landholders themselves. Since the Portuguese kings depended upon these enterprising landholders for both the economic productivity and the military security of their colony, one readily understands the vast power enjoyed by the great patriarchal families, the owners of sugar mills, immense tracts of land, and large numbers of slaves. It is doubtful whether, without these families, Portugal could have held her grip on the part of America that eventually became Brazil.

These patriarchal families were distinguished by the vigorous domination exercised by their head not only over slaves and tenants but also over wives, children, and grandchildren. The patriarch's power over his wife and offspring was absolute. But this power did not inhibit the coordinating and creative activities of the wives and mothers. They preserved and transmitted the domestic arts, gave social help and religious advice to slaves and tenants, so that European culture was not only preserved under the zeal and vigilance of these wise matrons, but enriched by Amerindian and African ways in such things as food and its preparation, homemade medicines, and tropical hygiene. These influences were mostly absorbed by the white mother of the family from her African servants and from her Amerindian domestics. The native and African values permeated the family in still other ways. They touched the white children whose playmates were Indian, African, or *mestizo*. Sometimes it was work, sometimes play, sometimes study, but from these childhood frolics, games, and studies there resulted a considerable cultural interpenetration. If the Portuguese patriarchal family structure had not been at the root of social formation in Brazil, I doubt that the European stamp would have lasted in Brazil.

What has been said of the family organization in sixteenth-century Brazil applies with equal force to the seventeenth century. The principal difference between them is that the seventeenth century was much more disturbed by invasions from Northern Europe —the French invasion of Rio de Janeiro led by Villegaignon, for example—even though there had been some invasions during the sixteenth century.

None, however, was as important in impact on the Luso-Christian family structure as the Dutch incursion into northern Brazil in the seventeenth century. In Pernambuco, a goodly number of the Dutch interlopers took daughters of influential rural families as their brides or they married widows of Luso-Catholic plantation owners, as the famous Dona Ana Paes.

The truth is that the patriarchal family organization, already developed in Brazil for more than a century by Portuguese Catholics and their descendants, with its stronghold in the mansions of the great sugar lords, not only resisted the Dutch-Protestant impact but was fully capable of absorbing the foreigners. Those who came closest to the system ended by becoming a part of it. Gaspar Van der Lei, for example, renounced his Protestant faith and finally became part of the Luso-Catholic family circle, all for the purpose of marrying a daughter of a Melo. And Van der Lei was a leading captain during the invasions and a prominent Dutch aristocrat as well.

It should be clear now that Luso-American society in general and the patriarchal Christian family in particular evolved and took familiar shape within the confines of the Catholic faith. No misguided or extreme xenophobia influenced or prejudiced it. We have records of marriages between North Europeans and Portuguese women born in Brazil. What was thought intolerable were marriages with heretics, Protestants, and Jews who continued their Judaic customs and beliefs. Actually, there were not a few Jews of this kind discovered by agents of the Inquisition in colonial Brazil. However, there must have been a considerable number who allowed themselves to be absorbed into the Luso-Catholic family complex.

The Jesuit system of catechizing the Indians and educating the children is part and parcel of the patriarchal family structure. Yet, the interests of the Jesuits and the patriarchal family were not always the same. Even so, many sons of colonial families, in the sixteenth and seventeenth centuries, were educated by the Society of Jesus. In their colleges, the Jesuits taught on a basis of perfect equality, giving instruction to Amerindian boys, sons of whites and *mestizos*, and sons of whites and socially prominent Amerindians. Mulattoes and, all the more so, Negroes could not enter these schools. In the seventeenth century, the King of Portugal spoke out in favor of the mulattoes in a letter severely reprimanding the Jesuits for this policy of exclusiveness. Jesuit colleges reached their apogee of splendor and importance in this century, the same century when the great priest, Antônio Vieira, lived his brilliant existence.

Another important element in the consolidation of the Brazilian family in the early stages of colonial life was the orphans who came from Portugal to take spouses already living comfortably in Brazil. Many settlers in Brazil during the pioneer period of colonization married orphans coming from Portugal, a fact that does not mean they refused *caboclas* (Indian girls) or Negresses as extramarital lovers. The proclivity for white skin evidently represented for them not a sexual or aesthetic preference but a purely social one, more against an individual of servile condition than against people of color. Prejudice against people of African blood began to diminish only after acceptance of the Amerindian. Some Portuguese merchant princes in Bahia in the seventeenth century were well known for their predilection for African women, black or brown, although they rarely married them. The jewels with which they bedecked their beautiful colored mistresses, and not their legitimate white wives, were famous—or notorious. These mistresses were usually Senegalese Negresses, who sometimes gave birth to handsome and winning sons and light-skinned daughters who would advance to a position of social prominence by their womanly arts and charms. The lawful wives were at home in chaste, Moorish fashion, only leaving the house in a palanquin to attend church and other solemn festivities. It was quite a different affair for the colored mistresses. They would be freely exhibited in the streets, at parties, and in processions. The jewels they wore proclaimed the wealth of the merchants who kept them.

In the sixteenth and seventeenth centuries, in fact during the whole splendid epoch of the patriarchal family, there seems to have been a considerable incidence of marriages of convenience, which, at times, probably even sprang from romantic notions and love. During the entire patriarchal age, marriages between cousins and even between uncle and niece were common enough. Not infrequently, a widowed man would marry his wife's sister—a sign that marriages were first among families and secondly between individuals. But regular marriages of white aristocrats and African women do not appear to have taken place during the first centuries of the colonial period. Marriages of socially prominent men with Christianized Amerindian women occurred rather often and, ultimately, under the Marquis of Pombal, they received official sanction by the Portuguese Crown.

Women of both the upper and the lower classes seem to have married at an early age—anywhere from thirteen, fourteen, and fifteen years old. The men, however, had already entered full manhood. Many sons waited for marriage so that they would be considered happy or normal and live up to the Christian idea of the orthodox patriarchal marriage. But many children died in their infancy and many mothers perished during the labors of childbirth.

The sixteenth century in Brazil was a time of diseases and plagues that the European was slow in learning to cure.

The Christian organization of the slave family in patriarchal Brazil apparently was unstable and precarious because husband, wife, and children were subject to sudden separations. If the slaves were Christianized, they could expect a degree of sympathy and moral and religious assistance from their masters.

Very early the patriarchal family developed as a system of protection and comfort for the slave when he was sick or injured. The slave-owner was encouraged to protect the slave because of the vital economic interest he had in the slave's physical well-being. The most favored slave was, of course, the domestic, but the *peón* was also covered by this protective system when ill, and he was relatively well fed by the wealthier rural families. The widespread godfather relationship (*compadrio*) linked more than one patriarchal lord to a tenant farmer or slave who, on the occasion of the baptism of a child, would adopt the name of the godfather's (*padrinho*) family. From this custom many children of lowly birth would come to bear the names of noble families.

The eighteenth century ushered in the intensive exploitation of mines discovered in the seventeenth century. The working of the gold mines and the diamond fields interrupted the development of Portuguese America as solely an agricultural colony with its basis in the monocultural regime of the large landed estates (latifundia). This new economic activity did not alter the fundamental growth of its social system with the patriarchal family as its keystone.

During the colonial period, the Portuguese government selected many Brazilians for posts of political and intellectual importance both in Portugal proper and in the overseas empire. Their descendants were to become, as soon as Independence was won, the principal leaders of the new Brazilian Empire—the barons and the marquises, the politicians, statesmen, bishops, generals, admirals, and members of parliament.

Nearly all these leaders came from a background that was strictly patriarchal in the most orthodox sense. Their families were the backbone of the agrarian and feudal aristocracy, which, in its turn, was the foundation upon which the Brazilian Empire stood. The empire itself, with Dom Pedro II as the supreme expression of patriarchalism, was the patriarchal family writ large. Its leaders were not only heads of great families but also in a general way "mothers and fathers" of the whole Brazilian people. This does not mean that there were no men of modest, plebeian origin among the leaders at that time. One finds men of stature who were self-taught, illegitimate children, some with Indian or African blood (often thought a source of pride among the many Europeans of that period), and some manumitted slaves. The Brazilian Empire was in this way an open society. Positions of importance were never inaccessible to men of lowly birth, once they had demonstrated their ability and their acceptance of the ingrained traditions of the patriarchal system.

Socially, colonial Brazil extended well into the national period without many real alterations. The middle of the nineteenth century was, in fact, no more than a mixture of colonial and national elements. Brazil kept many of her colonial vestiges while taking on the new, national characteristics.

In an essay I published many years ago, I cited the work of the Frenchman Emile Abet on mid-eighteenth–century Brazil as the most perceptive insight into Brazilian society made by any foreign observer. In his comments Abet emphasized the importance of family solidarity for all Brazilians. His observations can be profitably used by those who are concerned with the investigation of Brazil's past.

In an article written for the *Revue de deux mondes* and later translated for the excellent *Revista Universal Lisbonense* (December 25, 1851), Abet has this to say about contemporary Brazilian society: "After the United States, Brazil is the best organized power in the New World." And, then, underlining the conservative patterns of Brazilian society with its close-knit family and patriarchal system, he ventures this generalization: "It is a country in which the foreigner only after many years surmounts the barriers separating him from Brazilian families and the intimacy of their home life."

He did not miss the significant fact that Brazil is differentiated into many regional units and is definitely not a monolithic structure or a homogeneous state. He saw these differences and recorded them: "The people of Bahia and Maranhão are dominated by the cross of the equator . . . the creole's indolence is offset by fitful, but fruitful periods of work which show slow, but sure progress especially in intellectual undertakings . . . and the people in the area of Pernambuco are compelled by a revolutionary spirit and often lose their heads in hopeless causes."

The common psychological characteristics, however, were more important than these differences in uniting all the regions and giving a degree of unity to the people of north and south. All Brazilians were moved by the same religious feeling. They all lived within the ties of the patriarchal family. And they were always courteous and hospitable in their dealings with others. Religious feeling and an open spirit of hospitality were closely related to the family complex of Brazilian society that Abet wrote about. The private ethos of the patriarchal family projected itself into everyday public life, sometimes helping, sometimes harming, an individual's actions.

It is impossible to understand the Brazilian ethos without considering the impact of family, patriarchal, and godfather relationships upon national, or public, behavior. Its influence is still felt today, although the patriarchal family is practically extinct, without ostensible force upon the other elements in the Brazilian community.

The following question was put to me recently by a young student of Brazilian studies at Heidelberg University in Germany: "What are the repercussions of the patriarchal family in the overall social formation of Brazil, or what you have called the behavior and ethos of modern Brazil?" Similar questions had been raised by a North American postgraduate student doing work in the sociological interpretation of Brazil.

The patriarchal family still exerts an influence upon both the behavior and the ethos of contemporary Brazilians. It works in subtle, oblique, and unseen ways. Brazilians are, above all, a people whose background and history up to the end of the nineteenth century were heavily colored by a strong family organization.

The typical Brazilian is not known for deep friendship. Profound ties between friends are rare among Brazilians. Of course, they can be found, but they remain the exception rather than the rule. The rule is comradeship and cordiality. The typical Brazilian is expansive, given to good fellowship, cordial in the extreme, with a wide circle of acquaintances.

His deepest affections, however, are kept for his family. Usually he is a good father to his family even if his actions are not strictly monogamous, as so frequently happens. His bonds to his family are, for the average Brazilian, the most important bonds in the whole world, and he is usually faithful to relatives before he is loyal to his friends.

An interesting study, still to be undertaken, is that of the role of sons-in-law within the Brazilian family. The son-in-law (*genro*) often rises in the social, economic, and political echelons because of the ties to his wife's family. He take part in important activities because of his new status within the family. The son-in-law is one of the most characteristic figures of the Brazilian family. Rising in politics, in business, in law, or in teaching, at times in actual competition with the immediate scions of a family, he assumes positions of rank and importance. And all because of his new ties with another family.

The family is a significant fact even today in Brazil's political life. When a president is elected and installed in the Presidential Palace, it is not just one individual who becomes important around him, it is an entire family, a whole gamut of legal and consanguineous relationships (*parentela*). The same thing happens when governors, state ministers, and mayors are officially invested with fuller political power.

In the republican history of Brazil, certain figures became known for their nicknames, echoes of the preceding monarchal age. The patriarchal overtones were always clear. Empress Teresa Cristina had been known as the "Mother of All Brazilians." President Rodrigues Alves, surrounded by his sons and sons-in-law, was called *"Papai Grande"* ("Big Daddy"), and President Epitacio Pessoa was referred to as *"Tio Pita"* ("Uncle Pita") for the important posts he gave to his sons-in-law (he had no male issue), his many nephews, and further removed relatives as well. These epithets were the outward expressions of a patriarchalism and a feeling for family that crop up again as more or less discreet references to precedents in the republican era. A good example is the name people gave to

Getúlio Vargas: *"Nosso Pai"* ("Our Father"), or *"Getúlio, Pai dos Pobres"* ("Getúlio, the Father of the Poor").

The family complex reaches out into the whole fabric of society. It touches the law, the teaching profession, and the administration of justice. There have been examples where thoroughly honest men have had their reputations damaged by the thoughtless or unscrupulous acts of sons and sons-in-law. Ruy Barbosa is said to have been the victim of such thoughtless interference in his public career by his male relatives.

Another interesting aspect of patriarchalism still at work in twentieth-century Brazil is the decisive role of the patriarchal figure when whole family groups are converted from Catholicism to Protestantism. The patriarch really makes the decision and leads the entire family in a new psycho-social direction if that is his will. This is what actually happened with the Nogueira Paranagúa and the Gueiros families.

The institution of godfather and godchild (*compadrio*) still has a vigorous hold on Brazilian life. Godparents are close friends who are considered socially as parents. The godfather stands in society as a second father, and his godchild practically becomes his real son. There are any number of instances in which social, economic, and political success have been due to this relationship. The *compadrio* system is an essential element in Brazilian family life. Because of its social significance, further study about its nature should be made.

Professional advancement often takes place within the family framework. Judges are succeeded by judges, politicians by politicians, doctors by doctors, lawyers by lawyers, professors by professors, all within the realm of the family and its relatives. Godchildren, too, have followed in the footsteps of their godfathers' wealth and influence. Naturally, this system of preference for professional talent within the family orbit has not always produced the best results, intellectually or technically. Mediocre children have succeeded their brilliant fathers in the law or the university only because they were of the same family. On the other hand, there have been veritable dynasties of superior intelligence in many professional fields and in the Brazilian army and navy. A good example of family dynasty in the military are the Mena Barreto of Rio Grande do Sul.

The remnants of patriarchalism and strong family unity, the axis of Brazil's social formation, are still alive in contemporary Brazil. The families are no longer patriarchal, as they were a century ago. The majestic figures, the barons, the viscounts, the commanders of the empire, faded from the scene at the turn of the century. But their influence lingers and is seen still today in some of the provincial "colonels." Patriarchalism, the close unity of the family is, if not the substance of Brazilian society in this century, still an active force and explains much about the Brazilian, his ethos, and his social behavior.

9

Luso-Brazilian Kinship Patterns: The Persistence of a Cultural Tradition

CHARLES WAGLEY

The varieties of kinship systems in primitive societies and the role of kinship in channeling social norms and behavior have been favorite subjects of study on the part of social anthropologists for over a century. In primitive societies, the study of kinship is almost synonymous with the study of the *society*, so important are the rights, obligations, and expected patterns of behavior that are determined by kinship. Until recently, however, sociologists and anthropologists have all but ignored the role of kinship in our more complex modern societies. There has been considerable interest in and research on the family, but comparatively little attention has been given to the wider network of kinship. In fact, we have tended to view our modern institutions as essentially antagonistic to extended kinship bonds and obligations. It has generally been assumed that the social changes set off by the Industrial Revolution tend universally to isolate the immediate family from their kindred.

In recent years, however, anthropologists and sociologists have begun to suspect that this trend is not inevitable. Garigue, for example, found extensive kinship networks playing an important role in the social life of the French Canadians living in Montreal despite a high degree of urbanization and industrialization.[1] Raymond Firth and his associates found extended kinship ties important in the lives of Italians living in London.[2] And, to cite but one more

174

example, Young and Wilmott were "surprised to discover that the wider family, far from having disappeared, was still much alive in the middle of London."[3] It becomes apparent, then, that widely extended kinship ties are not entirely incompatible with our modern institutions and that kinship continues to have an important role in certain areas of our modern Western world.

The importance of kinship in the Brazilian tradition is well known. Gilberto Freyre in his now-classical studies has shown conclusively the importance of the patriarchal family in the development of Brazilian society.[4] These large and powerful patriarchal families are now, in the main, a thing of the past. As the agrarian society of yesterday gave way to the urban-oriented and more industrialized society of today, the large patriarchal families became disorganized. As one writer on the modern Brazilian family has stated, "The extended patriarchal family as an integrated social unit no longer exists."[5] Still another student of the Brazilian family today has it that "the family no longer is an economic and political group, nor is it any longer the all-important group in social organization."[6] There can be no doubt that the patriarchal family regime has come to an end; but this does not mean that kinship no longer has an important function in contemporary Brazilian society.

It is the thesis of this paper that, while the patriarchal family type of the agrarian past may have disappeared, a larger network of relatives, which I shall call the *parentela*, has persisted with modified but important functions in Brazilian social, economic, and even political life.

The Luso-Brazilian *parentela*, as I am using the term, means all those relatives traced on both maternal and paternal lines whom an individual recognizes as kinsmen. It also includes one's affinals as well as those individuals who are related by the ceremonial ties of the *compadrio*. I do not need to describe the system by which kinsmen of such *parentelas* are classified, for that system is shared generally by all European cultures. In this system of kinship, which is bilateral and includes both the matrilineal and patrilineal lines, literally hundreds of individuals may be considered relatives, as long as the genealogical connection can be remembered. In anthropological terms, the Brazilian *parentela* is a kindred.

The various community studies that have been carried out in

Brazil during the last decade provide us with rich data on the role of the *parentela* in Brazilian society. Most of the communities studied have been small; often they have been relatively isolated; and, in general, they were located in the more conservative north of Brazil. They admittedly do not provide us with a picture of the way of life in large cities or in the extreme south, where the influence of Northern European immigrants has been felt so strongly. It might be said that, in the main, the community studies we now have at hand reveal "traditional" Brazilian culture, which is being modified in larger centers and in the more rapidly changing rural zones of the country. Still, they offer a rich source of empirical data covering several regions of the country and a variety of ecological adaptations.

What do some of these studies reveal regarding the *parentela* and its functions? Not all of them discuss the *parentela* explicitly. As so often is the case, the term "family" is frequently used in several ways. It is used to mean the nuclear group of man, wife, and children; the household unit; a patriarchal extended family; and sometimes it refers to a large network of kin—the *parentela*. None of the authors of these community studies has made an exhaustive analysis of the *parentela* and its functions. Perhaps because there is nothing exotic or strange about the workings of our own Western kinship system, we have tended to overlook its importance in our own social structure. Yet, it seems clear from these community studies that kinship has an important role in Brazilian social relations.

There is neither time nor space to present all of the data regarding the *parentela* from the numerous community studies available to us for Brazil. In the pages that follow, however, I have summarized the data for seven communities on which data on the "family" has been published.[7]

Vila Recôncavo[8]

The community of Vila Recôncavo is situated on the Bay of All Saints in the region known as the Recôncavo, just 41 kilometers from the city of Salvador in Bahia State. The Recôncavo is perhaps the oldest sugar-producing region in all of Brazil, and sugar cane is still by far the most important economic pursuit in the region. (Petroleum is, however, now being pumped from the sugar-cane fields.) The community of Vila Recôncavo consists of a small town (a county seat) of 1,462 people and of the people living on the sugar-cane plantations and at the sugar factory in the rural zone. The inhabitants of the rural area number about 2,800, of whom 500 are concentrated near the sugar factory while the rest live on the sugar plantations. Hutchinson describes four social classes for Vila Recôncavo: Class A, an upper class of landowners who live on their plantations and spend part of each year in the city of Salvador; Class B, a middle class made up of local bureaucrats, merchants, and professional people who live in town, and plantation administrators, technicians, and specialists at the sugar factory and on plantations; Class C, a lower class of fishermen and artisans who live in the city and of mill workers and field hands in the rural zone; and Class D, a marginal lower class of servants, laundresses, and others lacking steady employment.

Many of the landowners in the Vila Recôncavo upper class are descendants of the *senhores de engenho* of the past, and they have clung to many of their aristocratic patterns of behavior. This class consists of "five family lines which own practically all of the sugar lands in the area"[9] and dominate the community politically and socially. "Two of these families . . . are closely interwoven by first-cousin marriage; a third . . . is related to these two by marriage."[10] From the point of view of any member of these three "families," they constitute one large kinship circle. Hutchinson reports only seventy-eight consanguineous relatives among the two closely interwoven "families" in the community; but it must be remembered that these people divided their time between Vila Recôncavo and the city, where they had numerous kinsmen. His description of family life (*vida em família*) among these upper-class kinsmen and their in-laws, both in the community of Vila Recôncavo and in the city, is reminiscent of descriptions of "family life" in the nineteenth century.[11]

The *parentela* of the other social classes differs strikingly, however, from that of the upper class. Although members of Class B take "as their pattern the older traditions of the upper-class families,"[12] they do not, with only one exception, have numerous kinsmen,[13] but "are conjugal units without local tradition of genera-tions in the area,"[14] for they are apt to be people from other communities or "newly arrived" socially. Little is said about the extended kinship relations of Class C, but it must be presumed that, like the slaves before them, wage workers on the plantations and the lower class in the town seldom have more than a few rela-tives. Yet, as in the past, the permanent field hands on the family-run plantations are, in a sense, attached to the "families" of the plantation owner, for a strong sense of paternalism persists in Vila Recôncavo. Class D is characterized by fragile marital bonds, often by women without husbands, and the kinship ties are few.

As might be expected, the members of the landowning class in Vila Recôncavo use the *compadrio* system to reinforce their already widespread kinship bonds.[15] On the contrary, Class C, lacking the support of kinsmen, looks for *compadres* in the upper class. "If possible, at least one of the godparents will be a member of the upper class, a patron who will help the child if necessary, especially if the godson when he grows up wants to go to school in the city or enter the army or navy."[16]

Cerrado and Retiro[17]

Cerrado, a small town of 2,425 inhabitants, is the county seat of a large *município* (county) of nearly 13,000 people. Retiro, where approximately 400 people live, consists of a group of ranches within this same *município*. Cerrado and Retiro are both situated in the upper São Francisco Valley in the state of Minas Gerais. The eco-nomic life of this community depends primarily upon the grazing of cattle, but there is also considerable subsistence agriculture (maize, beans, and rice), some production of cotton for export, and some mining of rock crystal.

Borges Costa makes a clear distinction between the household unit, consisting of the nuclear family in the majority of cases, and the *parentela*. The term *família* may be used for either unit, but often it is used to mean a subunit of the *parentela* (i.e., the nuclear family of ego, of his uncles and aunts, of his grandparents, of his cousins, and of his nephews and nieces). The *parentela*, he states, "is more cohesive than any other association such as political parties, economic associations, or cliques."[18] Such large groups are known by certain surnames (the Oliveiras, the Barbosas, etc.), but in the traditional manner, people are given surnames in a variety of ways, and mainly to indicate their kinship with a strong *parentela*.[19] Social life is intimate within such groups. Kinsmen back up kinsmen in crisis situations such as death, financial loss, and the like; and for birthdays and weddings "relatives . . . are always present to cooperate in the preparations."[20]

The cohesion of political parties depends upon the *parentelas* that make them up. "The Ferreira family always was of Party A," writes Borges Costa. "Recently, when one of its members had almost decided to vote for a candidate of Party B, he was reprehended severely by his godfather, who is the political leader [of Party A], and also by his uncle."[21]

Feuds still continue in Cerrado between "families"; two "family groups" have been for some years in open conflict, which is only periodically interrupted. Recently, there was a shooting in the streets between members of these "families."[22] Members of these families feel the responsibility of avenging offenses and even slights shown toward "family" members. Judicial and police authorities (often "outsiders") have been forced to leave the community in fear of their lives because they offended a member of a large *parentela*.[23] In Cerrado and Retiro, "it is dangerous to speak badly about anybody when others are standing nearby, because these might be kinsmen, however remote, of the person in question."[24]

The size of these *parentelas* is not given, although they would seem to be very large. Differences in kinship extension according to social classes are not mentioned, yet it is clear from the study that they are present in both the urban (Cerrado) and the rural (Retiro) areas.

Passagem Grande[25]

In this small community (population 3,713) in the northeastern state of Alagoas, the cultivation of rice is the principal basis of the economy. The majority of the population are wage workers on the rice farms, and this is a zone of heavy migration to the cities and to the rural areas of the "south" (mainly São Paulo). A large *pa-*

rentela, or "extended family" as Maynard Araujo calls it, is characteristic of only one "dominant family." The number of relatives of this kinship circle "adds up to more than a hundred members." Despite marriages between relatives (cousins with cousins), it is the family with the largest number of members.[26] There is, however, a division among them into "poor" and "rich" relatives—the "poor relatives" are the "children of a brother of the family head who dies—leaving his young children" in the hands of the widow, who does not know how to take care of their economic interests. The present "family head" owns several rice farms, which are administered by his three sons-in-law. "His sons . . . were not interested in the life of a 'hick' [*matuto*] and went to study in the capital, . . ." and after graduation evidently stayed there. Even among the upper classes who own considerable rural property, the size of the *parentela* is reduced by migration to large cities.

In Passagem Grande the *parentela* of the lower socio-economic groups suffers most intensely from migration and is thus relatively circumscribed. One man, a barber, was able to enumerate forty-five relatives in the community. Another lower-class man listed twenty-eight relatives including his "wife and eleven children" but added that "in the south, if they are alive, I have five brothers" and an unknown number of sisters-in-law and nephews and nieces. Still another informant had sixty-three local relatives but again spoke of his two brothers in the "south" of whom he "never had news." The desirability of a large *parentela* was made explicit by one informant who complained about his lack of kinsmen: "I am envious of Sebastião," he said, "that one has a *parentada* [kinship group] which is a 'beauty' [*beleza*]—I think almost a hundred."

Minas Velhas[27]

Minas Velhas is a small county seat in the mountain area of central Bahia State. It was once the commercial center of a prosperous gold- and diamond-mining region. Today, it is a bureaucratic and commercial town; subsistence farmers make up the surrounding population.

The *parentela* functions with much-diminished force in Minas Velhas, despite the fact that it is a relatively isolated community proud of its old traditions. The sharp decline of its old mining economy and the rise in social position of the local artisans have modified the old social structure. Yet the community still holds the remnants of a regional aristocracy consisting of three *famílias* represented by approximately 11 per cent of the population. This local upper class (which would be middle class in the city) has been "connected and reconnected" within itself and with other *famílias* in other communities of the region. It is still obviously the dominant group in local economics,[28] and it has traditionally dominated local politics, although one family called the Bomfims has split politically to the point "that first cousins meeting on the street fail to acknowledge each other."[29] Although the size of these *parentelas* of the local elite is not specified, they are large, extending into other communities and even to the city of Salvador, to which many of them have migrated.

Even among the average townsmen in Minas Velhas, the network of kin is relatively large. "Almost any townsman can name up to one hundred kin living in Minas Velhas or in the vicinity," among whom are many second- and third-degree relatives.[30] And close kin particularly "treat each other with special deference, visit each other, borrow and lend freely and count upon each other for mutual support in crisis situations."[31] Yet, in Minas Velhas, such kinship circles are often divided by political, economic, and social lines. Beyond the primary relatives (parents, siblings, grandparents, aunts and uncles, and first cousins), kinship ties are but weakly considered. However, in Minas Velhas, those same people who lack strong kinship ties make full use of the *compadrio* system in an effort to extend the realm of quasi-kin. Only among the upper class are *compadres* selected to reinforce kinship ties; among middle- and lower-class groups people select their children's godparents from among the influential elite who might tender assistance to the child and to themselves. Thus, 10 men, the heads of upperclass households, had a total of 336 godchildren (plus twice as many *compadres*) among them. Although as Harris points out, obligations assumed in *compadrio* systems are not taken in their full traditional meanings and are often "flimsy and artificial," kinship bonds are extended by the *compadrio* system.

Itá[32]

In 1948, the community of Itá consisted of a small town (a county seat) of approximately 600 people, and the surrounding rural population of about 2,000. It is situated on the lower Amazon River in the state of Pará. The town is an administrative and commercial center; the rural population is divided between subsistence farmers, who are mainly cultivators of manioc, and collectors of wild rubber. Before 1912, the town was a prosperous commércial center for the rubber trade; but with the end of the Amazon rubber boom, it declined in importance and in population. Most of the "traditional families," including that of the Baron of Itá, have left to seek a living elsewhere.

In 1948, Itá had a small "first class" (local upper class), which comprised remnants of the "traditional families," merchants, and public employees and officials. It had a lower class consisting of three segments—rural farmers, rubber gatherers, and the lower-class town dwellers who did manual labor of one kind or another. The "first class" explicitly expressed the ideal of large *parentelas* and told of the "old days," when local society boasted great "families" that controlled economic, social, and political life. But their kinsmen were few, since most of them had moved away.[33] Likewise, the lower-class townsmen had few kinsmen in the community, for many of their brothers and cousins had left for the city or other parts of the state to look for employment. Members of the rural population devoted to rubber collecting were known for their nomadic habits. They moved whenever possible to escape debts and with the hope of finding a more productive rubber trail to exploit.[34] Thus their local kinsmen were few. And since both of these lower-class groups were largely illiterate, they tended to lose contact with their kinsmen in other communities.

This situation, however, did not hold true for a settlement of small farmers. In the settlement of Jocojó, within the Itá community, a complex web of kinship united the inhabitants of the nineteen households. One man, the leader, claimed kinship with 80 of the 102 people; and another counted 50 as consanguineous relatives and many more as affinals. In Itá, only the relatively stable farming population, less affected by the ups and downs of the rubber market, had a large network of kin.

In the absence of large *parentelas*, the *compadrio* system functions to almost exaggerated proportions. People have the usual *compadres* of baptism, confirmation, and marriage. In addition, there are "*Compadres* of the Fire." Members of the "first class" had an average of 28.1 godchildren, while members of the lower class averaged only 4.2 godchildren. In addition, all of them had many "*Compadres* of the Fire," a less serious relationship. As might be expected, nonkin were selected as *compadres* in Itá in almost all cases.

Cruz Das Almas[35]

Cruz das Almas (pop. 2,723, of which 90 per cent live in the village), only twenty-four miles from the great city of São Paulo, is a village of relatively stable and homogeneous small farmers. In the past, a few plantation-owning families provided the community with an upper class, but they have either migrated or been reduced in status.[36] Thus, today, there is no local or regional upper class. In this essentially one-class community, the kinship ties are strong.

"In this community," writes Donald Pierson, "individuals are bound together in families with tenacious bonds of belonging, obligation, and affection, which by way of inter-family marriage extend throughout virtually the entire community."[37] The size of such groups is large. One twenty-four-year-old woman, cited as an example, recalled without effort 166 relatives. Among these relatives, sixty-four had the same surname as the informant, but sixteen other surnames, including the six most common surnames of the village, were found in her list. Furthermore, people extend their kinship ties through the *compadrio* system. Of twenty-five persons questioned as to how many godchildren they had, none had less than one and one person had forty. One villager, who prepared a list of *compadres* for Pierson, listed fifty-three, of whom seven were relatives and forty-six were nonkinsmen.

In discussing the functions of the "family," Pierson stresses the more immediate groups of the nuclear and patriarchal family of a man, his sons, and their spouses; yet, it is quite evident that the large *parentela* is of considerable importance in community affairs. One village leader made this quite clear in his statement referring to a coming election. "I have the key that controls the community," he said. "I have fifty-three *compadres*. Besides, there are my relatives, my children, my sons-in-law, my daughters-in-law, my nephews and nieces. Here in these parts, the Buenos and the Cardosos [the names of his own and his wife's families] *é mato* [are legion]. That's why no one here can win from me. Every election it is the same; if I go one way, you can bet they'll go with me and that we'll win."[38] Membership in a prominent family that has been a long time in the community is listed as one of the more important criteria that make for high prestige.[39]

Cunha[40]

Situated in the coastal range of São Paulo State, Cunha is the name of a county (*município*) and the county seat. The county contains over 25,000 people, of which only some 6,500 live in the "city." It is a region of subsistence farming, producing mainly maize and beans. In recent years, the exhausted soils have been turned more and more to pasture. The natural increase in population, combined with the inefficient agricultural system and the growth of grazing, has caused an exodus from Cunha to other communities and to the city of São Paulo. In nine "traditional" families selected at random, 25.9 per cent of the members lived outside the community. According to Emilio Willems, local society contains three socio-economic classes—an upper class made up of the "traditional families" as well as of some outsiders (even foreigners) and their descendants who have achieved a secure economic and social position; a middle class whose members are lower in the social and economic scale but who, because of their education, occupations, and manners, maintain cordial relations with the upper class; and finally the lower class made up of sharecroppers, renters, poor farmers, artisans, and manual laborers.

Both the older rural *bairros* (districts) and the city "were inhabited by families, largely related." Of the 296 individuals measured by Willems for his studies in physical anthropology, 127 carried but 17 traditional surnames, and there were 33 people known

by 1 surname and 27 by another.[41] And among the 9 families from
which he drew his data on migration, it is clear that each listed an
average of 135 relatives, over 100 of them in the community. One
family listed a total of 435 relatives from 6 generations, another
274 from 4 generations, and 1 only 10 relatives from 2 generations.[42] Willems notes the "respect" offered to relatives, even
though removed, and the solidarity among relatives that surpasses
that of mere neighbors.[43] Kinship seems to have provided a bridge
between the town and the rural zones. "Almost all the great families residing in the *sêde* [county seat] have ramifications in the
rural zone, forming not infrequently enormous kinship circles
[*parentelas*] in various districts."[44]

It seems clear that kinship was still important in Cunha society.
Yet, evidently, family oligarchies had, at the time the study was
carried out, lost control in local politics. The deterioration of a
traditional system of common landholding among siblings had
made for conflicts between relatives. The loss of what was called
locally *respeito* (literally "respect," but actually "a sense of solidarity") had produced disorganization in the family or *parentela*.[45]
And this was supplemented by the exodus of kinsmen from the
community.

It is evident from the data provided by these seven community
studies that kinship plays an important role in social, economic,
and even political affairs. Yet, it is equally apparent that not all of
the various social and economic classes that make up these communities share the large *parentela*. In the communities under review, three social segments seem to be characterized by widely extended kinship networks—the descendants of the landed gentry
(Vila Recôncavo), the local elite (Minas Velhas, Cerrado and
Retiro, Passagem Grande, and Cunha), and the stable subsistence
farmers (Itá and Cruz das Almas). It is the wage workers on
plantations, sharecroppers, rubber gatherers, and others whose economic condition is unstable and precarious who seem singularly to
lack kinsmen. Yet, even these lower-class groups are often connected with important *parentelas* in the communities in which
they live. Although the obligations involved have been attenuated,
the *compadrio* system is used more widely to secure protection by

those without kinsmen. In none of these communities, with the possible exception of Vila Recôncavo, does the *parentela* assume the form of the patriarchal family of the past, yet kinship ties retain many of their former essential functions.

Objective and empirical data as to the extension of kinship ties and the role of kinship are less readily available for those segments of the Brazilian population not included in the communities studied above. It would seem probable that kinship would be less extensive in recently settled frontier regions. The same would seem to be true also in great cities among lower-class groups, so many of which have migrated recently from small towns and rural zones. Yet, it is always possible that migration from one region to another and from rural districts to urban zones may involve not isolated individuals or nuclear families but whole *parentelas*. For one urban class, namely the urban upper class, however, there are clear indications that kinship has very important ramifications. In Salvador, Carmelita Junqueira Ayres Hutchinson reports one member of an important and traditional "family" who was able to name and give the precise genealogical relationship of 290 kinsmen (53 of whom were deceased). According to Mrs. Hutchinson, this is not unusual among the Baian upper classes.[46] A series of interviews carried out among the middle and upper classes in Rio de Janeiro shows that individuals maintain relations with between 100 and 200 relatives, and people related to wealthy and traditional *parentelas* often recognize even more numerous kinsmen.[47] And, in the city of São Paulo, Emilio Willems states that people "were able to distinguish between 30 and 500 relatives."[48]

In these large cities, crowded urban conditions have dispersed kinsmen throughout the city, but such conditions have not isolated them from one another. Regular telephone conversations, frequent visiting, and many "family" gatherings at weddings, baptisms, graduation ceremonies, birthdays, and the like maintain these large *parentelas* in an intimate and continuous relationship. And, there is a trend, often commented upon but as yet unstudied to my knowledge, for kinsmen to purchase or rent apartments in one building, uniting a segment of the *parentela* under the same roof. Large and elite kin groups still dominate Brazilian economics and are important in politics. An American economist writing about Brazil a few years ago said, "The power of the oligopolis and the duopolis is enhanced by the strong ties which exist among the few families that are strong in business and politics."[49] The other social classes of the great urban centers of Brazil do not share, in practice, the large *parentela*. Members of the middle class are often migrants from provincial cities and small towns. They often help their kinsmen to migrate to the city and they maintain contact with their kinsmen at home. The lower class in the big cities suffer most from the lack of kinsmen: They come from far away and they are often illiterate; thus they lose contact with their relatives on plantations and small farms. It is this segment of Brazilian society, more than any other, that seems to lack the support of a wide network of kinsmen. But even for these people, the large *parentela* persists as an image or an ideal—as the way people ought to behave and ought to live in Brazil. Whenever possible, they attach themselves to "families" and they extend their kin by the *compadrio* system. As one very astute Brazilian writer put it, "The patriarchal system still impregnates the minds of Brazilians, even when they are no longer able to live it out."[50]

This tradition of familism has deep roots in the Portuguese tradition. Jorge Dias comments upon this historical fact and describes the extended family (or the *parentela* in our terms) in modern Portugal in the following terms:

The relations between the members of families (i.e., *parentelas*) are always highly intimate and sometimes exclusive. Parents and children, brothers and sisters, uncles and aunts, cousins of both sexes form closed and confused networks into which an outsider penetrates with difficulty. Many of these *familias* meet together frequently. On birthdays—of the oldest as well as of the youngest—the whole *familia* comes together, often bringing with them servants to take care of the children. Christmas, New Years, Easter, and the other principal festivals of the year are always pretexts for "get-togethers" when the family is invited for lunch, for dinner, or for tea after which conversation goes on around the table or in other rooms when it is an upper-class family.[51]

Jorge Dias' description would be valid for the provincial upper class of small towns and cities of Brazil today as well as for many Brazilians who live in great metropolitan centers.

The persistence of the widely extended *parentela* in Brazil must be considered as the reflection of deep-seated Luso-Brazilian values. The patriarchal family system of the plantation era may have disappeared, yet the strong bonds of kinship have been re-formed in terms of contemporary conditions of life. The traditional emphasis upon the *familia* and the *parentela* provides a model for human relations that is an aspiration for even those segments of the society that cannot live in this way. The predominance of kinship in ordering social life explains the relative absence in Brazil of such voluntary associations as parent-teacher groups, garden clubs, civic clubs, and the like. People give greater value to kinship relations than to relations based upon common interest or even occupation.

Recently, Arnold Strickon has shown that the working-class rural *criollo* of Argentina depends strongly upon a large kinship group extending his relations horizontally by affinity—recognizing all of his *cuñados* and *concuñados* as well as all his *parientes* within the realm of his knowledge. He says, "Jobs and assistance of various kinds depend upon some kinds of kin tie to the person who has them to dispose, making it advantageous to extend one's kinship network as widely as possible."[52] He also points out that the Argentine elite extend their kinsmen vertically—that is, in a lineal system, deriving from some famous or wealthy man on the mother's as well as the father's side. This also makes for a large kindred similar to that found in Brazil. There is no doubt in my mind that the kindred rather than the more immediate family is one of the fundamental institutions of Latin American society. In each nation, it needs to be studied by economists interested in business enterprise, by political scientists interested in the actual function of government, by historians interested in regional or local developments, and by all of us interested in Latin American society. The persistence of kinship in Brazilian society, or in any Latin American society, should be viewed not as a social or cultural lag but rather as the continuation of a fundamental cultural value. There is a growing body of evidence that kinship relations and awareness of kinship need not disappear with industrialization and urbanization. Our own situation in the United States, where kinship is reduced to a minimum in channeling social relations, may be a result "of the presence of the small family in Northern Europe prior to the industrial revolution" and not a functional result of the industrialization or urbanization.[53] There is every reason to believe that, especially in those cultures where the tradition of familism has been strong, such as Brazil and other countries of Latin America, kinship will continue to play an important role in ordering social relations. A true comparative sociology cannot be based upon the United States and northern Europe alone; it must consider the different cultural traditions of the "new" countries.

10

Brazil and the Myth of Francisco Julião

ANTHONY LEEDS

i

In September, 1962, the "independent socialist magazine," the *Monthly Review*, published an English translation of a speech made by the notorious Brazilian, Francisco Julião, a leader of some of the equally notorious Peasant Leagues in the Northeast of Brazil. It is not necessary to repeat here how often the Brazilian Northeast has been alleged to constitute a "danger zone," a seat of "communist revolutionary ferment," a fervid locus of *fidelismo*, or even the possible site of origin of "another progressive socialist revolution" in Latin America. The Northeast is, in newspaper, journal, and magazine, virtually identified with Brazil, the axiom appearing to be, "As goes the Northeast, so goes Brazil," and Julião is represented as the prophet and leader of this revolutionary activity, a man who is likely to overthrow the stability of all Brazil.

It is my purpose, here, to present an interpretation of Brazilian socio-political conditions that is at variance with these views and that, I believe, better represents the present and long-term conditions than do most of the currently popular views. I make use of the speech published in the *Monthly Review* simply because it affords a convenient handle, one more convenient than most because of the expectations one might entertain that a socialist or Marxist interpretation of the situation would be different from a "capitalist" one—expectations that strikingly were not fulfilled in the

Review's presentation of the speech, at least as far as one can infer from their omissions of relevant information.

Julião's speech was delivered in Ouro Prêto, State of Minas Gerais, on April 21, 1962. The English version published in the *Review* was made from a Spanish translation from the Portuguese and appeared in Montevideo. It is presented without comment, but with a brief footnote to which I return below. That a socialist journal publishes the speech in this manner, especially in view of the letter and apparent intent of the footnote, seems to indicate general accord with the thought or content of the article—certainly no disclaimers were offered. It is fruitful, therefore, to examine some of the facts relevant to Julião's speech and also the larger realities of Brazil, because the journal appears to make the same basic assumptions and misinterpretations as the rest of the—nonsocialist—American press. Hopefully, the discussion that follows will rectify some of these misinterpretations and shed light on the socio-political structure of contemporary Brazil.

ii

Let us turn first to the footnote that accompanies the published speech.[1] It is there asserted that Julião is "head of the Peasant Leagues of Brazil." This statement, reflecting a view virtually universally held in the United States, is at least misleading, if not quite erroneous. In the first place, there are a variety of types of peasant leagues in various states of Brazil: Paraná, São Paulo, Pernambuco, Paraíba, and elsewhere. In each of these states there are leagues that are being organized by representatives of the Catholic Church, e.g., Padre Melo in Cabo, Pernambuco; Bishop Eliseu Simões Mendes in Maringá, Paraná; and a number of others in several other states. It is my strong conviction that these organizing activities, socially progressive as they may be, are directly encouraged by the position expressed in the papal encyclical, *Mater et Magistra*, and by the Church hierarchy itself, and are, in part, directed at reviving the Church as a popular power in Brazil (an attempt also being made elsewhere in Latin America). Some of the leagues are in fact official expressions of Church interest and activity.[2] These activities, in some areas, are also directly sup-

ported by the secular central-state power—the presidency itself—
which has cooperated with the Church officials of the northeast in
various ways[3] in encouraging their work among the rural people.

The Catholic-encouraged leagues have no connection at all with
Julião's and have been created specifically as counterpoises to
allegedly Communist-dominated leagues, and, in some cases, also to
Julião's. The latter, in turn, strictly avoid the supposedly Communist-dominated leagues. The opposition of the Church's leagues
to Julião exists, at least as far as the fostering agents are concerned,
despite Julião's appeal to the Christianity of Brazil as expressed in
the speech and many other utterances.[4]

In passing, it is important to note that most of the leagues
spontaneously began, and many continue, as informal groups
without jural recognition in the Brazilian polity.[5] That is, they
cannot operate as legal persons for their members. Though some
have been given legal status, there is apparently considerable delay
in and resistance to doing so.[6] When they are recognized, they
officially become syndicates. Besides the leagues, however, organizations have been developed in various parts of the country
with the explicit intention of achieving legal recognition as syndicates—that is, of being juridically established associations or legal
persons *ab initio*. These have been particularly characteristic of
the Catholic-sponsored groups, though these, too, have experienced
delays in recognition by the Ministry of Labor.[7] These groups aim-
ing at jural syndication are being formed especially in areas where
peasant leagues have sprung up, specifically to create legally organized counterweights to the so-called Communist-led organizations.[8] In Alagoas, for example, representatives of urban Catholic
and civic groups have joined together to foster the organization
of such syndicates in the rural hinterland.

Thus, the entire mass of rural workers concerned is being split
into groupings of mutually antagonistic organizations whose formation is, in large part, being encouraged in a paternalistic manner by representatives of the controlling and more powerful media-
torial elites of the country.

A second matter of importance that must be noted is that
Julião is connected with peasant leagues, not in Brazil at large, but
almost exclusively in Pernambuco, though he possesses some in-

fluence in the neighboring states of Alagoas and Paraíba. It is in Pernambuco that he holds political office. As far as I know, there are no peasant leagues at all in Ouro Prêto, the site of his address, nor in the general region of southern Minas Gerais, which is pre-eminently a mining area. Thus, as far as his organizational roots are concerned, he is localized in a small, though influential, part of the northeast, and has, according to informants from all other parts of Brazil, virtually no influence outside of the Pernambuco-Paraíba area. In order to extend his influence, he has initiated a newspaper, A *Liga* (*The League*), which has as its primary distri-bution center Rio de Janeiro, not the northeast at all. It appears quite irregularly and seems to be inconsequential in circulation and influence, especially in that stronghold of conservatism or even reaction which is presided over by Governor Carlos Lacerda.

Two other facts should be recognized. First, though it is not known in detail, the *distribution* of the northeast peasant leagues of all kinds appears to be quite limited socially and geographically. The northeast is divided into three major ecological bands more or less paralleling the coast. Along the coast itself lies the *zona da mata* (forest zone), the wet, sugar-growing area characterized by great mechanized and industrially organized latifundia, run with large numbers of wage workers, a rural proletariat. Inland and parallel to the *zona da mata* occurs the *zona do agreste* (roughland zone), a strip of mixed farming, for the most part in small hold-ings. The third area comprises the *zona da sêca* (dry or drought area), or *sertão* (backland), the famous dry northeast, parts of which are devoted to large cotton farms, parts to huge cattle ranches, and parts to peasant subsistence planting.

As far as the very scanty information goes—and it is indeed strange that no precise material is available—it indicates that the peasant leagues of all sorts, and the syndicates as well, are re-stricted to the *zona da mata* and parts of the *zona do agreste* and to the rural proletariat and sharecroppers and tenants on large holdings.[9] That is, peasant holders, probably the majority of the laboring classes in the northeast, appear not yet to be significantly included in any sort of organization and, in fact, are largely outside both the body politic and the body economic. This fact means that the peasant leagues are limited to the effective political, electoral portions of the northeast—that is, to the industrially organized coastal sugar belt, and thus appear to be a function of the operations of the political system of the controlling elites, a point returned to below. Julião's influence and activities are even more restricted, being limited to only a small segment of the northeast of Pernambuco.

Second, as I have suggested above, the leadership comes from outside the "masses" who comprise the peasant leagues. I am aware of no instance in which a leader of a peasant league or even a syndicate has arisen from the masses themselves, and informants were unable to name one. Undoubtedly, there are such cases, but they are clearly in the minority in number and influence. The leaders and organizers, including Julião, as I shall show, have almost exclusively been representatives of urban-centered interests and politics, even when agricultural products and landholding have been involved.[10] Their orienting interests have necessarily been urban-directed and industrial-commercial ones.

I believe, moreover, that the urban-industrial orientation extends to the rural proletariat itself.[11] I have seen no evidence that they actually *want* the land to be divided among them into small peasant holdings, other than in the slogans of the "leaders," especially Julião. One does receive the impression, however, that they, as well as the sharecroppers and tenants, want a greater share of the proceeds of the agricultural products produced for the commodity markets and the improved conditions of living that go with such increases in real wages.[12] These are fundamentally urban and politico-economic ends, to be achieved by political means and characteristic of societies organized in basically industrial-urban rather than rural patterns.

In sum, with respect to the items of information given in the footnote—so similar to information generally given about Julião in the American press and reflecting its basic axioms and distortions—Julião's influence has neither the national scope usually attributed to him nor the total inclusiveness with respect to working-class interests usually pictured of him, even in his own northeast. He is one of several paternalistic representatives, or ostensible representatives, of popular and semipopular social movements of great complexity in a small part of the very large northeast, which is, itself, only a subordinate part of that vast, diverse, and complex country, Brazil.

The foregoing discussion concerning the faulty information given in the footnote to the *Monthly Review's* version of the speech and characteristic of the American press at large may be illuminated further by some facts about Julião himself that have no currency at all in the American press reports about him and are virtually unknown among the public, though they are of great significance.

First, it is quite necessary to know that Julião is a large plantation owner (latifundista). Second, all his "organizing" activities are done in territories physically separated from the location of his own *latifundium*, which is *not* organized. Third, he is by profession a lawyer, and law is a highly regarded profession in Brazil, and one that provides a crucial springboard (*trampolim*) into political life. It is also largely an occupation of the higher classes.

Fourth, he was a state legislator and now has succeeded in getting himself elected as a federal deputy (for Pernambuco)— that is, he is sufficiently connected with, and not antipathetic to, the political machinery (i.e., the organs of the Brazilian controlling elites) to maintain himself in political positions that are of considerably greater importance than comparable positions in the United States. As a holder of political office, especially the higher one, he not only enjoys immunities but has access to an ostensibly national platform from which to expatiate. Julião regularly travels about, as do all other ambitious politicians, making political speeches. Just such a speech was that at Ouro Prêto, given on the Day of Tiradentes. Tiradentes, the equivalent, perhaps, of Nathan Hale in Brazilian national symbolism, was a hero executed after an abortive revolutionary independence movement in the late eighteenth century. Julião's speech, it may be noted, was not specifically addressed to peasant leagues at all but simply to the people, the masses perhaps, and even to potential voters.[13]

In passing, one may note that a careful reading of Julião's speech reveals a facile manipulation of a set of symbols that bear comparison with those of President Getúlio Vargas' speeches and his suicide note of 1954, as also, perhaps less neatly, with President Jânio Quadros' letter of resignation of 1961. Their charismatic and inspirational Christian-nationalistic symbols, which help reinforce the paternalistic relationship of vertical dependence discussed below, occur throughout Julião's speech: "redemption," "the patriotic" (to the state composed of members of Julião's own class?), "the kind and friendly 'campesino' John XXIII," etc. Elsewhere, too, for example: "Thou givest the soldier to defend the Fatherland. And the Fatherland forgets thee," etc.[14]

The manipulation of symbols is clear also in the linking of the Day of Tiradentes (including all the obfuscating nationalistic significances elicited at the expense of possible important meanings to the laboring class by Julião's way of using Tiradente's name) with today's stereotyped nationalistic symbols used for the mystification of the people, notably the disproportionate attacks on American imperialism that often conceal the imperialism of the Brazilian controlling elites themselves from what has been called the "internally colonized" masses.

Thus, Julião is distinctly a member of the controlling class even if he represents a somewhat aberrant and individualistic but not, properly speaking, dissident faction of it. He has moved into the political power positions of interest to members of his class by means of attaching himself to, fostering, and controlling a social discontent already present among an aggregate—and potential electorate—of the landless and the impoverished. To stir these to true revolution would be to destroy himself; to use them is in his best interest. Among many others who use the masses, Julião has distinguished himself by uniqueness in his method of manipulating them while operating in the political system of the elites.

One may well ask whether such uniqueness will bear Julião even further forward toward revolutionary behavior, such as actively redistributing land in the face of opposition of his own class or carrying on guerrilla warfare. Symptoms of such behavior are at this time absent. Alternatively, one may ask if that uniqueness will dissolve into greater conformity to the political system as he becomes increasingly embroiled in it or as the pressures against uniqueness increase. My opinion veers toward the latter course in view of the absence of symptoms, his not having run afoul of the law, his increasing enmeshment in the political system, the general indications of careerism I have discussed, and the increasing importance of the Labor Party and other bodies in the organization of the rural and urban working populations.

iii

This situation can be properly interpreted, I believe, as one in which the masses concerned are being "organized," as I remarked above, from outside in a markedly paternalistic manner. This kind of organizing, along with appropriate ideological reinforcements, provides one of the best mechanisms for the management and maintenance of virtually impenetrable class boundaries and a practically nonrevolutionary lower mass—a mass of perhaps 60 per cent of the Brazilian population flowing around, beneath, and outside even the great, progressive, but largely "middle-class" labor unions.[15] Virtually all peasant leagues—Julião's, the Catholic ones, or others—as well as the rural and urban unions and those other parts of the masses, organized or not, entering into relation with such large-scale socio-technical development agencies as SUDENE (Superintendência do Desenvolvimento do Nordeste), are in just such paternalistic relationships. They guarantee a vertical dependence upward, ultimately to the presidency of the nation—the nodal center of political and economic power for the entire sociopolitical and economic system.

Whether consciously or not, what in fact Julião has done is to fashion his own myth, a self-mystifying myth,[16] and create a political aggregate among the "masses" that serves as an electorate for the advance of his career as a politician within the body politic, i.e., the "classes," of Brazil.

It is a striking phenomenon that this sort of career procedure is relatively standardized in Brazil.[17] A certain stance with a manifest meaning is adopted, usually early in the career. But the manifest meaning is merely an empty form. The latent and true meaning may be totally different from the apparent one. This true meaning, the careerist's private and, apparently, often unformulated set of goals, only appears once the foundations of the career are firmly established. Thus San Thiago Dantas, recently Minister of Foreign Affairs and then of Finance, and accused by the United States of being leftist, in the early stages of his career belonged to the

Fascist Party (Integralistas); Carlos Lacerda, Governor of Guanabara State and oft touted as the "democratic" friend of the United
States (though by most ordinary standards his behavior, especially
the relatively arbitrary use of police power, would be judged demagogic and near-fascist), was a Communist in youth.

Cases of such extreme shifts, or having taken extreme positions
in early phases of careers, are ubiquitous. Such behavior ensures an
audience, a following, many connections, a claque (called in
Brazil a *rotary* or an *igrejinha*, "little church"), on the basis of
which the rest of the career can be built. The behavior constitutes
standard procedure in the operations of members of the politically
controlling elites and opens the road to political and economic
power.

iv

It is significant that, despite all of Julião's talk of agrarian reform, the stage of active political implementation has never been
reached.[18] Of course not. Why, as person or as class, commit suicide? One of Julião's most diagnostic remarks was quoted in *The
New York Times*: Unless the army steps in to keep order and
disarm the great landowners (who were ostensibly shooting peasants), "the desperate masses will be thrown into an insurrection
without a fixed course."[19] The implications of the quotation are
quite curious. On one hand, he appears to be teasing the peasants
into the threat of violence against landlords, thus making, to the
former, a representation of his interest in and identity with them,
and, for the latter, creating a socio-political pressure. But, on the
other hand, he is calling for the army (which was, in fact, in the
region at the time, blocking a workers' march of protest) to maintain the peace lest the situation get out of hand and become a
"disorderly" insurrection or revolution.

One may well ask why a man who, judging by his public utterances, wishes to be considered a revolutionary, who calls upon Che
Guevara, Mao Tse-tung, Fidel Castro, and Christ as models of rebels
(*rebelados*) for the people to follow, and who visits postrevolutionary Cuba, should be disturbed by an insurrection that appears
to have been favorable to his stated aims, and calls upon the army,

already interfering with the *peasants*, to maintain the peace, and, further, why he asserts that the "insurrection," hypothetical in any case, should have no "fixed course." Can the insurrection not find a revolutionary leader who would give it a fixed course, or are there no such leaders now present? Why, in view of his public proclamations regarding, say, agrarian reform and the like, is Julião not such a leader? Agrarian reform, as an action program, would presumably supply the core of a "fixed course."

One must infer that his aim is not revolution or insurrection among the masses at all, but rather the use of the masses (and the military, be it noted) against the great coastal sugar interests and the older class of *coroneis* ("colonels," i.e., local politico-economic *caudillos*). If this is a revolution at all, it is one pertaining to a newly rising segment of the controlling classes and it is firmly in the control of the Julião's, the Brizzolas, the Goularts, the Furtados—all of whom are excellent examples of the career process I have spoken of. Though representatives of this type of men may be split among themselves, they are all ranged against the older entrenched interests. At the same time, they are all of them also firmly conservative, consciously or unconsciously acting to preserve the basic aspects of the system as they find it, making only such ameliorations (on whatever scale) as will foster that preservation. They all also enter into various paternalistic arrangements with large aggregates of the masses who contribute to their political ends.

These are exceedingly able and intelligent men, often of great vision, given their assumptions about the proper nature of Brazilian society. They are what we may call the "liberal-conservative" wing, or new guard, of the great controlling class of Brazil, the wing that is presently fighting the arch-conservative or strongly reactionary old-guard wing of the same class.

Today, the battle is being carried out, at the topmost level, between the new-guard president and the old guard in the Congress. The former has recently succeeded, by means of a series of manipulated crises, in re-establishing the relatively liberal presidentialism that has been evolving slowly since Vargas' revolution of 1930; since the defeat of the reactionary São Paulo coffee and industrial powers in the attempted counterrevolution of 1932; since the overthrow of the dictatorship; and since the various episodes of military support to legitimate electoral succession.

On the other hand, the congressional majority, made up to a large extent of great commercial-landed interests and older industrial groups (the 1932 reactionary interests), as well as a number of *coroneis,* in a recent stage of the struggle (1961–63) seized the opportunity of President Jânio Quadros' resignation to create the fiction of a parliamentarianism. This strictly pseudo-parliamentarianism is under no circumstances to be understood as a democratization of the political process, but rather as a strengthening of old-guard control by means of limiting the effectiveness of the presidency.

I call it "pseudo" because the institutional structure of parliamentarianism was never complete in Brazil, since the prime minister was named by the president and the cabinet appointed by the minister had to be satisfactory to the president. Dissatisfaction with the prime minister's appointments could lead inevitably and intentionally to the resignation of the prime minister, an event that indeed occurred, as a move in making the conflict overt, during the crisis of July, 1962.

Space does not permit more than to remark that, in the struggle, various segments of the military, carefully split by Quadros by means of his resignation; major segments of labor; elements of the Church; significant sections of the rural masses, especially the political rural proletariats; and a great number of allied political powers were, and are, being most skillfully maneuvered in a great strategy, each of whose major battles has been largely won by the new guard[20] or, at worst, fought to a tie. For example, in Goulart's two years in office, he succeeded in creating an electoral climate that was to make significant "progressive" shifts in key governorships and federal deputyships; he forced the Congress to accede to the plebiscite; he achieved a steady return of powers to the presidency, culminating in the plebiscite vote (January, 1963) against parliamentarianism and for the return to presidentialism; he succeeded in appointing a wholly new cabinet characterized by nationally impeccable respectability and very strong reformist tendencies; he has massively propagandized the public without having appeared to do so. In short, he was increasingly in control of

vast sources of power—more total power than the old-guard opposition—and continued to use it effectively to break the old-guard
control exercised by means of the occupation of numerous key
administrative, bureaucratic, and congressional positions.

Each of the recent Brazilian political "crises," which, significantly enough, have never gotten out of hand—that is, become
"disorderly"—has moved toward the sharper definition of this
struggle and the strengthening of the new guard. The old guard
has been forced into open obstruction of the governmental process by Vargas' suicide, by the clamor surrounding Kubitschek's
succession, by Quadros' resignation, by the establishment of the
unworkable parliamentarianism, by old-guard resistance to the
plebiscite, and so on.

v

In summary, though the data for the foregoing discussion are
numerous and varied and cannot be presented fully here, they
point, I think, indubitably toward the lines of interpretation I
have given. Even though detail may vary, many Brazilian interpretations also tend in this general direction—and are systematically
overlooked by American interpreters of all political complexions,
including the socialist commentators.[21]

In the context of total Brazilian political, social, economic, and
geographical organization, Julião can be seen as only one of many
elements constituting an exceedingly complex structure of various
kinds and degrees of power and their manipulations. With respect
to major bureaucratic-administrative and economic power, forces
are aligned in two major groupings, the new and the old guard,
around which cluster in varying, though fairly stable, alignments
the political parties and parliamentary coalitions, the major agencies (such as the national social security agencies) and bureaucra-
cies, and the major associations (such as banks, businesses, and
labor unions). The rural labor unions and the peasant leagues are
among these and are primarily linked with the expanding new-
guard forces, especially as represented by the Partido Trabalhista
Brasileiro.

Julião, in his speeches, presents a somewhat mystical form of

the aims and interests of the new guard and hence is taken as representing the laboring groups whose interests are better served by
new-guard goals than by old.[22] Some of these groups have, consequently, attached themselves to him. But they have also attached
themselves to numerous other groups also representing such aims
and interests and even explicitly backed by the paternalistic state
itself. Both the new guard and the old guard have, in the exercise
of class maintenance, however, also encouraged factionalism in the
rural proletarian mass, so that organized groups emerging from it
are locked in combat at each other's expense and to the advantage
of the exercise of socio-political controls by the controlling elites.
Julião, by virtue of the relatively extreme forms of his utterances,
has tended to isolate his leagues more sharply from the rest of the
rural proletariat, but at the same time has won himself a more
secure electorate with which to advance his political ambitions.
This isolation is reflected also in his position in the Congress. Thus,
his interests are linked to the leagues' but are far from identical
with their members' aims. Francisco Julião is neither a prophet nor
one potentially to overthrow the Brazilian state, though I wish explicitly to state that the unintentional effects of his activities might
ultimately contribute to revolutionary upsurge.

More widely viewed, Juliãoism is a phenomenon characteristic
of Brazil in change. It seems to me basically the same phenomenon, at least until recently, as the relationship between a Vargas or
a Goulart and the urban labor movement, or certain of the military and civil authorities and the line soldiers.[23] The aim in all
such cases has been the manipulation of the mass and its harsh
experience of life to convey a threat to the old guard, which is
resisting the political ascendancy of the new guard. Over the past
third of a century, the threat has been generally successful. The
main power of the old guard today is in their continued grasp of
the juridical means of resistance, especially the resistance against
progressive constitutional change, where the next major battles will
find their locus.

The resistance to change is increased by the multiplicity of
types of groups, localizations of groups, geographic differentiation
of groups, administrative levels (municipal, state, and federal) of
groups, and the distribution of various types and quantities of

power among them. The complexity of power oppositions in Brazil comprises both a source of control for the political elites and a source of stability and equilibrium for the socio-political system as a whole. The loci of power, great power, are many, and the peasant league northeast has only a small part of the total power. Were a revolutionary upsurge to occur in that part of Brazil, many, if not most, of the other great loci of power would be mobilized by the controlling elites, which are geographically and economically dispersed but institutionally centralized, to repress the movement effectively. The resources to do so are highly varied and very great. Thus, the axiom "As goes the Northeast, so goes Brazil" seems to me basically false, if not actually silly, and can only give an erroneous portrait of Brazil.

I consider Brazil today one of the more stably conservative, albeit strongly reformist and nationalistic, polities in Latin America. Despite recent events, it seems to me one of those least liable to a violent revolution, the one intrinsically most sympathetic to the reformist aims overtly expressed in American foreign policy, and one of the least understood societies in Latin America.[24]

I would go further and say that, in regard to the ostensibly desired ends of American policy, Brazil represents America's best friend and strongest ally against revolution in all Latin America. The United States' officialdom has not understood this any more than has the press, including the socialist opinion, so that both have been operating on false premises and to their own disadvantage. They have not understood this because they have not understood the meanings behind forms such as calls for agrarian reforms by landowners like Julião, Brizzola, and Goulart. They have not understood such gestures as the pseudo-democratic moves of a Lacerda who constantly attempts to destroy democratic process by the arbitrary use of police force (as against the students striking for change in the privileged structure of Brazilian universities, or against workers striking for a progressive return to presidentialism).[25] They have not understood the significance of such actions as expropriations (essentially a mode of strengthening the controlling elites who make demagogic noises of liberation from oppression that are conveniently blamed on outsiders—a constant, only partially justified change, repeatedly used in Brazilian politics, and expressed,

for example, by Vargas, Kubitschek, Julião, Brizzola, Quadros, etc.).
They have misunderstood the real nature of the pre-eminently
pseudo-democratic form of the so-called parliamentarianism, the
establishment of which brought into the open (quite possibly a
long-term strategic intention of Quadros' resignation) the petrifica-
tion that the reactionary wing of the controlling class had produced
in the more progressive governmental process represented by the
presidentialism of the liberal wing of the same conservative class.

The prognosis seems to be the eventual emergence of the new
guard and the concurrent relegation of the old guard to a position
considerably more peripheral to the main political and economic
resources than is occupied by similar groupings in the United States
such as the Conservative Republicans and the Southern Democrats, who also, to a large extent, represent old commercial landed
interests and older forms of capitalist-commercial enterprise.

There will continue in Brazil the headlong economic development that has characterized the new guard's policy for thirty years,
possibly at an accelerated rate and with a marked expansion into
new areas. The effect will be, politically, to strengthen the "liberal"
wing still more; economically, to carry Brazil nearer our general
kind of finance-monopoly capitalism, but one more strongly state-
centered; and socially, to transform ever larger proportions of the
great masses of peripheral peasantries into proletariats within the
body politic in a social system wherein the outward forms of
democracy will be fostered, while the veiled, hierarchic, socio-
political controls characteristic of democracies will be created and
maintained by the development of a mass culture in a mass society.

IV

CHALLENGES TO THE
WESTERN HEMISPHERE

11

The Problem of Color in Foreign Relations

JOSEPH MAIER

The cost of race prejudice has always been heavy. It is forbiddingly so at the present moment. Spring, 1963, will long be remembered as a time when the faces of American foreign-policy officials were grimmer and wearier than at any period since the Cuban missile crisis of October, 1962. The threat to America's image abroad was stark and striking. All lands of "color" followed the sorry spectacle that bounded from Arkansas, Mississippi, and Alabama to the metropolitan centers of the North. The scenes pictured on the front pages of newspapers in all capitals of the world were incredible and unforgettable. There was the Negro woman pinned to the ground by armed policemen, one of them with his knee resting on her throat. There was the Negro man rolling across the pavement as firemen hosed him with torrents of water so strong that they could tear bark off trees. There were the Negro youths with their arms raised to ward off the vicious dogs, and the electric cattle prods wielded by white-helmeted, dark-glassed cops and troopers. And there were the little Negro children dressed in white and waving tiny American flags, singing "We Shall Overcome" and "Freedom, Freedom" while being packed into garbage trucks to be rushed off to prisons and improvised detention centers.

The racial clashes taking place in this country strike not only at a vital domestic problem but at an equally vital aspect of United States foreign policy. Our treatment of minority groups receives world-wide attention. During World War II, we "relocated" Americans of Japanese ancestry behind barbed-wire fences in various internment camps. Their only crime was their ethnic origin. Japan was quick and thorough to exploit this as propaganda among the colored peoples of the world. Even Nazi Germany, whose whole philosophy and practice was racist with a vengeance, played upon the theme of American hypocrisy. It goes without saying that the propaganda was often exaggerated or distorted and that Americans at their worst should not be mentioned in one breath with those who made it their purpose to incinerate "inferior" people by the millions. But there have been enough instances of brutality and injustice that the enemies of our country needed only to cite our own newspapers for evidence.

The world today is not that of a hundred years ago, when slavery was officially abolished and the American Negro granted the equality that should have been his under the Bill of Rights. A hundred years ago this was largely a domestic problem. It is no longer. The globe's political balance has changed since the end of World War II. The peoples whose skins are pigmented differently from that of our majority have moved into their place in the sun. Their representatives speak with increasing authority in the United Nations. Their cooperation and friendship are objects of open contention and rivalry among the superpowers. In a world grown thoroughly interdependent, their numbers and power are increasing at a fast rate. For decades, and probably centuries, to come, they will constitute a progressively larger part of the world's population. The future of both the Western and the Communist blocs may well depend on who wins the competition for the trust and sympathy of the peoples of color.

Latin America is an area where race prejudice and discriminatory practices are especially expensive luxuries for the United States. Most of the Central and South American populations are complex mixtures of Indian, Negro, and white stocks. Race lines are relatively unimportant. Race prejudice is looked upon as an insult to the individual and the nation. More than 200 million people of color live south of our borders. And by the end of this century, if the conservative estimates of our demographers are correct, there will be 600 million. Our problems with them are numerous and complex. Some of them are, no doubt, economic and political. The single most crucial problem, however, is neither economic nor political. What divides us is a moral issue. "I have sometimes wondered," says Frank Tannenbaum,[1] "why American writers trying to account for the resentful feeling in Latin America toward the United States have failed to point to the most serious source of our difficulties—the treatment of Latin Americans as inferiors. . . . In this world of ours it is necessary to face up to the fact that our treatment of the Negro is the single most serious obstacle to our role of leadership in a world of nations which are inhabited mostly by 'people of color'."

The Alliance for Progress and the Good Neighbor Policy before it have been an important part of American foreign policy. What kind of fruit they will bear depends in no small measure on how vitally they are affected by prejudice and discrimination. Our protestations of friendship and solidarity do not sound very sincere to the peoples of Latin America when accompanied by manifestations of racial superiority either against them, against citizens from other lands, or against the colored residents and citizens of the United States itself. The fact remains that Latin Americans feel that we are treating them as we treat all men of color—as lesser people.

How, then, do we persuade our neighbors to the south that as a democratic and multiracial society we reject racialism as an ideology and a practice utterly alien to, and incompatible with, the very idea of America? It will not do to point to the tremendous progress of American Negroes since Civil War days. To be sure, this progress has been real enough. In the two decades following World War II, enforceable laws forbidding discrimination in public and private employment were passed in twenty-one states. About 98 per cent of the nonwhite population north of the Mason-Dixon Line is now covered by such a law. At the same time, sixteen states enacted legislation prohibiting discrimination in housing and public accommodations. The United States Supreme Court invalidated racially restricted juries and forbade segregation in the public schools and in public transportation. Segregation is no longer a serious problem in the U. S. armed forces. If education alone is taken as an index of upward social mobility, the American Negro has come a long way indeed. There are now more Negroes in American colleges and universities than there are university students in all of Latin America or Europe.

But none of these arguments will convince anyone that we have really succeeded in righting the wrongs of slavery and that the sins of the fathers are no longer visited unto this generation of Americans. On the contrary, such claims as to the legal gains that have been made in putting an end to discrimination in places of public accommodation, housing, schools, transportation, and jobs are more likely to be seen as reinforcements of white complacency—designs of the whites to soothe themselves and the colored folk in the comforting belief that "these things take time. Progress is being made. The Negro is better off and will one day come into his own." The slowness with which racial barriers are crumbling even in our northern cities lends not a little plausibility to the reproach of American hypocrisy in race relations. For, despite the proliferation of governmental regulations forbidding discrimination in housing, the vast majority of our colored population live in areas that are exclusively or predominantly Negro or in the process of becoming so.

The ghetto pattern in housing is reflected in the ghetto pattern in the public schools. Prejudice and educational deprivation combine to limit Negro job opportunities, and Negro unemployment is twice that among white workers. As President Kennedy summed up the situation:

> The Negro baby born in America today, regardless of the section or the state in which he is born, has about one-half as much chance of completing a high school as a white baby, born in the same place, on the same day; one-third as much chance of completing college; one-third as much chance of becoming a professional man; twice as much chance of becoming unemployed; about one-seventh as much chance of earning $10,000 a year; a life-expectancy which is seven years shorter; and the prospects of earning only half as much.

We should be wary of reminding Latin Americans of their own shortcomings on the racial frontier lest they point the accusing finger at us. Of course, there is race prejudice in Latin America—claims to the opposite by many Latin Americans and North American observers notwithstanding. It exists against both the Indian and the Negro. "Perhaps it is necessary to be a Negro, an Indian,

or an Asiatic," writes Eugenio Chang-Rodriguez, a well-known
Peruvian author of partly Chinese descent,[2] "to measure the degree of this cruel reality, which many whites and mestizos do not
notice. In the diffusion of the false belief which could be called
the White Legend, many factors have served to blind the vision of
even discerning scholars."

But there is a huge difference between Latin American racial
conditions and our own. Whatever prejudice there is in Latin
America, it has no sanction in the law. "It is social and economic
and cultural. It is determined more by social status than by a sense
that people of color are inferior in nature."[3] It is a question of individual attitudes rather than the mores of the group. And while
pecuniary matters are high on the American scale of values,

> . . . the fact is that in the land of Lincoln racial prejudice is
> stronger than the admiration of money. In Latin America, on the
> other hand, in spite of the Ariel thesis of Rodó, respect and con-
> sideration for money and culture is stronger than racial prejudice.
> Furthermore, money and culture raise the social category of their
> possessor and consequently the rich and cultured Indian or Negro
> comes to merge with and get lost in the ethnic group and social
> class in power, acquiring its virtues and its vices.[4]

There is in Latin America little of our nonsense about "racial
purity" and none of our fear of "mongrelization." There are no
barriers to intermarriage in Brazil either in the law or in the mores
of the land. To have a color line like the one that exists in the
United States would be impossible because it would split the Brazilian family. The colored people are both acculturated and assimi-
lated Brazilians. They think of themselves as Brazilians and Latins.
The Negroes of the United States are acculturated but not assimi-
lated. Bearing in their personality the mark of oppression, they
think of themselves as Negroes first and only secondly as Americans.[5] It is with considerable, and justified, pride that Gilberto
Freyre speaks of Brazil as "a racial democracy, characterized by an
almost unique combination of diversity and unity," where one
thing is certain: "The regions or areas of greatest miscegenation
are those which have been most productive of great men."[6]

This is not the place to examine in detail the long history of the contrast between the legal and social positions of the Negro in the United States and in Latin America. In his *Slave and Citizen*, Frank Tannenbaum has shown how, in the legal structure of the United States, the Negro slave became property and how, as property, he became a chattel without the rights to marriage, to children, to the products of his labor, or to freedom; while in the Iberian Peninsula, as in the colonies of Spain and Portugal in the New World, where the slave was endowed with a moral personality long before emancipation, long before he achieved legal equality, "there was never the horrifying spectacle so often invoked in the United States of admitting a morally inferior and therefore, by implication, a biologically inferior people into the body politic on equal terms."[7]

Clearly, in the area of race relations we have long been irritants rather than models for Latin Americans to emulate. What, then, can and must be done to reshape our public image, to make them feel they are not lesser people in our eyes? We can enact new, broad laws against discrimination. By implementing them with zeal and vigor at home, our government can earn the reputation of fighting against the evil rather than abetting it. It must be admitted that, until the spring of 1963, our government moved too slowly and with too little evidence of deep moral commitment. But then, by sending a program of new civil rights legislation to the Congress, the President demonstrated a genuine sense of urgency about eradicating racial discrimination from our national life. By initiating and pressing for the implementation of such policies at home, official society can do that much to change the image of America abroad. It can do that much to justify its claim as the land of the free and as the leader of the free world.

Past history and present incidents in American race relations have given a genuine advantage to Communist policymakers and propagandists. That racism was inevitable under American capitalism, that inaction by official society was tantamount to support of the racists, that racial tensions exposed the hypocrisy of American claims to world leadership, and that attitudes toward Negroes in the United States were indicative of attitudes toward colored peoples everywhere—these themes, as Secretary of State Dean Rusk testified, have been of inestimable value to the Communists in winning friends among the peoples of color. The Communists, he said, would have been able to exploit the racial incidents in our country even more effectively were it not for the race prejudice encountered by nonwhite students in Soviet bloc countries, the loyalty of nonwhite Americans to the United States, and the progress being made toward full equality.

By supplementing the efforts of the executive and judicial branches of the government, the Congress can do its part to counteract Communist propaganda and to meet the doubt abroad as to the real convictions of the American people. There are many more things that can be done. Private foundations, universities, and church groups might join the government in inviting such articulate Americans as James Baldwin, Ralph Bunche, Lena Horne, John H. Johnson, Martin Luther King, Jr., Louis Lomax, Thurgood Marshall, and Roy Wilkins on speaking tours through Latin America, Asia, and Africa, and at the same time sponsor visits by distinguished Latin Americans, Asians, and Africans to our country, to discuss their problem and ours with the candor and honesty befitting a free society. We might expand the program and the activities of the Peace Corps. Surely, that much can be done by official society.

But let us not delude ourselves. "That much" is not enough. The job that needs to be done is not the President's or official society's alone. True, there are military and diplomatic aspects to race relations in the Western Hemisphere (as elsewhere). We have a ring of bases in the Caribbean area and in Panama. For our common defense we require the cooperation of the surrounding people. The race attitudes of our military commanders and personnel are thus matters of some importance to our security, matters of special concern to the government. And legal and legislative redress can be initiated and enacted by wise government in such situations. The problem of race relations, however, is much broader than the question of discrimination, which it includes. It is primarily a moral issue and a problem in the effective functioning of our society. It is, first, a question of whether all citizens are to be afforded equal rights and equal opportunities. For generations, Attorney General Robert F. Kennedy has said, "Americans have prided themselves on being a people with democratic ideals, a people who pay no attention to a man's race, creed, or color. This very phrase has become a truism. But it is a truism with a fundamental defect: It has not been true."

When the Attorney General made this statement, he also cited Lord Acton to the effect that laws should be adapted to those who have the heaviest stake in the country, for whom misgovernment means want and pain and degradation and risk to their own lives and to their children's souls. He was right in doing so. But he focused his attention, as he had to in the circumstances, on only one aspect of the problem. The broader question is this: "How do we reshape the attitude, feeling, gesture, tone, and manner of a people raised in the belief that colored people are inferior by nature and that the white European and especially the American are superior? . . . How do we keep all of our built-in mechanisms of resistance, defense, and repulsion from coming to the surface when faced with colored people, when it has always been natural, right, and proper to behave, talk, believe, act, and do just the way we are, better and superior? How can we be different from what we are, and how long will it take us to be changed?"[8]

In other words, the question of race relations in our society is not only one of equal opportunity and desegregation but one of equal achievement and integration. Of course, it would be foolish to expect any civil rights legislation automatically and swiftly to deliver equality of achievement and integration to our colored citizens. Custom and habit are not broken fast or easily. That does not mean that legislation is not essential or only of secondary importance. On the contrary, those who argue that "you cannot legislate morality," and have nothing but the counsel of patience to offer to the deprived, only leave themselves open to the reproach of callousness; it is they who are unrealistic. For they do not seem to realize that, in President Kennedy's words, "the fires of frustration and discord are burning in every city, North and South"; that "a great change is at hand, and our task, our obligation, is to make that revolution, that change, peaceful and constructive for all"; and that "those who do nothing are inviting shame as well as violence, while those who act boldly are recognizing right as well as reality."

We might add that those who argue the superiority of education versus legislation in the area of race relations are apt to underestimate the *educative* effect of the law. And there is enough social science research to indicate that once desegregated and nondiscriminatory conditions have been established—willingly, reluctantly, or unwillingly—attitudes and emotions will reform themselves in the crucible of those new conditions.[9]

Foreign policy is largely a function of domestic policy. We have discussed only a few of the costs and consequences of race prejudice to America. While the greatest cost by far is the loss of purpose and solidarity we inflict on ourselves as a nation, what we lose in the eyes of the world—a world that is increasingly one of color—is not negligible either. Spring, 1963, will long be remembered. It could be remembered as the time when America missed her great opportunity to deal with colored people on the basis of equality; when the race pride and the race prejudice of people of color was still mostly a defensive mental device, a secondary reaction built up to meet the humiliations of white supremacy; when this not only was apparent in the case of the American Negro but probably held true even for the other colored people who had not yet had a taste of power. It could be remembered as the time when America failed to realize that "when colored nations have once acquired power but still sense the scorn of white superiority and racial discrimination, they are likely to become indoctrinated by a race prejudice much more akin to that of the whites—a race prejudice which can be satisfied only by the whites' humiliation and subjugation."[10]

But history is never irredeemable. If America moves now to make good on her own promise, if she acts as the model and the leader in abolishing color prejudice and extending the realm of freedom, she would, as Myrdal says,[11] "have a spiritual power many times stronger than all her financial and military resources—the power of the trust and support of all good people on earth. America is free to choose whether the Negro shall remain her liability or become her opportunity." We can still see to it that spring, 1963, will be remembered as the time when America improved her image abroad by beginning in earnest to set her own house in order.

12

A New Approach:
Alliance—Not Aid

GERMAN ARCINIEGAS

"Underdeveloped" is an inappropriate word. It puts countries of very different histories and standards of living, and even of distinct grades of development, in the same category. All of America would gain if the word "aid" also were eliminated from our present political vocabulary. Both words, in fact, are frankly misleading. Under "foreign aid" programs, people have lost much of their dignity and enterprising spirit. Each country facing a difficult situation feels itself obliged to ask for aid from the United States. If the "aid" is not forthcoming in an almost fabulous sum of millions of dollars, the country requesting it suddenly feels frustrated and as if it had been shunted aside in the rightful claim it feels that all countries of the world have on the "common funds" of the United States.

What is new about President Kennedy's plan for Latin America, and what makes it basically different from the monotonous routine of "aid," is the very word "alliance." "Alliance," here, does not mean the *diktat*, like the Monroe Doctrine, of one man; it does not connote a simple feeling of friendship, as was the case with Roosevelt's Good Neighbor Policy; nor is it just another aid program of the United States. In a true alliance, the signatories of the pact that unites them stand on exactly equal footing. What Mr. Kennedy's Alliance proposed was the adoption of some extraordinary measures to accelerate Latin America's progress and overcome her relative backwardness. If the Alliance is really ambitious, as it must be, it must not merely provide loans of several million

216

dollars to offset momentary crises without attacking the basic evils. Its primary aim must be the elimination of the difference in living standards between the two Americas.

As long as the great disparity in standards of living continues and, even worse, if the extremes continue unrelieved, if there is always to be a rich America living next door to a poor America, the poor America will be a seed bed of resentment, discontent, and attempts at subversion. We shall go on witnessing a kind of class war in which the indigent and revolutionary class is not within the borders of the United States but rather in the neighboring apartment of the same house. There will be a poor class, the Latin Americans, and a rich class, the North Americans; and on the basis of such blatant inequality, we shall never be able to build a stable structure of peace and cooperation—especially in a world like ours, where news travels fast. The Alliance will have to make possible the ultimate extension of industrial productive capacity from the Río Grande to the Patagonian wilderness. I am speaking of that capacity of well-being which begins in the Great Lakes area around Chicago but which does not reach beyond the borders of what might be called the "Common Market of the United States."

An aid program that only lessens the shock of falling prices on the world coffee market is of little avail. Every day, fewer men are needed to till the fields and harvest the crops. To make the land yield more, it is no longer the peasant who is the important factor; it is machines, advanced techniques, modern science, and chemistry that play the dominant roles. The problem lies not so much in the rural areas, where the population falls off daily. It lies in the cities, which are inundated by relentless waves of peasants drawn there precisely because the city is *not* underdeveloped, because the attractive opportunities of progress and advancement are to be found in urban life. The Alliance will have to come to the old cities and the new industrialized centers alike, but not with the old plans of loans and aid. It must be based upon the progressive growth of a world that is to become the impregnable outpost of democracy with real freedoms. A strong America, a truly strong America from North to South, is the only way to make the whole world believe that it is possible to attain social justice without destroying everything, unlike what the movements of violent revolt offer as their radical solution to existing evils.

We should not forget that the human and historical factors of the Americas allow solutions on a somewhat higher level than those that may be expected in Asia and Africa. Nor should we overlook the fact that America has a democracy of surer foundations than the various attempts at democracy in Europe. Four-fifths of the Americans living today in the Western Hemisphere have European blood in their veins. The remaining fifth is composed of Indians, descendants of some of the most advanced civilizations the world has known, and Negroes, who, while still facing formidable problems of social integration in the United States, have, nevertheless, shown aptitudes for mature citizenship in a free society.

The way of life in American cities can in no manner be compared to the crowded sites of human living so common in China. The two largest cities where Spanish is spoken are not in Spain, but in Latin America: Buenos Aires and Mexico City. And the two largest Portuguese-speaking cities are not Lisbon and Oporto but Rio de Janeiro and São Paulo in Brazil. This world of rapid growth, which has such importance from the point of view of culture and urban development, must not be thought of simply in terms of the peasant's existence, or treated as a continent whose sole resources are coffee, cocoa, bananas, copper, tin, and oil. In the brief span of fifty years, cities that once had populations ranging from 100,000 to 200,000 now have more than a million inhabitants. The rate of industrial development must keep pace with the relentless speed of urbanization and population growth.

It is in such terms that the problem of the Americas must be seen. The progress of the Americas—that is, toward higher standards of living—is really nothing new in the history of the Western Hemisphere. One hundred years ago, for example, the disparity between North and South was just the reverse. When Mexico City was the largest city and was considered the "capital" of North America, Washington, D.C., had yet to reach the blueprint stage. New York and Philadelphia were much smaller than Mexico City, and Los Angeles and San Francisco were not even dreamed of by the men who were to settle them. A century ago, the whole broad expanse of the United States had more buffaloes than men and was rather like the plains described in Rómulo Gallego's *Doña Bárbara* or like the Argentine *pampas* in *Don Segundo Sombra.* Politics in the time of the "Big Four" who built the railroad joining the East coast with the Pacific Ocean were as corrupt as any during the *peronista* dictatorship. At the beginning of the last century, Humboldt said, there was no other city in all America to compare with Mexico City in its scientific institutes, museums, and splendid university. Thus, if we establish a common standard of well-being for the North and the South and if we can achieve it in the course of the next few decades, all of America will serve as the great example and bastion of democracy for the world.

The new realities now in the Western Hemisphere, as President Kennedy very clearly saw, are the Alliance for Progress signed in Montevideo and the physical presence of Russians in Cuba. Revolutionary and mutually exclusive events, they point up the fact that the great battle for democracy is being waged right here in the Americas. Moscow's discovery of America dates only from yesterday. When the first Russians arrived in Havana, invited by Fidel Castro and Ernesto Guevara, that moment must have been for the Soviet government something like the first American landfall of October 12, 1492. Russia entered, or thought she was entering, Cuba just the way Spain had come to Mexico with Cortes' soldiers. The aptness of this comparison may be seen if we recall that there was no one further removed from the struggle against the Batista tyranny than Russia herself. As a matter of fact, Batista fell because green bills with the faces of Washington, Lincoln, and Jefferson underwrote the cause of Fidel Castro's insurgents. Not one kopeck, let alone one ruble, was contributed to the fight against Batista.

Castro's funds were raised in New York, Caracas, Costa Rica, and Mexico. Men like Betancourt, Figueres, and Juan Bosch gave Castro the most active support. The Communist Party of Cuba had been an official part of the Batista dictatorship and its head, Juan Marinello, was a minister in Batista's cabinet. Just as Cuban Communism collaborated with Batista, Russian Communism eagerly came to Castro's aid when it saw how much could be attained with hotheaded shouts against the North Americans and by executions along Havana's waterfront. Russian aid was then at least one-half military, as befits Moscow's view of the world. The extent of Russia's military embroilment in Cuba is made clear by Khrushchev's withdrawal of weapons and missiles and his pledge to evacuate Russian troops from the island.

Russia knows that if the Alliance for Progress becomes the source of continental strength, all of America will thereby become invulnerable to Communism; not because it is anti-Communist but rather because it is affirmatively democratic. The Alliance has come into being, not as a response to Communist machinations, but because it is native to the character of Americans. Latin Americans, more especially, have always been vehement in their preference for a radical policy of change that would not sacrifice man's spiritual values at the very moment of enacting social reform.

The North Americans have a better and more exact knowledge of Latin America than the Russians. We are, after all, tenants of the same house. Latin American independence was inspired by Jefferson's ideas, and Sarmiento revolutionized Argentinian education on the basis of Horace Mann's reforms. To be sure, then followed the sorry history of "manifest destiny," military interventions when the Marines were sent to the Caribbean, and Theodore Roosevelt's depriving Colombia of that part of her sovereign domain where the Panama Canal now links the Caribbean to the Pacific. What is more, American companies created in Latin America the image of "Yankee imperialism" that has so damaged continental relations. The Russians, for their part, have learned magnificently well how to exploit all these themes. Against this background, Kennedy's attitude represents a profoundly new approach and a much more promising policy for his country.

The systematic violence employed to sabotage the very idea of the two Americas united by an alliance is more characteristic of Latin American Communism than it is of the Muscovite variety, but, withal, the origin of both is the same.

The Cuban Communists find their inspiration in China, but their lifeblood comes from Moscow. They have been taken in by Chinese propaganda that there is really only a Nazilike tradition in North American life. Thus blinded, they have opted for the Chinese way of increasing the well-being of the masses rather than for that of the United States, even though the Chinese now live without rice and without liberty. It seems the Cuban Communists have come to prefer the yellow to the red revolution.

Fundamentally, the Alliance conceived at Montevideo must be considered a turning point in hemispheric relations and world history, the final outcome of which we cannot now foresee. If we probe the idea of the Alliance a little more deeply and if we strengthen this very concept of "alliance," we shall be able to present, especially to Europe, an imposing defense of the free world. For England, it would represent something like a political and social Webster's Dictionary, uniting the whole English-speaking world. And for the Latin nations in Europe, the Alliance would mean a "new world" in which their oldest and best ideals could again flourish.

The problems of the Alliance show clearly that the old standards for extending aid will no longer suffice to deal with such new and sudden issues as the drop in prices of basic commodity exports from Latin America, or the development of an African market in Europe that undercuts traditional Latin American ties with the Old World. Colombia, for example, has been one of the countries most favored with United States loans and grants. However, all the money entering that country is not sufficient to offset the loss to the economy created by the drop in coffee prices. The steady increase of African export products at lower price levels and in competition with Latin American exports threatens to push Latin America into severe economic crises. These two examples show, first, that the Alliance must be armed with instruments to prevent these economic upheavals and, second, that the processes of industrialization and diversification must be accelerated to accomplish in a few years what would ordinarily take generations to achieve.

The plan of the Alliance is put forward, moreover, in a time when miracles seem to take place in the most diverse countries. Russia is today on the list of the most industrialized nations of the world, when, forty-five years ago, at the fall of the Czars, it was no more than an underdeveloped empire. When Lenin ascended the red throne, some of the Soviet Socialist Republics, such as the Ukraine, to mention only one of the more important ones, were no more advanced than Bolivia or Paraguay. And one example above all others is startling: Israel, where, to the surprise of every visitor, the luxuriance sung in some of the more idyllic passages in the Bible has miraculously taken the place of dry and stony deserts, unproductive for millennia.

The Alliance should not be taken as a purely defensive reaction to the momentary pressures of economic problems and political upheavals. It is an act of faith in America's resources, an affirmation of what free people can plan and do if they take advantage of their opportunities and amend the many errors of recent history and the erroneous policies of the past. It is the struggle for democracy that the free world has to wage and which five years ago no one thought would be upon it in such stark terms. Above all, the Alliance rests upon common human values. It is man who has been put in the foreground so as to redeem, educate, and train him, and thereby convert him into the first factor of a new America.

13

Some Misunderstandings on the Alliance for Progress

VÍCTOR L. URQUIDI

If, as many claim, the Alliance for Progress is an attempt by the United States to respond to Latin American demands for adequate assistance in development, and it stands also for the kind of constructive concern with welfare and development on the part of Latin Americans that the United States has frequently called for, the pervasive feeling of frustration, skepticism, distrust, and even cynicism on both sides is profoundly disquieting. Is the Alliance failing? Or, more to the point, can it succeed? If not, what are the alternatives to this "vast cooperative effort"? Are the aims and methods of the Alliance even properly understood on either side?

The expression "either side" is used here deliberately, to indicate that they are separated by a powerful barrier that is stronger than tariffs, immigration policy, distance, or ordinary language: the difficulty, almost the failure, of understanding. I shall try to deal with this question in the light of different aspects of the Alliance as seen, as far as I am able to judge, from the United States and from Latin America.

What might be termed the more "vulgar" viewpoint is that of money. According to some Americans, taxpayers' money is being used by the United States government to bail out Latin American governments, or, more elegantly, congressional appropriations are being requested to make grants and soft loans to enable Latin American countries to spend more than they could normally afford on their development programs. The Latin American misconception is that, because of worsening trade conditions and various fiscal and other shortcomings in Latin America, the United States is under some kind of obligation to make available large sums of money, on easy terms, to finance a variety of projects, or for general purposes. There are a number of variations on these themes: on the American side, that taxpayers' money is being used to create "socialism" in Latin America (should *private* American funds be employed for that purpose?); on the Latin American side, that more aid funds should be forthcoming because foreign private investment has fallen off (is not foreign private investment relatively unwelcome?); in the United States, that aid funds are only serving to replace what wealthy Latin Americans put in Switzerland for safekeeping—on which simply fantastic figures, based on vague "sources," have been quoted; in Latin America, that not enough aid is given to offset the capital flight and create confidence.

Obviously, the problem is not merely a financial one. But the success or lack of progress of the Alliance is being measured by the amount of aid funds appropriated, committed, or actually disbursed each year. According to convenience, different data are used. An American source will add up every possible loan, grant, and food program to show that the United States government has lived up to its commitment to make available to Latin America a billion dollars per fiscal year—roughly half of the assumed *average* of $2 billion of foreign-capital funds that the Charter of Punta del Este implies (i.e., $20 billion over a 10-year period). However, the annual billion since mid-1961 includes grants that many Latin Americans have considered to be outside the framework of the Alliance, and emergency loans negotiated bilaterally with some countries without specific reference to Alliance programs. But are not all loans negotiated bilaterally, with each country signatory to the agreement sovereign in its decision to enter into it? The Punta del Este commitment cannot be—and is not—so rigid as to preclude emergency action. Whether or not they are emergency loans to avert a crisis, they increase the external purchasing power of the recipient country and enable it to go on with its development programs.

There is something of a controversy over what constitutes Alliance for Progress aid. The text of the Charter of Punta del Este does not lend itself to an indisputable interpretation. However, some sort of calculation must apparently have been made indicating that, in order for Latin America to achieve an average of 2.5 per cent annual per-capita growth in national product over a decade, some $20 billion of foreign-capital funds would be required to supplement domestic savings (assuming tax reforms, improvements in the financial structure, etc., are carried out). Now it is not at all clear whether the $20 billion is to be gross or net, that is, total disbursement of loans, grants, and privately financed investment or net transfer of capital after repayment of past loans has been deducted. In the latter case, the gross lending would have to be of the order of $30 billion or more over the decade.

Economists, calculating on the basis of a simple "model," are apt to interpret that the Alliance for Progress' foreign-capital need of $20 billion is *net*. The reasoning is as follows: In order to increase per-capita output at the rate of 2.5 per cent per year, with population growth of 2.8 per cent, and assuming an incremental capital-output ratio of 2.5 (which is slightly optimistic), a net investment ratio of 13.25 per cent would be needed. Assuming, hopefully, that a net domestic-savings ratio of 10 per cent will be achieved, the net foreign capital required (equal to the import surplus of goods and services) would add up, over a 10-year period, to some $28.5 billion. To keep this figure down to $20 billion net, the domestic-savings ratio would have to rise to about 11 per cent, which is not impossible. If, not unreasonably, the capital-output ratio were assumed to be 3 instead of 2.5, a total of $20 billion net foreign aid would call for an average net domestic-savings ratio of close to 14 per cent, which would be quite difficult.

These are not merely arithmetical exercises based on varying assumptions. The orders of magnitude involved have important implications; for instance, to raise the net domestic-savings ratio from 10 to 14 per cent of net product means increasing the tax burden, and with it the amount of public savings, rather sharply, as well as inducing higher business and personal savings in relation to income. This may be expected under the Alliance for Progress, though not assured. On the other hand, if it did actually occur, there is nothing to guarantee that $20 billion of net external capital would be forthcoming over 10 years. So far, spokesmen for United States aid—and, generally, people involved in the Alliance program and public-information media—talk of the $20 billion apparently as *gross* disbursements. In net terms, this may mean something less than $10 billion, which is only slightly more than the amount Latin America derived from all foreign-capital sources in the 1950–60 decade, when private investment in petroleum and mining played such a large role, foreign-trade prospects were incomparably better, population growth was less, and general conditions were perhaps more favorable.

A significant source of misunderstanding is therefore hidden in the $20 billion figure. American opinion is bound to consider it as an upper limit in *gross* terms, whereas Latin American opinion will more and more regard it as a minimum in *net* terms. But the misunderstanding goes further. The Punta del Este Charter vaguely embraces every source of foreign finance in the over-all amount, and this was supported by a statement made in September, 1961, by the U.S. Secretary of the Treasury in a speech at the World Affairs Council in Los Angeles, California, when he indicated that the $2 billion annual capital transfer might roughly be made up as follows: $400 million from the Eximbank, $250 million under the Act of Bogotá for social development through the Inter-American Bank, $150 million under the Food for Peace program, $75 million from the U.S. Development Loan Fund, $75 million from technical-cooperation sources, $750 million from international financial agencies (World Bank, Inter-American Bank, etc.) and various public and private sources in North America, Europe, and Japan, and the remaining $300 million as private foreign investment in Latin America. Realistic or not in the breakdown of the total—and the U.S. government is to supply one-half —the statement obviously reflects the view that these are to be gross disbursements and, furthermore, that every source (except, naturally, Soviet bloc aid) is to be put under the Alliance umbrella, including loans, say, from the French government or from an Italian or a Swiss banking corporation.

However, this is not what many Latin American circles understand. If country X, it is argued, has successfully negotiated loans from the World Bank or a European consortium or a Canadian supplier of heavy equipment, and continues to do so in the ordinary course of business, why should these loans be attributed to the Alliance program or even be computed as part of the Punta del Este aid funds? They would have been obtained anyhow, whereas as loans under the Alliance they may be harder to get. And if country Y issues long-term bonds on the international financial markets, in what way is the successful placement of the bonds due to anything other than the country's good credit, its ability in preparing the issue, and the skill of the underwriters? Officials in many countries will not be inclined to regard these transactions as Alliance "aid"; if told that this proves their countries do not need aid in the ordinary sense of the term—grants, soft loans, emergency financing—they might reply that, in view of housing, educational, health, agricultural, and other structural problems, their countries are entitled to nonconventional loans under the aid programs and the Charter, and that without such loans or grants the Alliance for Progress would have to be regarded as a "failure."

There is, no doubt, a good deal of confusion concerning the definition and extent of Alliance "aid." Taken as a whole, the Charter of Punta del Este should increasingly lead potential lenders and investors—national and international agencies or private sources—to scrutinize the policies of the Latin American countries and appraise them as conditions relating to the transaction; at the same time, their own policies are bound to gradually become more flexible and favorable as a reflection of the United States position. Therefore, in a broad sense, all forms of foreign-capital assistance are influenced by the Alliance; if country X obtains better terms from the World Bank or a German supplier, this will be the result of Punta del Este, and so on.

Nevertheless, "aid" is a bad term—almost a dirty word in some circles—and a suitable substitute for it will have to be found. The American taxpayer treats as "aid" both a ten-year Eximbank loan at 6 per cent—an ordinary banking operation—which, besides, is spent on United States electrical power equipment, and an appropriation for the Peace Corps, which in helping a poor country might enable a few American citizens to gain a down-to-earth knowledge of people and problems in a particular Latin American area. The Latin American considers the Eximbank loan not as "aid" but as a repayable credit, and is likely to treat the Peace Corps—even when he accepts it—not as part of financial aid but rather as a good-will gesture. An American might well-meaningly think of United States private direct investments in Latin America as "aid"—and as still the best form of aid; the Latin American, even when he might conditionally accept that private foreign investment would be beneficial, will under no circumstances call such investment "aid." The possibility of misunderstandings on aid are thus multiple. And the Latin American, when he hears that aid is a burden to the United States taxpayer, is likely to dismiss the argument by simply pointing to the very much larger tax burden created by defense expenditures, rockets-to-the-moon projects, and the like. A \$4 billion United States aid program—for the whole world—amounts to less than 1 per cent of the United States national income; one-fifth of that aid, or less than .2 per cent of American income, is allocated to Latin America, and a large part is recoverable.

Trade problems aggravate Latin America's financial difficulties. Despite possible impressions to the contrary in uninformed United States circles, Latin America has always paid for most of its imports by means of exports: 90 per cent in the 1950–60 decade. And 80 per cent of Latin America's imports have been capital goods, raw materials, semimanufactures, and fuels rather than expensive automobiles and gadgets. While imports tend to rise with development, the value of exports is stagnating—and in some countries declining—because of falling world prices due to the oversupply of basic commodities and/or import restrictions by the developed countries. According to the Economic Commission for Latin America (ECLA) estimates, Latin America's terms of trade in 1960 were 11 per cent below the 1955 level, 18 per cent below the 1950–51 peak, and even 7 per cent under the 1948 ratio (not only have export prices declined, but import prices have increased). Americans are prone to adopt a curious attitude that amounts to favoring protection for the domestic supplier and leaving the foreign supplier at the mercy of free-market forces. It must be admitted that few Latin Americans can understand this position. If United States production of lead, beet sugar, or petroleum is uneconomic, why not benefit the American economy with imports from lower-cost Latin American suppliers, who in turn will spend the export proceeds on American manufactures? If farm-support programs operate in the United States, why cannot this principle, with necessary modifications and even on a limited scale, be applied internationally? Not only are most Americans strongly against such an idea, but economists and others will tell Latin Americans that such a program should not exist even in the United States. But in fact it does.

American economists usually deny or qualify in all sorts of ways the terms-of-trade problem; many believe the terms of trade will improve. But in the absence of some kind of commodity arrangements, such as the coffee agreement, and/or compensation or insurance schemes such as those recently considered by U.N. expert groups, there is nothing that can lead a Latin American to believe that there is a reasonably good outlook for export prices or that foreign-exchange proceeds will be maintained. On the other hand, he feels that import prices of equipment, steel, chemicals, and the like are certain to go up. The whole question of the terms of trade is looked at with much too little sophistication on both sides: The truth is neither that the American housewife could not tolerate a slightly higher coffee price nor that the Latin American exporting country is entitled to a "just" price ratio, whatever this may mean, or that it should be compensated for theoretical losses calculated by multiplying the price decline by the number of tons of exports. Economics is not that simple. The only truth, rarely appreciated in the midst of emotional verbiage on either side, is that world supply-demand maladjustments are very hard to correct and that policies of both importing and exporting nations need to be modified in order to expand demand and restrain excess supply. Little progress is being made, and the Punta del Este Charter treats commodity problems as something to be kept in the background while the aid and social-reform problems are being worked out. Increased trade is essential to Latin America, and is preferred to increased aid. (Could it be that, if both Latin Americans and North Americans were opposed to expanding aid, some progress might be achieved on trade?)

The Latin American Free Trade Association (LAFTA) and

the emerging Central American common market are seen from opposite angles. To Latin Americans, these arrangements, unorthodox
as they may sound, are part and parcel of development policies. A
preferential and, eventually, tariff-free area will facilitate industrialization by supporting larger-scale industry and speeding up the
growth of manufacturing capacity. The Punta del Este Charter
gives its support to these free-trade programs and, though not all
Latin American countries are involved in them, the two schemes
—the nine-country LAFTA and the five-country Central American
common market—have been safely launched. But there are underlying suspicions on the part of Americans that these programs are
designed to "divert" trade—there is even academic backing for
this view—and thus cut out U.S. exports, and worse, foster pro-
tected manufactures to the detriment of "free competition."
At the same time, Latin Americans fear that the giant American
industrial trusts are maneuvering to get inside the preferential
tariff on a large scale in order to forestall Latin American competition. In other words—so the Latin American argument runs—
Americans would want "free competition" to enable entry of
United States subsidiaries, which would become monopolies and
take over domestic industry. Evidently, there is need on both sides
for clarification of the concept of competition, as well as of the
role of foreign capital in Latin American manufacturing development. Otherwise, a serious divergence of views will affect judgment
of the over-all results of the Alliance for Progress. (So far, the
evolution of LAFTA and the Central American scheme is widely
regarded as outside the scope of the Alliance.)

A common way of measuring progress under the Alliance is to
figure out whether or not the per-capita growth in national product
in Latin America has been at least 2.5 per cent in the preceding
year, since the Charter states this rate as a minimum quantitative
objective. The Charter actually requires it of "any" country, but
only as an average (compound rate) over a ten-year period. It
should be recalled that only two years have elapsed since Punta
del Este. If, due to bad crops in country A, a stabilization program
in country B, a power bottleneck in country C, and a further decline in export prices in country D, Latin America's per-capita gross
product rises by only 1.2 per cent, is the Alliance a failure? If the

following year there is a rapid recovery from the previous year's low level, is the Alliance a success? Obviously, this kind of simplistic criterion approaches nonsense. What is important is that while per-capita output, according to ECLA estimates, was increasing by 3.3 per cent per year—not in each and every country—in the late 1940's, the rate dropped to about 1 per cent in the late 1950's, and recently to even less. The problem is then to reverse the trend, which requires a number of favorable conditions, including stable commodity prices, foreign financial assistance, increased productivity, a higher rate of investment and better programing, and so forth; in other words, the objectives of the Punta del Este Charter. A single index—per-capita increase in over-all output—in a single year is meaningless. At least five years will be needed to judge whether the trend has been successfully reversed and whether the 2.5 per cent target, as an average, is being attained.

Another frequent manner of measuring progress is to compute the number of schoolrooms, hospital beds, housing units, acres under irrigation, number of farm loans, miles of highways, and so forth, added in the preceding twelve months, and to enumerate the number of countries that have put through tax reforms, adopted land-reform legislation, or set up planning boards. This sort of presentation surely can only be intended for children and would hardly merit any comment, were it not that this sort of thing is apparently used to "sell" the United States aid programs to the United States Congress and to the American public. If North Americans are going to decide that Latin American development is slowing down because in a particular year fewer hospital beds are installed than in the previous one, or because only three more countries set up planning commissions instead of five more as in the year before (nineteen is clearly the limit), the annual rate of misunderstanding is going to increase—and by more than 2.5 per cent per capita! Latin Americans believe that a valid judgment must be based on a comprehensive evaluation that takes into account the specific achievements as well as the long-standing obstacles that have to be overcome, including foreign ones. Not only quantitative but qualitative information is necessary; not only statistics but information as to problems and trends, subtle changes in the alignment of political forces, and so forth. But this means that more should be known in the United States generally about Latin America, through education and by means of communication media. This is a long-term proposition.

There is, however, the other side to this, namely, the failure of Latin Americans to understand that they make little impact on United States public opinion by merely proclaiming certain principles of policy and announcing patriotic intentions regarding economic and social development. To "sell" Latin American progress to North Americans, serious efforts will have to be made to show, in what the latter consider to be practical terms, that the programs of the Alliance are going ahead. Lack of knowledge by Latin Americans concerning the United States and its ways is seriously impeding a proper evaluation; to which must be added the bias of sensationalism and misinformation that fills most of the United States press on events in Latin America.

All this is particularly apposite to the question of social reform in Latin America. The Alliance for Progress is distinguished from earlier proposals of cooperation like Operation Pan-America by its stress on the need for social change originally brought out in the 1960 Act of Bogotá. There is considerable information today, compiled by international agencies as well as by individuals. on social conditions in Latin America, particularly regarding land tenure, education, health, housing, and social security; and surveys on population trends and characteristics, social strata, rural conditions, urban slums, etc., are under way. Both North Americans and Latin Americans accept the facts of these appraisals and are equally appalled by them. The question is how to improve such conditions, and how to decide on priority and speed of execution.

The Punta del Este Charter sets up fairly concrete ten-year goals for education and health, but is not specific on land reform, housing, labor relations, or other social conditions. Housing is largely a problem of financial resources, and a creditable effort has been made with the help of aid programs to increase the volume of low-cost housing and get new projects under way. But the impression is widespread that land reform is advancing slowly. And no wonder! Since meaningful land reform attacks one of the cornerstones of a static society, such as prevailed in much of Latin America until 1960, it is bound to be resisted by those who, under

an economic and social structure based on the unlimited ac-
quisition and ownership of property, have held economic and
political power in their own narrow interests and have been unable or unwilling to understand historical trends. The profound
rigidity implied in land concentration, with its linkages to commercial, banking, and insurance business and foreign enterprise,
could only be broken in one fell swoop, as in the violent stage of
the Mexican Revolution, the rapid-fire Bolivian upheaval of 1952,
and the missile-age drastic Cuban entrance into the Soviet bloc;
or gradually and rationally, by legislative process and the pressure
of new political forces, as is being attempted in Venezuela, Colombia, Peru, Brazil, and other countries today. Land reform implies a change in the internal balance of power. To achieve it by
consent, that is by asking landowners to distribute their own holdings, is not something that can be proclaimed one day and put into
effect the next. Many Americans underestimate the difficulties of
putting through legislation on land reform against strong and represented vested interests (though, judging from parallel events in
the United States, perhaps no one should be surprised), which are
compounded when other social reforms, as well as tax reform, are
being carried out. American impatience over delays in Latin
American reforms is understandable, but the delay is not all a
question of resistance on the part of the oligarchies. It is also a
matter of preparation and organization, of financial resources (for
farm improvement, credit, training, resettlement, etc.), and of
balancing one program against another. Land reform and tax reform together cannot but shake a country's social and political
structure, and they must be pursued carefully and intelligently.

On the other hand, the Latin American attitude in many countries lacks clear thinking and is somewhat unresponsive to United
States preoccupation with social change. Too many Latin Americans believe that token reforms will satisfy the Punta del Este requirements sufficiently to induce gullible Americans to pour in a
torrent of foreign aid. One of the great misconceptions in Latin
America is that, at heart, the United States is interested not in the
human welfare of the Latin Americans, but only in material gain.
Many feel that Americans are not sincere in favoring social improvement, and they resent American insistence on the need for it.

Since United States pressure on the social front will be regarded as interference in domestic affairs, in many countries of Latin America an extremely prickly problem is posed that eventually can only be solved by domestic pressures against the powerful landed, commercial, and industrial propertied groups. Much of all this applies equally to fiscal reform.

A further area of misunderstanding is the extent and nature of planning required to accelerate economic and social development under the Alliance. The Charter of Punta del Este is clear on the need for "comprehensive and well-conceived national programs," but not on the specific form of planning, which is left to the introduction or strengthening of "systems for the preparation, execution, and periodic revision of national programs . . . ," and so forth. Undoubtedly, planning is a rational means of using scarce resources to achieve a number of stated objectives. However, it is easy to mistake the plan for the policies. There is a tendency in the United States government agencies, the Inter-American Bank, and the so-called "Committee of Nine Experts" in the Organization of American States (who are charged with evaluating the plans) to extol the virtues of a fully documented medium-term development program in country A, even if six months later it becomes, because of unforeseen events and policy changes, an almost academic exercise, and to criticize the well-rounded and fully operative development programs and policies of country X because they are not put down in great detail in a 600-page report with every quantity projected to the precise decimal point. Of course, for many Americans, "planning" means "creeping socialism," and they would be against it and against the Alliance's insistence on it anyhow. Nationalization of foreign properties is opposed, and public investment—which is not even an item in the national accounts of the United States—is not widely approved, no matter what the extent of planning, though in Latin America it is necessarily an important component of a development program. As the debate moves forward, and in spite of the shortcomings of planning in Latin America, the Latin Americans are going to be damned for not doing enough planning and damned for doing too much.

Confusion also arises on the relationship of the Alliance for Progress to democratic evolution in Latin American countries.

The Charter starts out as follows: "We, the American Republics, hereby proclaim our decision to unite in a common effort to bring our people accelerated economic progress and broader social justice within the framework of personal dignity and political liberty." (This, of course, applies to the United States as well as to Latin America.) Further on it is stated that development programs must be "carried out in accordance with democratic principles." The Declaration to the Peoples of America, which precedes the Charter, mentions "the institution of representative democracy," and the strengthening and improvement of democratic institutions. Since a working representative democracy is an ideal that cannot be created overnight and is subject to various interpretations, whereas economic progress and social justice must go on uninterruptedly, there is danger that the Latin American propensity to upset an established government by unconstitutional methods will lead most Americans to believe that the Alliance is failing. No doubt it is difficult for Americans to understand why one apparently democratic government will be considered by Latin Americans to be a dictatorship, while in another country a dominant-party system is actually democratic; or why a military junta under particular circumstances may do more for democratic evolution than the deposed elected government. Latin Americans are perhaps becoming concerned more with the substance than the forms of democratic evolution, and much of the unrest and upheaval in many parts of the hemisphere is the struggle for a new balance of power that may be truly representative and that will, precisely, permit economic development and social justice to be properly achieved. To deny or suspend aid to a country whose president has been ousted by force is a much more serious lack of compliance with the Punta del Este Charter than is the unorthodox action undertaken by the political group coming to power. This is not a justification of military or any other take-overs—most of which have to be judged on their own merits—but a statement of the position that, basically, the Alliance programs are for the benefit of the people and that any delay in carrying them out not only puts off the attainment of the economic targets but also weakens in the long run the democratic process, since poverty does not breed representative democracy. This is an admittedly difficult

and ticklish matter on which it is to be hoped Americans will
show patience and some understanding, as well as tolerance of the
fact that there is in Latin America a strong left-wing sentiment,
particularly among the younger generations, that under democratic
institutions is bound to express itself and obtain representation,
however much the United States may look with suspicion on
the Left.

Far from having a clear-cut organization, the Alliance for Progress program is divided up into a number of different authorities.
European reconstruction under the Marshall Plan was by comparison very efficiently handled: There was, on the one hand, the
Organization for European Economic Cooperation and, on the
other, a special United States government agency that went under
different names. The United States Congress acted in a statesman-
like fashion. When Secretary of State George Marshall made his
famous speech at Harvard University in June, 1947, the response
of the Europeans was to convene and draw up statements of their
situation, requirements, and future plans. Foreign Secretary Ernest
Bevin, on behalf of sixteen countries, presented Western Europe's
programs to the United States government for consideration in
September, 1947. There is no parallel in Latin America, nor perhaps is there even the same sense of urgency. It is hardly conceivable that one country could speak on behalf of the others, and it
is premature to expect full understanding among the Latin American governments as to diagnosis of the situations, requirements,
and future plans. Even on diagnosis, the ten-year efforts of the
ECLA Secretariat were hardly heeded, when not obstructed. For
better or for worse, inter-American economic relations, including
the Alliance for Progress, are dealt with within the framework of
the unwieldy and ineffective machinery of the Organization of
American States, created originally for purposes quite different
from those involved in the Punta del Este Charter.

On the other hand, it appears that the Alliance program in the
United States administration has no clear authority: It has a
Coordinator, under an over-all foreign aid agency inside the State
Department, whereas several of the other agencies presumably have
their own lines of authority under various government departments.

The Organization of American States has tried to deal with the

Alliance through annual meetings of the ministers of finance as members of the Inter-American Economic and Social Council, preceded by meetings at the expert level as well as by the work of special committees. But this apparatus is in fact only a sort of assembly to review progress and discuss policy. The decisions regarding the amount and type of financial assistance to Latin America are taken unilaterally by the United States government (under Congressional authority), without consultation with the Latin American governments as a whole. And the various financial agencies follow their own policies and criteria, although no doubt influenced by the Alliance. The Committee of Nine Experts of the OAS, appointed to evaluate development programs, in turn feels that it is quite autonomous.

The frustrations and disappointments, real or imagined, of this complicated machinery, have led to the recommendation of yet another inter-American body. Under a resolution adopted in October, 1962, by the ministers of finance, including the United States Secretary of the Treasury, former presidents Lleras Camargo and Kubitschek, of Colombia and Brazil respectively, prepared two reports advising the creation of an Inter-American Development Committee. Although the authors could not agree on the precise functions and composition of this agency, it would be charged with deciding how the Alliance aid programs (only funds from the United States government, or also from the Inter-American Bank, etc.?) should be divided up among the countries, and would also act on behalf of the Latin American governments in negotiations with international agencies, European capital sources, and so on. The São Paulo meeting of ministers of finance, in November, 1963, had these proposals before it.

Given the manifold difficulties inherent in the Alliance for Progress, it is doubtful that any new machinery, whether it cuts across the old or not, will make much difference. It remains to be seen if the United States Congress will agree to "multilateralizing" decisions on its Latin American aid programs, and if Latin American countries will delegate to representatives of other governments matters that they have traditionally treated as exclusive to national sovereignty. If nationalism is declining in Western Europe, it is still rising in Latin America. It would be foolish for anyone, on either side, to believe that the underlying problems of the Alliance will be straightened out by a new committee when the difficulties lie, fundamentally, in the often divergent views held by Americans and Latin Americans on the many issues.

There is, however, no easy alternative to the process of trial and error under the Alliance for Progress. A great deal of ignorance prevails on both sides, which only education, responsible public information, direct contact among peoples, and continuous discussion at all levels can gradually erase. Latin Americans are accused of being emotional about their problems and their relations with the United States. Looked at from the other side, the attitude of the Americans is far from cold and rational. And, what is wrong with being emotional, if forbearance, intelligence, and purposeful action are also exercised? Countries, like children, have a way of growing up and knowing their own minds.

Notes

NOTES TO CHAPTER 1: *Traditions of Conflict in Latin America.*
By Richard W. Weatherhead

1. José Vasconcelos, *La raza cósmica* (Paris, n.d.); and *Indología* (Paris, n.d.).
2. Víctor Raúl Haya de la Torre, *¿A dónde va Indoamérica?* (Santiago de Chile, 1935); and *Aprismo y filosofía* (Lima, Peru, 1961).
3. Raúl Prebisch, "Joint Responsibilities for Latin American Progress," *Foreign Affairs*, XXXIX, No. 4 (July, 1961), 622–33; and *Introducción a Keynes* (Mexico City, 1960).
4. José María Luis Mora, *México y sus revoluciones* (3 vols.; Paris, 1836).
5. Lucas Alamán, *Historia de Méjico* (5 vols.; Mexico City, 1849–52).
6. Arturo Humberto Montes, *Morazán y la Federación Centroamericana* (Mexico City, 1958).
7. Juan Bautista Alberdi, *Bases y puntos de partida para la organización política de la República Argentina* (Buenos Aires, 1933).
8. Domingo Faustino Sarmiento, *Facundo, civilización y barbarie* (5th ed.; Buenos Aires, 1952).
9. José do Manoel Bomfim, *O Brazil na América* (Rio de Janeiro, 1929).
10. Manuel González Prada, *Horas de lucha* (Buenos Aires, 1946); and *Prosa menuda* (Buenos Aires, 1941).
11. Eugenio María de Hostos y Bonilla, *España y América* (Paris, 1954).
12. William Benton, *The Voice of Latin America* (New York: Harper & Bros., 1961).
13. Jesús de Galíndez, *La era de Trujillo* (Santiago de Chile, 1956).

NOTES TO CHAPTER 2: *Crosscurrents in New World History.*
By Richard M. Morse

1. José Gaos, *Pensamiento de lengua española* (Mexico City: Stylo, 1945), pp. 77–78; Octavio Paz, *The Labyrinth of Solitude* (New York: Grove, 1961), pp. 119–20.
2. Juan Larrea, *Rendición de espíritu (introducción a un mundo nuevo)* (2 vols.; Mexico City: Cuadernos Americanos, 1943).
3. Edmundo O'Gorman, *La idea del descubrimiento de América* (Mexico City: Centro de Estudios Filosóficos, 1951); and *La invención de América* (Mexico City: Fondo de Cultura Económica, 1958).
4. *Ibid.*, pp. 98–99. A new version, *The Invention of America*, has appeared. (Bloomington: Indiana University Press, 1961.)
5. Louis Hartz, *The Liberal Tradition in America* (New York: Harcourt, Brace, 1955), p. 29.
6. Walter Prescott Webb, *The Great Frontier* (Boston: Houghton Mifflin, 1952), pp. 87–88.
7. John Leddy Phelan, *The Millennial Kingdom of the Franciscans in the*

New World; a Study of the Writings of Gerónimo de Mendieta (1525–1604) (Berkeley: University of California Press, 1956).

8. Jack H. Hexter, *More's Utopia: The Biography of an Idea* (Princeton: Princeton University Press, 1952).
9. Silvio Zavala, *Filosofía de la conquista* (Mexico City: Fondo de Cultura Económica, 1947), p. 112. See also his "La 'Utopía' de Tomás Moro en la Nueva España," *Memoria de El Colegio Nacional*, IV, No. 4 (1949), 49–78.
10. Roger Bastide, *Brésil, terre des contrastes* (Paris: Presses Universitaires, 1957), p. 27.
11. Sérgio Buarque de Holanda, *Visão do paraíso, os motivos edênicos no descobrimento e colonização do Brasil* (Rio de Janeiro: Olympio, 1959), p. 148.
12. Sérgio Buarque de Holanda, *Raízes do Brasil* (3d ed.; Rio de Janeiro: Olympio, 1961), pp. 217, 219.
13. Second ed.; New York: Alfred A. Knopf, 1956.
14. New York: Alfred A. Knopf, 1963.
15. *Ordem e progresso* (2 vols.; Rio de Janeiro: Olympio, 1959), I, xxvii.
16. The reviewer of a recent book by Freyre goes so far as to charge him with necrophilia: "The perfervid regionalist who once exhumed the colonial past seems now enamored of a corpse." Stanley J. Stein in *The Hispanic American Historical Review*, XLI, No. 1 (February, 1961), 113.
17. Freyre, *Ordem e progresso*, I, xxiii–xlvi.
18. Oscar Handlin, *The Uprooted* (New York: Grosset & Dunlap, 1951), pp. 3–5.
19. Örnulv Ödegaard, *Emigration and Insanity, a Study of Mental Disease Among the Norwegian-born Population of Minnesota* (Copenhagen: Lerin & Munksgaard, 1932), p. 120.
20. Carle C. Zimmerman, "The Evolution of the American Community," *The American Journal of Sociology*, XLVI, No. 6 (May, 1941), 809–17.
21. See Richard M. Morse, "Language as a Key to Latin American Historiography," *The Americas*, XI, No. 4 (April, 1955), 517–38.
22. That is, the pronunciation of *z* or of *c* before *e* and *i* as an *s* rather than, as in most of Spain, a voiceless *th*. Amado Alonso, *Estudios lingüísticos, temas hispanoamericanos* (Madrid: Gredos, 1953), pp. 102–50.
23. In Vera Rubin (ed.), *Caribbean Studies: A Symposium* (Kingston: Institute of Social and Economic Research, 1957), p. 62.
24. Luis Recaséns Siches *et al.*, *Latin-American Legal Philosophy* (Cambridge: Harvard University Press, 1948), xxxv.
25. The Marxist-Leninist doctrine prescribed for Castro's Cuba is little more than a spontaneous by-product of Cuba's precipitous plunge into world power politics. It is no outgrowth of the pre-1959 writings of the revolutionaries themselves.

NOTES TO CHAPTER 7: *Mexico: The Preferred Revolution.*
By Stanley Robert Ross

1. *New York Times*, July 1, 1962.
2. *Denver Post*, July 1, 1962. Italics mine.
3. Frank Tannenbaum, *Mexico, The Struggle for Peace and Bread* (New York: Alfred A. Knopf, 1952), p. 249.

4. Frank Tannenbaum, *Peace by Revolution* (New York: Columbia University Press, 1933), pp. 115 ff.
5. Daniel Cosío Villegas, *Change in Latin America: The Mexican and Cuban Revolutions*, Montgomery Lectureship on Contemporary Civilization, 1960 (Lincoln: University of Nebraska, 1961), p. 30.
6. *Ibid.*, pp. 41–42.
7. Although most of the basic principles were anticipated earlier in Mexican history, it was Carranza who first avowed them during the revolution and gave them systematic expression. Some facets of the so-called "Carranza Doctrine" were rather clearly stated as early as 1913 and 1914, but all were formulated in his message to the Mexican Congress on September 1, 1918. His one-time Acting Secretary of Foreign Affairs, Isidro Fabela, summarized the Carranza Doctrine as follows: "I. Mexico does not accept the Monroe Doctrine because it represents an arbitrary and forced tutelage imposed on countries which neither requested nor needed it; a tutelage which caused difficulties for the Hispano-American countries by violating their sovereignty. II. All nations are equal before the law. Consequently they ought to respect scrupulously each other's institutions, laws, and sovereignty, submitting themselves strictly and without exceptions to the universal principle of nonintervention. III. Nationals and foreigners ought to be equal before the sovereignty of the State in which they find themselves; consequently, no individual ought to seek a situation better than that of the citizens of the country where he goes to establish himself, nor make of his status as a foreigner the basis of protection or privilege. IV. The legislations of the States ought to be uniform as far as possible, without establishing distinctions on the basis of nationality except in regard to the exercise of sovereignty. V. Diplomacy ought to watch out for the general interests of civilization and for the establishment of universal brotherhood; it ought not to serve the protection of private interests nor to put at their service the force and majesty of nations. Neither ought it to serve to exert pressure on the governments of weak countries for the purpose of obtaining modifications of laws which do not suit the subjects of the powerful nations." Isidro Fabela, *Paladines de la libertad* (Mexico City: Populibros de La Prensa, 1958), as cited in *Homenaje a Isidro Fabela, Al hombre, al escritor, al revolucionario, al internacionalista, al maestro* (Mexico City: Universidad Nacional Autónoma, 1959), I, 579–83.
8. The "Estrada Doctrine" of recognition was announced in September, 1930. Although directly prompted by the overthrow of several South American governments, the experience with the United States in the early 1920's and before clearly influenced this effort to eliminate the granting or withholding of recognition as a form of intervention.
9. Carranza objected to intervention even when its immediate purpose tended to favor his movement's interests: "Any occupation of foreign territory, even when inspired by the highest motives, constitutes a hostile invasion and a violation of sovereignty."
10. *Cf.* E. David Cronon, *Josephus Daniels in Mexico* (Madison: University of Wisconsin Press, 1960).
11. Obregón, on September 1, 1921, explained to the Mexican Congress his rejection of the Treaty of Friendship and Commerce proposed by Secretary of State Hughes: "This proposed treaty contained stipulations contrary to some of our constitutional precepts; their adoption, therefore,

would have led inevitably to the creation of a privileged position in favor of Americans resident in Mexico. . . . The Government of Mexico has concluded that it is neither possible nor appropriate nor necessary to sign such a treaty . . . considering that the signing of said treaty could imply or mean, at the same time, the renewal of diplomatic relations between the two countries [which] would have given to the recognition a conditional character and would have gravely injured the sovereignty of Mexico." *Diario Official,* September 5, 1921.

12. Tannenbaum, *Mexico, The Struggle for Peace and Bread,* p. 284.
13. M. S. Al'perovich, "Ocherki zhurnalov [Surveys of Journals]: *Historia Mexicana,* 1951–1958," *Voprosy istorii* (February, 1962), No. 2, pp. 184–85, as cited in J. Gregory Oswald, "The Mexican Revolution in Recent Soviet Historiography," p. 3 (MS prepared for delivery at the meeting of the Pacific Coast branch of the American Historical Association, August 28, 1962).
14. *Cf.* S. R. Ross, "Aportación norteamericana a la historiografía de la Revolución Mexicana," *Historia Mexicana,* X, No. 2, (October–December, 1960), 282–308; and "Historiografía mexicanista: Estados Unidos, 1959–60—México independiente," *Historia Mexicana,* XI, No. 2 (October–December, 1961), 299–313.
15. Juan A. Ortega y Medina, *Historiografía soviética iberoamericanista, 1945–1960* (Mexico City: Universidad Nacional Autónoma de México, 1961), p. 24.
16. M. S. Al'perovich, B. T. Rudenko, and N. N. Lavrov, *La Revolución Mexicana, cuatro estudios soviéticos* (Mexico City: Edición de las Insurgentes, 1960); also Al'perovich and Rudenko, *La Revolución Mexicana de 1910–1917 y la política de los Estados Unidos* (Mexico City: Fondo de Cultura Económica, 1960).
17. Ortega y Medina, *op. cit.,* p. 38.
18. *Ibid.,* pp. 9–11.

NOTES TO CHAPTER 9: *Luso-Brazilian Kinship Patterns.*
By Charles Wagley

1. Philip Garigue, "French Canadian Kinship and Urban Life," *American Anthropologist,* **58,** No. 6 (1956), 1090–1101.
2. Raymond Firth (ed.), *Studies of Kinship in London* (Monograph of London School of Economics, 1956).
3. Michael Young and Peter Wilmott, *Family and Kinship in East London* (Glencoe: Free Press, 1957), p. xvi.
4. Gilberto Freyre, *Casa grande e senzala* (4th ed.; Rio de Janeiro, Olympio, 1943); and *Sobrados e mucambos* (Rio de Janeiro; Olympio, 1936).
5. Carmelita Junqueira Ayres Hutchinson, "Notas preliminarias ao estudo da família no Brasil," *II Reunião Brasileira de Anthropologia* (Bahia, 1955), pp. 261–74.
6. Antonio Candido, "The Brazilian Family," in *Brazil, Portrait of a Half Continent,* ed. T. Lynn Smith and Alexander Marchant (New York: Dryden Press, 1951).
7. The studies of Minas Velhas and Vila Recôncavo were part of the program of community studies sponsored by Columbia University and the

State of Bahia and directed by Thales de Azevedo, of the University of Bahia, and the author. The studies of Passagem Grande, Cerrado, and Retiro were carried out under a similar program sponsored by the São Francisco Valley and directed by Donald Pierson.

8. Harry W. Hutchinson, *Village and Plantation Life in Northeastern Brazil* (Seattle: American Ethnological Society, 1957).
9. *Ibid.*, p. 127.
10. *Ibid.*
11. *Ibid.*, pp. 128–35.
12. *Ibid.*, p. 137.
13. *Ibid.*, p. 135.
14. *Ibid.*
15. *Ibid.*, p. 130.
16. *Ibid.*, p. 147.
17. Esdras Borges Costa, "Relações de família em cerrado e retiro," *Sociologia*, XVII, No. 2 (1955), 132–46.
18. *Ibid.*, p. 141.
19. *Ibid.*, p. 146.
20. *Ibid.*, p. 142.
21. *Ibid.*, p. 144.
22. *Ibid.*, p. 143.
23. *Ibid.*
24. *Ibid.*, p. 142.
25. Alceu Maynard Araujo, "A família numa comunidade alagoana," *Sociologia*, XVII, No. 2 (1955), 113–31.
26. *Ibid.*, p. 113.
27. Marvin Harris, *Town and Country in Brazil* (New York: Columbia University Press, 1956).
28. *Ibid.*, pp. 107–8.
29. *Ibid.*, p. 151.
30. *Ibid.*, pp. 148–49.
31. *Ibid.*, p. 149.
32. Charles Wagley, *Amazon Town. A Study of Man in the Tropics* (New York: Macmillan, 1953).
33. *Ibid.*, p. 148.
34. *Ibid.*, p. 149.
35. Donald Pierson, *Cruz das Almas. A Brazilian Village* (Publication No. 12, Smithsonian Institution of Social Anthropology) (Washington, D.C., 1948).
36. *Ibid.*, p. 202.
37. *Ibid.*, p. 127.
38. *Ibid.*, pp. 184–85.
39. *Ibid.*, p. 202.
40. Emilio Willems, *Cunha. Tradição e transição em uma cultura rural do Brasil* (São Paulo; Secretaria da Agricultura, 1947).
41. *Ibid.*, pp. 56–57.
42. *Ibid.*, p. 52.
43. *Ibid.*, p. 56.
44. *Ibid.*, p. 77.

45. *Ibid.*, p. 55.
46. Carmelita Hutchinson, *op. cit.*, p. 268.
47. Wagley, Personal notes.
48. Emilio Willems, "The Structure of the Brazilian Family," *Social Forces*, 31 (1953), 343.
49. Henry Spiegel, *The Brazilian Economy; Chronic Inflation and Sporadic Industrialization* (Philadelphia: Blakiston Co., 1949), p. 228.
50. Hernane Tavaris de Sá, *The Brazilians: People of Tomorrow* (New York: John Day Co., 1947), p. 10.
51. Jorge Dias, "Algumas considerações acêrca da estrutura social do povo portugues," *Revista de Antropologia*, III (1955), 13.
52. Arnold Strickon, "Class and Kinship in Argentina," *Ethnology*, I, No. 4 (1962), 514.
53. Sidney Greenfield, "Industrialization and the Family in Sociological Theory," *American Journal of Sociology*, LXVII, No. 3 (1961), 322.

NOTES TO CHAPTER 10: *Brazil and the Myth of Francisco Julião.*
By Anthony Leeds

I thank Dr. Mário Paes de Barros for commenting on this entire paper in several phases and for keeping me from gross errors of fact. In the notes below, the following abbreviations are used: Brazilian Northeast—BN; Editôra—Ed.; Fundo da Cultura—FC; Institute of Current World Affairs—ICWA; Instituto Superior de Estudos Brasileiros—ISEB; *New York Times*—NYT; Rio de Janeiro—Rio; São Paulo—SP.

1. Francisco Julião, "Brazil, A Christian Country," *Monthly Review* (September, 1962), pp. 243–50 (hereafter cited as Julião, MR).
2. "Unions Compete in Rural Brazil," *NYT*, April 30, 1963 (hereafter cited as *NYT*, 1963). Padre Melo is reported often to have referred specifically to *Mater et Magistra* as the foundation stone of his work.
3. *Cf. NYT*, 1963. Also, President Jucelino Kubitschek addressed the first two Conferences of the Bishops of the Northeast in 1956 and 1959 (a third was held in 1962 in SP), called by the Brazilian Episcopate. He later issued several presidential decrees based on the resolutions of the Conferences regarding colonization, rural social service, etc. He created at the Presidential Palace a special secretariat for these matters only. Indirectly, SUDENE, created December 15, 1959, developed from these and related activities.
4. *Cf.* Julião, MR; Julião, *Que São as Ligas Camponesas?* (Rio: Ed. Civilização Brasileira, 1962) (hereafter cited as Julião, 1962); also Gondin da Fonseca, *Assim Falou Julião* . . . (SP: Ed. Fulgor, 1962) (hereafter cited as Fonseca, *Assim*).
5. There was apparently at least one league in existence as a popular movement before Julião or Padre Melo became involved. *Cf.* James W. Rowe, "The BN I: The *Zona da Mata*," Letter No. JR–4 to the ICWA, New York, February 11, 1962 (hereafter cited as Rowe, BN I), pp. 6–7.
6. *Cf. NYT*, 1963; also extensively and sardonically mentioned in Julião, 1962.
7. NYT, 1963.

8. *Cf. NYT*, 1963. These data were confirmed by informants, especially an Alagoan organizer for the Catholic groups who reported the case described in the paragraph.

9. NYT, 1963; "Peasants' March Blocked in Brazil," *NYT*, April 11, 1962 (hereafter cited as *NYT*, 1962); Julião, 1962, pp. 69–80, *passim*; Rowe, BN I, pp. 6–7.

10. A probable exception to the statement in the paragraph is mentioned in Note 5, above. For leaders of this urban-oriented type, *cf. NYT*, 1962, which mentions "Assis Lemos, a professor at the Paraiba University School of Agronomy and president of the Federation of Peasant Leagues in Paraiba. . . ." Padre Melo and Julião are other examples. Their interests are urban-oriented respecting agricultural products because these products are essentially industrially produced commodities entering into commerce in the dollar market; and, respecting landholding, because land, in large holdings, is used either by landowners to produce for the commodity market; by persons who have multiple industrial and financial interests including factory-style land-production of a product; or by commercial persons who have bought land, which automatically appreciates in value even without improvements, as a hedge against the inflation pressuring their urban businesses. *Cf.* A. Leeds, *Economic Cycles in Brazil: the Persistence of a Total Culture Pattern; Cacao and Other Cases* (Ann Arbor: University Microfilms, 1957, especially chap. 5); A. Leeds, "Brazilian Careers and Social Structure: A Case History and Model" (paper read before the Anthropological Society, Washington, D.C., 1962; hereafter cited as Leeds, "Careers").

11. With respect to the urban-orientation of people of the interior and especially the working classes, see Marvin Harris, *Town and Country in Brazil* (New York: Columbia University Press, 1956), and Leeds, *Economic Cycles in Brazil*, especially chaps. 6 and 7.

12. This is made especially clear in *NYT*, 1963; Rowe, BN I, p. 6; Julião, 1962, *passim*.

13. Under Brazilian law, he could run for office in Minas Gerais, although he is not a resident of that state. It appears probable, also, that he has presidential ambitions.

14. Julião, 1962, p. 69.

15. Among the most important Brazilian unions are the bank workers', the airline pilots', and the students'—all eminently "middle-class" unions. Strong proletarian unions are few and largely undeveloped. Most important are the stevedores' and the transport workers'. These proletarians are enmeshed in the politico-economic sectors of Brazil, unlike the peasantry, still largely outside the country's political and economic life. The peasant leagues and syndicates are poised between the peasant "masses" and the working (and "higher") classes.

16. *Cf.* Julião, *Cachaça* (Recife: Ed. Nordeste, 1951); Julião, *Irmão Juazeiro* (SP: Ed. Francisco Alves, 1961); Julião, 1962; Julião, MR; various issues of *A Liga* (newspaper), edited by Julião from 1962 on; also Fonseca, *Assim*.

17. *Cf.* Leeds, "Careers."

18. Even at the national level, implementation has been very slow, though the changes in personnel at the ministerial level in late June, 1963, suggest

that the process will be expedited. Not one of the persons who has spoken of agrarian reform has taken direct action in the matter: There is no parallel that I know of to the role of the unions in land redistribution in Colombia and Venezuela.

19. NYT, 1962.

20. For example, Vargas' weakening of the state militia power, his nationalization of political parties, his creation and giving life to the Brazilian Labor Party; Jucelino Kubitschek's establishment of Brasília against great outcry; Quadros' establishment of the new Brazilian internationalism, especially with the Soviet Union, over great opposition particularly from the Catholic Church; Goulart's reinstatement of presidentialism, creation of the agrarian, tax, and administrative plans, and the initiation of their implementation.

21. Most American interpretations, of course, commence from the standard premises of an industrial-finance capitalist outlook and with that far-reaching disregard for socio-cultural differences so typical of the American world-view. However, the few American socialist or Marxist attempts at understanding Brazil and other Latin American countries have suffered similarly, since they start from the Marxist critique of industrial-finance capitalist societies rather than of semicapitalist or epi-feudal societies such as Brazil, Colombia, Peru, and others. Their analyses have consequently been placed on the wrong basis from the start. Though, in general, classical Marxist principles are quite useful to interpret Brazil and are widely used by Brazilian scholars today, in the hands of the unwary they also tend to obscure unique features of great importance in Brazil. For special adaptations of these principles to Brazilian circumstances, cf. the more or less Marxist treatments in: Celso Furtado, *Formaçao Econômica do Brasil* (Rio: Ed. FC, 1959); C. Furtado, *Desenvolvimento e Subdesenvolvimento* (Rio: Ed. FC, 1961); Octávio Ianni, *As Metamorfoses do Escravo* (SP: Difusão Euopéia do Livro, 1962); Hélio Jaguaribe, *O Nacionalismo na Atualidade Brasileira* (Rio: ISEB, 1958); Jaguaribe, "A renúncia do Presidente Quadros e a crise política brasileira," *Revista Brasileira de Ciências Sociais*, I, No. 1 (1961), 272–311; Jaguaribe, *Desenvolvimento Econômico e Desenvolvimento Político* (Rio: Ed. FC, 1962); Caio Prado, *História Econômica do Brasil* (Sp: Ed. Brasiliense, 1945), and *Evolução Política do Brasil* (SP: Ed. Brasiliense, 1947); Guerreiro Ramos, *Condições Sociais do Poder Nacional* (Rio: ISEB, 1957); G. Ramos, *Ideologias e Segurança Nacional* (Rio: ISEB, 1958); G. Ramos, *A Crise do Poder no Brasil* (Rio: Zahar, 1961); Ignácio Rangel, *Dualidade Básica da Económia Brasileira* (Rio: ISEB, 1958); Nelson Werneck Sodré, *As Classes Sociais no Brasil* (Rio: ISEB, 1957); N.W. Sodré, *Raízes Históricas do Nacionalismo Brasileiro* (Rio: ISEB, 1960). Many of these and other authors published numerous other books in the ISEB series, including Júlio Barbosa, Josué de Castro, Roland Corbisier, A. L. Machado Neto, Gilberto Paim, etc.

22. The surprising election, in October, 1962, of the Pernambucan Brazilian Labor Party candidate for governor, Miguel Arraes, an alleged leftist, against the concerted efforts of the combined factions of the old guard as well as the election of Francisco Julião to the Federal Congress as deputy must both be attributed to just this linkage. The old guard would be

comprised especially of those persons engaged in the so-called *indústria da sêca* ("drought industry"), that is, the exploitation of the emergency of the droughts for profit by extortionary pricing, selling emergency free goods, embezzling, etc. Persons most adversely affected by the *indústria da sêca* are the poor, the *flagelados* ("drought refugees"). *Cf.* A. O. Hirschman, *Journeys Toward Progress: Studies of Economic Policy-Making in Latin America* (New York: Twentieth Century Fund, 1963); James W. Rowe, "The BN II: Through the Backlands," Letter No. JR-5 to the ICWA, New York, February 11, 1962, p. 5.

23. The recent instance (April, 1963) of Leonel Brizzola, Federal Deputy from Guanabara State, in connection with the Army sergeants' manifesto is a case in point.

24. It is interesting to note regarding this similarity of interest but lack of understanding, especially on the American side, that Julião is quoted (by informants; *cf.* also James W. Rowe, "The BN III: Voices of Despair and Hope," Letter No. JR-6 to the ICWA, New York, February 11, 1962, p. 6) as admitting that some of the best boosts for his career have come from the American press, whose hysteria saw him meddling in "dangerous" areas as a revolutionary figure. He later deliberately established contacts with this press to see to it that it kept up the good work of helping him advance his career. In other words, Americans, including the *Monthly Review*, have fostered his controlling-elite career while understanding him as a revolutionary. As remarked in the text, not a single publicly known leader has come from the masses; they are, of course, unrepresented in any direct sense in the agencies of the state. There are no Juárezes, Zapatas, or Pancho Villas in Brazil, nor anyone remotely resembling them. This seems to me of the highest significance as a symptom of the true present condition of the masses in a country with a basically powerful and ubiquitous central state.

25. *Cf.* Governor Carlos Lacerda's attack (end of March, 1963) on the present government as criminal, traitorous, surrendered to foreign interests, Communist, interventionist (in state prerogatives), etc. Also *cf.* then Foreign Minister Hermes Lima's vigorous and balanced response of April 5, 1963, to this attack, reaffirming basic juridical values.

NOTES TO CHAPTER 11: *The Problem of Color in Foreign Relations.*
By Joseph Maier

1. Frank Tannenbaum, *Ten Keys to Latin America* (New York: Alfred A. Knopf, 1962), p. 176.
2. Eugenio Chang-Rodriguez, "Peru país adolescente," *Hispania* (September, 1960), quoted in Robert J. Alexander, *Today's Latin America* (New York: Doubleday & Co., 1962), p. 49.
3. Tannenbaum, *op. cit.*, p. 50.
4. Chang-Rodriguez, *op. cit.*, pp. 50–51.
5. E. Franklin Frazier, *Race and Culture Contacts in the Modern World* (New York: Alfred A. Knopf, 1957), pp. 316–17.
6. Gilberto Freyre, *The Mansions and the Shanties* (New York: Alfred A. Knopf, 1963), pp. 430–31.

7. Frank Tannenbaum, *Slave and Citizen* (New York: Vintage Books, 1963), p. 100.
8. Tannenbaum, *Ten Keys to Latin America*, p. 177.
9. Earl Raab (ed.), *American Race Relations Today* (New York: Doubleday & Co., 1962), pp. 23–55. Cf. also Harold R. Isaacs, *The New World of Negro Americans* (New York: John Day Co., 1963).
10. Gunnar Myrdal, *An American Dilemma* (New York: Harper & Bros., 1944), p. 1018.
11. *Ibid.*, p. 1022.

Glossary

The following words, which have been used in the essays of this book, refer to basic concepts of Latin American society and culture.

abrazo
embrace, the customary Latin American greeting of welcome and farewell by close friends and relatives; sign of cordiality and friendship. The mere handshake, in contrast, seems as intimate and personal as a military salute.

altiplanicie
the highland plain, often cold and arid, fringed by the mountain peaks of the Andes.

antifictionía
Bolivar's idea of a hemispheric assembly for the Americas, harking back to a similar assembly of states in ancient Greece, to deal with and resolve common problems.

ayllu
the Peruvian Indian village, similar to the *ejido* (*q.v.*) in Mexico, deriving from the Inca period. Its lands were held in common by the village, not by individuals.

barrio (Sp.) *bairro* (Port.)
quarter, section, area; also generally construed as that part of a city where poverty, filth, and restiveness abound. Loosely, it is the slum areas of a large city.

cacique
originally an Indian term from the Caribbean region, meaning a tribal chieftain; now the title applies to any local boss who controls the political conduct of his dependents; he is in the personalist tradition of managing political affairs; loosely, a ward heeler.

249

cajetilla

pejorative epithet given to the "city slicker" or "dandy," especially in Argentina and referring to a certain type in Buenos Aires.

campesino

the peasant, the destitute worker of the countryside, poor but still of a better condition than the *peón* (*q.v.*); roughly, with the *peón*, the rustic counterpart of the city slum dweller.

caudillismo

the rule or dictatorship of a *caudillo* (*q.v.*).

caudillo

a military leader, the provincial dictator who imposes his rule upon the whole nation. His rule was the basis of the apparent stability of the traditional order in the nineteenth century and a good part of this century.

civilista

referring to civilian rather than military rule.

comuneros

literally, commoners, townsmen; refers to revolts of the townspeople against the regal authority of Spain. There were three principal *comunero* rebellions: against Charles V in Spain, in 1520; in Paraguay against the Spanish Crown in 1721, and in Socorro, Colombia, in 1781. The people rebelled because of infringement of their civil liberties and what they thought to be crushing burdens of unjust taxes imposed by the metropolis.

compadrazgo

the system and practice of cofathership between godfather and natural father in Latin America, commonly signifying close and sure friendship.

compadre

a person who as godfather has a special relationship to the natural father; a term implying trust, spiritual affinity, and easy companionship; a buddy.

conquistador	conqueror and warrior, akin to the knight and crusader of the Middle Ages; a Spanish popular hero of the sixteenth century, as Cortés, Pizarro, Valdivia, who subdued the Indian civilizations and secured the Spanish conquest and rule in the New World.
constituyentes	a constituent assembly convoked to formulate the constitution and the basic laws of the land.
cordillera	from the Spanish *cordel*, cord or rope, and applied to the mountain chain of the Andes, the geographical spine of Latin America.
corregidor	a lesser official in the Spanish bureaucracy of colonial times; often abusive of his authority over his Indian charges and notorious for his cruel disregard of their interests and welfare.
corrido	a popular ballad, with imaginative and real elements recounting the exploits of a people or its leaders; e.g., in Mexico the *corridos* of Felipe Angeles, la Valentina, Juana Gallo, and la Adelita.
creole	the special patois and practically official language of Haiti, combining French and African tones and words; also, the English version of the Spanish word *criollo* (*q.v.*).
criollo	creole, generally a white person born in the New World; specifically, a social class deprived of the rank and privileges of the *conquistador* by the Spaniard in colonial times; sometimes applied to a class characterized by rancor and arrogance, while at other times simply meaning "American" or "native."

cuñado (concuñado)	brother-in-law, important as a link in the great chain of kinship so pervasive in Latin American society.
desacato	disrespect and defiance of authority; term employed by some governments to silence local enemies and a critical press; legal statute used by Perón against his opponents.
descamisado	literally, "the shirtless one," a member of the poor classes or the urban proletariat; refers especially to the *peronista* rank and file in Argentina.
Don Segundo Sombra	a classic Argentine novel, published in 1926, by Ricardo Güiraldes, dealing with the *gaucho* in generally romantic and idealized terms.
Doña Bárbara	A classic Venezuelan novel, published in 1929, by Rómulo Gallegos (1884–), portraying the ways of the Venezuelan rancher and the customs, sinister and folkloristic, of the plains (*llanos*).
ejidatario	the farm worker of the collective or communal lands of the *ejido* (*q.v.*).
ejido	originally a Spanish and indigenous Indian concept referring to lands inalienably held in common by the village and subsequently developed into an agricultural cooperative settlement by the Mexican Revolution, similar to Israeli *kibbutz*.
encomendero	during the colonial periods of the Spanish Empire the individual to whom was entrusted the welfare of Indians in return for their services and labor; historically, the *encomendero* is the predecessor of the *hacendado* (*q.v.*).

estanciero	the Argentine version of the *latifundista* (*q.v.*) or *hacendado* (*q.v.*); he is the proprietor of the *estancia*, as the large estate is called there.
falange	name of the contemporary Fascist party in Franco's Spain.
fazenda	the Brazilian counterpart of the *hacienda* (*q.v.*).
fiesta	the popular celebration of religious and secular holidays; a time to release human energy in explosive and social ways: fire and drink, dance and song, exuberance and excess, are characteristics of the *fiesta*; it is an observance, traditional and ritual, a spiritual attitude of a people, and an excuse for a hearty spree of diversion.
gaucho	the Argentine cowboy of the plains (*pampas*); an uncouth, tough person, but with the romantic aura of the rebel and the outcast; he is also found in southern Brazil.
golpe de estado	*coup d'état*, forceful seizure of power, usually by the military or one of its cliques; the traditional solution to parliamentary impasse and traditional alternative to the legal transfer of power.
hacendado	the owner and master of the *hacienda* (*q.v.*).
hacienda	the large tract of land held by one person or several individuals, like the entailed estate in English law or the cotton plantation in the antebellum South of the United States; principal social and economic institution of the traditional order in Latin America.

ingenio (Sp.) *engehno de açucar* (Port.)	the sugar-producing factory and its environs; a dominant economic factor and social determinant in the Caribbean, Central America, and northern Brazil.
jefe máximo	the absolute leader of party, government, and nation; the embodiment of political power and the virtues of manhood and masculinity (*machismo*) (*q.v.*).
justicialismo	literally, the doctrine of "justice for everyman," the political slogan coined by Perón to attract popular support of his regime.
latifundio	a large estate or landed property.
latifundismo	the system of land tenure in which land is concentrated in a few huge estates controlled by the traditional landed gentry.
latifundista (Sp.) *latifundiário* (Port.)	the owner of a large estate, the *hacendado* (*q.v.*).
libertador	a title meaning "the liberator," the founding father of Latin America and guarantor of its independence; specifically granted to Simón Bolívar by the Venezuelan people.
llanero	the Venezuelan plainsman and rancher.
llanos	the Venezuelan plains.
machismo	the cult of virility and the exultation of the virtues of manhood; the leader, whether in society or in politics, must somehow embody these attributes.
macho	literally, the human male; the epitome of manhood and masculinity.
mestizaje	the procreation of a mixed race of Indian and white; also, the culture or way of life of *mestizo* society, and one of the special

	traits of Latin American culture in general.
mestizo	person of Indian and white mixture and his or her offspring.
Nacional Financiera	Mexican governmental organization designed to direct and in part finance economic enterprises in both public and private sectors.
padrinazgo	the system and practice of godfathership in Latin America.
padrino	godfather, sponsor, with legal and affectionate bonds to his godchildren or wards, an important link in the extended kinship system in Latin America.
pampas	the wide fertile prairies and grazing lands that stretch inland from Buenos Aires. The "bread basket" and beef center of Argentina.
papiamento	dialect spoken on the island of Curaçao, a mélange of Dutch, French, Spanish, Indian, and English elements.
parentela	kinship relations, a significant aspect of familial and individual life in Latin America.
patria	cognate of the French *patrie*, the fatherland, carrying all the emotional overtones of nationalism and love of country.
patria boba	the "silly country," suggesting local chauvinism, the province one feels to be one's true nation instead of the actual national state.
patria chica	"the small fatherland," one's native soil, suggesting the deep attachment to the small, immediate community of one's birth.

patrón

master or employer, a term indicating complete authority over the lives and occupations of his subordinates.

pensador

corresponding to the *philosophe* of the French Revolution, political thinker, the Latin American intellectual who fights for his ideas in essay or in exile.

peón

unskilled laborer of rural areas, bound by debt to his *patrón* (*q.v.*); often close in status to the serf in the feudal system of the European Middle Ages; without land or rights and almost totally dependent on the *hacendado* (*q.v.*), he is reduced to the condition of a chattel.

personalismo

the doctrine and practice of government by the influence of and the dependence upon one man (e.g., the *jefe máximo*, *caudillo*); thus, political party adherence is defined in terms of loyalty to the person of the leader rather than to principles and programs of the party.

pipiolo

literally, a novice or youngster; in Chile the word has a political connotation referring to members of the Liberal Party, especially in the nineteenth century; it was applied to them by the conservative class in a derogatory manner.

política de campanario

politics within the purview of the belfry, political life controlled by the clique and the cabal.

porteño

resident of a port city, specifically of Buenos Aires.

puna

bleak, chill tableland common along the Andean mountain chain.

reconquista

the attempt in Spain by the embattled Christians to counterattack and reoccupy their lands, seized by the Moors after their invasion of the Iberian Peninsula in 711.

reivindicación

literally, replevin or recovery of something lost; term charged with revolutionary intent for the nationalist who seeks to discover and recover the true greatness of his nation.

rurales

the Mexican federal police created by Porfirio Díaz, dreaded instrument of the traditional order, hence one of the first casualties of the Mexican Revolution.

senhores de engenho

the sugar-mill owners in Brazil who were lords of the land and the factory, and the class that dominated political and economic life until the middle of the nineteenth century.

terruño

one's native soil, the land that touches one's heart, the place where one is born and dies.

Notes on the Contributors

ROBERT J. ALEXANDER, Professor of Economics at Rutgers University, is the author of *Latin America Today* and other works on this area.

GERMÁN ARCINIEGAS, Colombian scholar, journalist, and former Ambassador to Argentina and Italy, has written on many Latin American subjects, and is presently editor of *Cuadernos*.

DANIEL COSÍO VILLEGAS, Mexican educator and economist, former Director of the *Colegio de México*, is an eminent historian and the author of *Historia Moderna de México*.

GILBERTO FREYRE, Professor and Director at the Institute of Social Research at the University of Recife, Brazil, is author of *The Masters and the Slaves*, and *The Mansions and the Shanties*.

ANTHONY LEEDS is Associate Professor of Anthropology, Institute of Latin American Studies and Luso-Brazilian Program (NDEA), University of Texas.

JOSEPH MAIER, Professor of Sociology at Rutgers University, is the author of *Sociology: The Science of Society*.

RICHARD M. MORSE is Professor of Latin American History at Yale University and the author of *From Community to Metropolis*, *A Biography of São Paulo, Brazil*.

STANLEY ROBERT ROSS, Professor of Latin American History at the State University of New York at Stony Brook, Long Island, has written widely on the Mexican Revolution.

VÍCTOR L. URQUIDI, Mexican economist and government adviser, is author of various books on Latin American economics, including *The Challenge of Development in Latin America*.

ARTURO USLAR-PIETRI is a Venezuelan man of letters, statesman, and political scientist at the University of Caracas.

CHARLES WAGLEY, Professor of Anthropology and Director of the Institute of Latin American Studies at Columbia University, is the author of *Amazon Town: A Study of Man in the Tropics*.

RICHARD W. WEATHERHEAD is Lecturer in History at Columbia University.

ARTHUR P. WHITAKER, Professor Emeritus of Latin American History at the University of Pennsylvania, is the author of *The United States and Argentina*, and other studies on Latin America.